THE CULTURE OF THE MEIJI PERIOD

The Culture
of the Meiji Period

IROKAWA DAIKICHI

Translation edited by
Marius B. Jansen

PRINCETON UNIVERSITY PRESS

PRINCETON, NEW JERSEY

Copyright © 1985 by Princeton University Press

Published by Princeton University Press, 41 William Street,
Princeton, New Jersey 08540
In the United Kingdom: Princeton University Press, Chichester, West Sussex

Library of Congress Cataloging in Publication Data

Irokawa, Daikichi, 1925-
The culture of the Meiji period.

(Princeton library of Asian translations)
Translation of: Meiji no bunka.
1. Japan—Civilization—1868-1912.   I. Title. II. Series.

DS822.3.I7613 1985 952.03′1   84-42889
ISBN 0-691-06634-5
ISBN 0-691-00030-1 (pbk.)

First Princeton Paperback printing, 1988

Publication of this book has been aided by a grant
from the Paul Mellon Fund of Princeton University Press

This book has been composed in Linotron Caledonia

Princeton University Press books are printed on acid-free
paper, and meet the guidelines for permanence and durability
of the Committee on Production Guidelines
for Book Longevity of the Council on Library Resources

Printed in the United States of America

Meiji no bunka (The Culture of the Meiji Period)
by Irokawa Daikichi
Copyright © 1970 by Irokawa Daikichi

Originally published in Japanese by Iwanami Shoten,
Publishers, Tokyo, 1970

5   7   9   10   8   6

CONTENTS

CONTENTS

V
THE HEIGHTS AND DEPTHS OF POPULAR CONSCIOUSNESS, 151

VI
CARRIERS OF MEIJI CULTURE, 196

VII
MEIJI CONDITIONS OF NONCULTURE, 219

VIII
THE EMPEROR SYSTEM AS A SPIRITUAL STRUCTURE, 245

PREFACE TO THE ENGLISH TRANSLATION

I wrote this work, *Meiji no bunka*, The Culture of the Meiji Period, in the fall of 1969, when the concept of "people's history" had yet to win acceptance among Japanese historians. The hold of Marxism was still so strong then that it fettered most of us and stifled scholarly creativity. Most of us were trying to explain our nation's past from the material base of society by studying land ownership and other economic relationships, or else through a thesis of class conflict by analyzing clashes between ruling elites and opposition leaders. The methods that French social and cultural historians of the *Annales* School had long used to write "total history" were wholly beyond our ken, locked away as we were in our own narrow compartments of specialization. A few of us, however, were trying to provide a breath of fresh air by applying the findings of Yanagita Kunio and other folklorists to our studies of social history by writing about the everyday life of common people of Japan.

My first experiment at writing an analytic history of popular Japanese thought was published in 1964 as *Meiji seishin shi*. The work that is translated here represents a second attempt, one in which I raised basic revisionist questions for the field at large. It was my aim to discredit the prevailing mode of Japanese cultural history, which was centered on intellectual elites—great thinkers, scholars, educators, and men of arts and letters. In its place I sought to produce a cultural history conceived from the standpoint of the common people—a deep social stratum that was in basic opposition to intellectual elites—by exploiting methods used by Japanese folklorists and historians of popular thought. My goal was nothing less than a paradigmatic change in the field of Japanese cultural history.

Hindsight now shows that I did not achieve that goal. *Meiji*

vii

no bunka made a forceful impact on the minds of young Japanese readers, but it failed to change the scholarly world in any drastic way because its thesis lacked sufficient coherence, lucidity, and theoretical formulation. Chapter VIII, in which I had hoped to supply this formulation, proved disappointing; "The Emperor System as a Spiritual Structure" was at best an imperfect critique of Professor Maruyama Masao's scholarly approach.

My efforts to establish a new paradigm in cultural history did not fully succeed, but the pioneering zeal that spurred me to write *Meiji no bunka* is evident on every page. That zeal, I believe, won the hearts of many nonspecialists. It gradually helped gain acceptance for the concept of "people's history" in the academic world, and it enhanced the status of Yanagita's folklore studies among professional Japanese historians. Ever since the publication of *Meiji no bunka*, I have done everything I could to formulate more clearly the revisionist questions I raised and to answer them more cogently.

I visited Princeton's Department of East Asian Studies in September of 1970 at the kind invitation of Professor Marius B. Jansen, and I arrived with copies of *Meiji no bunka*, fresh off the press. I recall fondly how we read it in Jones Hall seminars with Professor Jansen's bright young graduate students in Japanese history. One of them, Ronald Morse, participated in this translation. Travels to other campuses brought me in touch with Carol Gluck, Stephen Vlastos, Tony Namkung, and other young specialists. Of those who took part in this translation Professors Gluck and Vlastos have also worked with me in Japan, while Noboru Hiraga and Eiji Yutani are former students recruited by Professor Jansen. It is a great pleasure to express my heartfelt appreciation, both to them for undertaking to translate my book, and to Professor Jansen, who coordinated and edited this volume. It has been a long and arduous enterprise, undertaken in a spirit of warm friendship. Sincere thanks also go to Princeton University Press for publishing the manuscript.

Tokyo, 1984   Irokawa Daikichi

EDITOR'S INTRODUCTION

With very few exceptions, Japanese historians are known abroad only through references to them in other scholars' works. They can seldom control or know the context in which they appear, nor can most non-Japanese have any idea of the way these scholars address their Japanese readers. We have prepared this translation because we believe that some figures deserve to be seen in the context in which their Japanese readers see them.

Irokawa Daikichi, Professor of Japanese History at Tokyo University of Economics, is one of the most popular Japanese historians of recent years. The volume translated here, *The Culture of the Meiji Period*, has gone through ten printings and circulated in some 58,000 copies to become a modern classic. Professor Irokawa is also the author of one of the twenty-six volumes on the History of Japan published by Chūō Kōronsha, *The Launching of the Modern State (Kindai kokka no shuppatsu)*, which has sold close to a million copies, as well as an influential work titled *The Spiritual History of the Meiji Era (Meiji seishin shi)*. His discovery and publication of a locally drafted constitution dating from the 1880s has provided the subject matter for additional books. It was therefore logical and natural for him to emerge in 1981 as a leader in a movement to defend the "Peace Constitution" of 1947 by commemorating the centennial anniversary of the Movement for Freedom and People's Rights of the early Meiji period.

History, politics, and values intersect in contemporary Japan to guarantee a wide hearing for an able and articulate historian. Irokawa and his friends characterize their approach to history as "people's history," and an understanding of its goals requires some understanding of the trends of historical writing in modern Japan.

With the overthrow of the Tokugawa shogunate in 1868

and the construction of the Meiji state, Japanese writers tried to locate their country's experience in the larger patterns they discerned in world—and especially European—history. The emergence of a popular democratic movement led by elements of the old elite, and the accommodation of those leaders by the new government in its constitutional structure in the 1890s, seemed to give English historical writing, especially the Whig interpretation, promise and relevance.[1] A generation of writers found it meaningful to place the events of the recent past in this apparently useful setting. Japan entered the stage of full national power in the 1890s with victory in war over a backward Ch'ing empire in China and went on to establish its dominance over Korea by defeating Russia, which was still without a constitution, in 1905, with the encouragement of England, which had become an ally in 1902 and would continue as one until 1922. Japan seemed securely tied to trends of Western liberalism and enlightenment. The acquisition of Taiwan and Korea appeared to parallel the growth of imperialist sentiment in the Western democracies and to impart a regional mission as well. As the influential publisher-historian Ukita Kazutami put it, Japan seemed squarely placed within Western patterns of modernity.

This interpretation had to coexist with a strongly particularist strain on the part of writers who reflected a vibrant new nationalist ideology by the end of the nineteenth century. The Meiji Restoration represented the return of power to the throne, and for these writers the sovereign was proof of the legitimacy and superiority of the regime. Its purposes were shaped by the sovereign's supposed will and authorization, and history had to play its part. Major compilations of historical documents were directed by boards representing equally the domains that had cooperated in bringing about the Restoration. The return of power to the throne was placed in a context of increasing affection for the sovereign, whose re-

---

[1] See Peter Duus, "Whig History, Japanese Style: The Min'yūsha Historians and the Meiji Restoration," *Journal of Asian Studies* 33, no. 3 (May 1974): pp. 415-36.

gime took on the heroic dimensions of a morality play. This version of the past also dominated the teaching in the public schools. By the turn of the century some popular historians found it desirable to revise works they had written in the 1880s to bend to this new wind of official patriotism. Pride in Japanese achievement sometimes competed with the need to place Japan in a larger setting. Tokutomi Sohō, for instance, had long advocated the wisdom of Spencer's stages of history that led to mercantile superiority over military rule. With the defeat of China he realized, however, that the government he had attacked was in fact his own, and that Japan could achieve equality with the West only if it learned to flex its muscles. The philosopher-aesthetician Okakura Tenshin put it more succinctly by writing that the West had accepted Japan as civilized only after Japan had shown its ability to engage in mass slaughter on the battlefield.

World War I and the end of empire in many states led to doubts; Japan suddenly found itself distrusted as an imperialist holdout instead of praised for its mastery of modern trends. The Anglo-Japanese alliance gave way to a new international system that few Japanese fully trusted. Postwar ills of unemployment and social discord, and the Russian revolution, provided new international examples that other Japanese found meaningful for their country. By the late 1920s Marxism was powerfully entrenched in Japanese intellectual circles, and evaluations of Meiji changes turned on the question of whether Japan had fully entered the bourgeois arena or some intermediate stage of absolutism based on an imperfectly developed capitalism under feudal leadership. The problem of fitting Japan into world history remained pressing, and Marxism provided new and more inclusive alternatives to emperor-centered history.

The extremism of the 1930s brought Marxist and nationalist enthusiasms to the fore. The Marxist approach gained in power and persuasion because of the tactics of the advocates of national perfection and uniqueness. War, defeat, occupation, and reform left the Marxists in command of the field. The nationalists were silenced and discredited. Some had the agility to cleanse their prewar writing of nationalist traits and join the new camp, but for a decade or more advocates of uniqueness and mission retired in confusion and silence. Nonetheless, the newly sovereign Japan of the 1950s and 1960s did not seem to conform to the Marxist vision. Full civil and political rights had been extended, freedom to organize was at hand, and yet the masses did not seem to make use of them. The great campaign to prevent ratification of the United States—Japan Security Pact peaked with the street riots and demonstrations of 1960 and left Japan no closer to a Marxist model. Gradually the arguments and the politicians who used the leftist slogans appeared to be dated and irrelevant prewar relics. A history that spoke to Japan's new urban masses had to find new things to say.

Irokawa Daikichi was born in 1925. He is a 1948 graduate of the Department of National History at the University of Tokyo. His brief experience there in prewar days convinced him of the shoddy nature of wartime thought, and the service in the Imperial Navy that interrupted his university education provided a setting calculated to produce a radical student. Well before Japan's defeat, diary entries and correspondence quoted in his personal history of contemporary times reveal Irokawa's distrust of Japan's leaders and what they said. For him and millions of others, defeat brought a sense of betrayal to the fore. From now on prewar ideology would be his target. Together with most of his generation, Irokawa dedicated himself to the creation of a new and healthier spirit of doubt, free from the self-imposed blinders of the "emperor system" that had been like a "weight upon the eyes." Health could not be sought in slavish conformity with Western patterns, for Japan's problems inhered in the flood of Western culture that had changed the equilibrium of Japanese thought and culture, even in the remote villages on the western edge of the Tokyo plain that Irokawa knows best. Postwar Marxist scholarship was a history without people, whereas prewar scholarship had been a history of the wrong people. History had to be about ordinary people. Prewar and postwar intellectuals had gone to school with Westerners, distanced themselves from their own countrymen, and forgotten how those countrymen lived and thought.

Irokawa and a number of other historians have devoted themselves to what they call "people's history" or *minshūshi*.[2] Irokawa, in particular, examines the formative years of Meiji statism in order to understand why people submitted so willingly to the malignancy of the official "emperor system," an evil so pervasive that it resembles for him a floating miasma. Contemporary Japanese move in a very different atmosphere, but it is by no means certain for practitioners of people's history that a country led by a modernizing bureaucratic elite, and lectured by a Western-oriented intellectual class, can develop the resources to enable it to avoid future crises.

Irokawa's desire to understand and communicate with his countrymen has led him to investigate the deep and silent stream of Japanese consciousness and sensibility. For him and his counterparts the influence of the folklore specialist Yanagita Kunio, who devoted his life to collecting information about the everyday life of ordinary people, offered hope. *Meiji no bunka* begins with an evocation of Yanagita's account of village life and values. It also draws on the work of Yasumaru Yoshio, a specialist in popular religion, whose ideas of "conventional morality" (*tsūzoku dōtoku*) treat a realm seldom pursued by academic historians or moral philosophers. Thus *The Culture of the Meiji Period—Meiji no bunka—*is not cultural history of the Burckhardt or Huizinga school. It is much closer to the *Annales* historians' concern with daily life and ordinary people, but it makes no efforts to achieve the sort of encyclopedic coverage that Paris specialists produce. Instead, Irokawa looks for what he feels are representative individuals and builds from that. Understandably, the discovery of a treasure-trove of materials about such people in Itsukaichi was of tremendous importance.

Irokawa's theme, and that of the people's history school, is

[2] A full discussion can be found in Carol Gluck, "The People in History: Recent Trends in Japanese Historiography," *Journal of Asian Studies* 38, no. 1 (November 1978): pp. 25-50.

that the centuries of Tokugawa rule produced important changes that made the early modern village of the early nineteenth century something quite different from what it had been and was to be. Obsequious deference to the military caste had disappeared during centuries in which the samurai were collected in castle towns and kept from entering the countryside. A countryside that administered itself had developed a natural elite of local notables whose education and concerns led them to think in terms of responsibility and public order. Government relied on a traditional morality that argued for the responsibility of leadership, and village notables responded with a conventional morality that made it their duty to defend and articulate local needs and expectations. They were supported by the broad consensus of the community as a whole. A sort of "moral economy" prevailed in which diligence and propriety were the expected response to legitimate authority, whereas oppression and greed could properly bring resistance. By the nineteenth century class differentiation was changing the countryside as capitalist agriculture for urban markets had penetrated major areas of Japan, but conventional morality still operated to systematize and articulate a loose constellation of moral assumptions. The diffusion of these assumptions—themselves an echo of the more schematized morality of upper-class values—made for self-awareness, self-discipline, and responsibility.

This largely autonomous country village, which Irokawa describes as a "commune" of sorts, changed under the pressures of capitalism into something much more exploitative by the century's end. Fixed tax rates, legal recourse and police protection for lenders, and a state monopoly on force changed the balance of power in the villages. Japan itself became more grasping and exploitative, both of its own citizens and even more so of its neighbors in Korea and China.

Irokawa tries to determine how this came about. In large measure, it would seem, he finds his answer in the desperate rush for modernization that the Meiji leaders inaugurated in their fear of Western incursions. Conventional custom, morality, and norms had to be sacrificed to the new urgency of national salvation. For that campaign nothing was more useful than the aura of the sovereign in whose name conventional morality was gradually replaced by a much more oppressive "higher" morality.

To undo the evil that was done to Japanese character and psychology, Irokawa argues, the readers—his countrymen—must return to the start of the process, enter once more into the values and morality of late Tokugawa Japan, and anticipate and head off the blight at the point of its creation. On doing so they will discover reserves of education, intelligence, and courage in the village that will show how ill-placed and counterproductive it has been to associate wisdom with the elite and follow that elite in dismissing the masses as ignorant. Japan has had, and still has, internal resources that make slavish acceptance of Western modernity unnecessary. No imported methodology or theory—neither Marxism nor modernization—will suffice. For Irokawa, Marxism builds on conflict and dispute, and modernization is concerned with ends rather than means. Rapid modernization led to popular traumatization and war. There were forces in the mid-nineteenth century that could have led to other outcomes.

This schema, although not Marxist, is indebted to the Marxist view of capitalism. Far from traditional, it nevertheless takes an optimistic and even romantic view of early nineteenth-century Japan. Intensely political, it is yet far removed from the sort of political history that chronicles statesmen's deeds and institutions to explain the past. Above all, Irokawa's work is beautifully written history: evocative, challenging, conversational, emotional, and at times sentimental in its surge of language. We have done our best to convey that quality in this translation and hope that we have served its author adequately.

ABOUT THE TRANSLATION:

Over a decade ago a group of us began plans for the translation of *Meiji no bunka*. Some of the group—Stephen Vlastos (University of Iowa) and Carol Gluck (Columbia University)—had come to know Professor Irokawa well during periods of research in Tokyo; others—Ronald Morse (East Asia Program, Woodrow Wilson Center, Smithsonian Institution) and the editor—during Professor Irokawa's stay at Princeton in 1969-1970; and others—Eiji Yutani (East Asian Library, University of California, Berkeley) and Noburu Hiraga (University of Washington)—knew him through his writings. In the formal division of labor Ronald Morse prepared translations of the Introduction; Noburu Hiraga of chapters I, II, VI, and VII; Stephen Vlastos, chapter III; Eiji Yutani, chapters IV and V; and Carol Gluck, chapter VIII. This began the process, but the end product was still several years away. There were problems of unifying the whole with regard to usage and style, and of adding footnotes of explanation and identification to the sketchy leads the author felt it necessary to provide for his Japanese readers. In these, and throughout the texts, names have been given in the Japanese order, with surname first. In going through the entire manuscript Bob Tadashi Wakabayashi of Princeton performed yeoman service; he, Michael P. Birt, David S. Noble, and Constantine Vaporis of Princeton caught further problems in the course of processing the text on the computer, as did Thomas Schalow and David Howell in preparing the index. I thank my colleagues for their patience in waiting to see the product of their work and am greatly saddened that Noburu Hiraga, who translated four of the book's eight chapters, died just as it went to press. We are grateful, too, for the enthusiastic support of Miriam Brokaw and her associates at Princeton University Press, and we are pleased that this work of contemporary historical writing has found its place in the Princeton Library of Asian Translations.

All of us are grateful to Irokawa Daikichi for his tolerance and encouragement during the decade that has passed. We feel with him that the book shows a side of Meiji Japan that has not been apparent to those whose reading has been limited to the usual sources; its judgments afford a perspective on contemporary Japan that would surely have surprised the citizens of Meiji Japan a century ago.

Princeton 1984   M.B.J.

THE CULTURE OF THE MEIJI PERIOD

INTRODUCTION

Japan: A Very Strange Country

Japan is a peculiar country. Seen from above, it resembles a long, narrow, arc-shaped chain of islands floating on the eastern edge of the Eurasian continent. In terms of Europe these four islands, which are veiled in mists and fog for the greater part of the year, would extend from England to the tip of the Italian peninsula, or from the Russo-Polish border to the Franco-Spanish border. A central spine of rugged mountains divides the islands into two extremely different climatic zones. The little valleys into which the islands are divided by seas and mountains prove to have paddy after emerald paddy, and little toy-like tractors move along their surface. Houses and villages resemble a miniature garden. The tranquillity of the fields and hills and the white sands of the beaches against which the waves roll all contrast sharply with the clusters of factories that fill the sky with black smoke.

But what is strange about Japan is not that this overpopulated, resource-poor Asian island country has managed to compete for a place as the world's second or third largest industrial power. The fairy-tale aspect of this small island is to be found in its history. Despite its location a mere four hundred miles off the coast of China that boasts Asia's oldest and greatest culture, Japan has never once throughout its two-thousand-year history been incorporated within that empire; it has consistently maintained its national independence, and it has by and large preserved its distinctive culture.

The people who built the great Maya and Inca civilizations have been destroyed. The splendors of the Nile and Tigris-Euphrates are now nothing more than objects of tourist curiosity. On the island of Crete, on the isles of the Aegean, in Ceylon, in Indo-China, and in the oases of Central Asia cultures developed that dazzle the eyes of modern man, cultures

3

that still sustain the spirit of their present inhabitants. But those are not part of a single web of history and culture that has somehow survived intact to become part of the modern life of a nation, to be absorbed into its industrial, scientific, and artistic strength, as is the case with Japan. In that sense, Japan seems a country filled with a strange wonder, at once ancient and new. There is not another case like it in the history of the world.

The fact that Japan has never been subjugated by a large continental power cannot be credited just to the accidents of geography or to the martial spirit of the Japanese people. It is probably a blessing derived from the monsoon climate. The wet rice cultures of monsoon Asia created a peaceful international environment of gentle and persevering peoples. The Chinese and Korean people constituted a defensive barrier, and they protected monsoon Asia against the warlike horsemen of the continent for so many centuries. Those peaceful neighbors in China and Korea never once directly opposed Japan; the Mongol invasions of the thirteenth century were part of a Mongol, and not a Chinese, effort to conquer all of East Asia. In contrast, the Japanese have had a long history of repaying this neighborly friendship with enmity. This was a violation of the morality of the East, contrary to the teachings of love and benevolence of the Buddha and of Confucius respectively, even though the Japanese themselves have revered both of them as spiritual teachers. This behavior has been especially true in the century that began with the Meiji era, during which Japan invaded and plundered her Asian neighbors without any provocation. I cannot overlook the fact that our country's leaders have still not given this contrast the critical self-reproach they should.

When this protective setting, in which the Japanese lived free from the threat of aggression from neighboring peoples for two thousand years, is contrasted with Europe's blood-stained history, it is not difficult to see how unusual Japan's environment has been, and how large a part it has played in the formulation of Japanese cultural sensitivity, modes of life, and social attitudes. It is of decisive importance that Japanese

culture developed within the insulated environment of an island country. Watsuji Tetsurō's approach to this problem in
his *Fūdo*[1] does not suffice. What is required is a much more
comprehensive theory of environment that will bring into play
the range of considerations anthropologists employ in recent
historical treatments of comparative culture, as well as the
results of research in folklore, history, and ethnology. Nevertheless, because Japan managed, despite internal conflicts, to
preserve its national independence over a very long period of
time, it developed its own distinctive culture resulting in homogeneous patterns of race, language, religion, food, clothing, and shelter, as well as a unique consciousness, attitude
toward nature, spirit, and sensibility. We need only compare
Japan with India, China, or Southeast Asia to see how sin-
gular and homogeneous it is. There is hardly another country
outside Asia that has preserved—the way Japan has—all the
elements that make up a people. The old shibboleth about "a
single (imperial) line unbroken throughout history" is only
one symbol of these special historical characteristics.

Attempts to comprehend the particularities of Japanese
culture according to the conceptual categories established for
the cultural history of the West have not been successful. It
is even less profitable to apply the analytic methods of Western "modernism" to the study of Japan and to try to use them
to distinguish the rational and irrational, and the modern and
premodern, elements in Japanese culture. Most Japanese intellectuals may think such an approach is valid, but it is one
that is far removed from the psychology of the ordinary Japanese. I think that in Japan's modern period the formation of
thought and culture has assumed two essentially different
patterns and methods, each informed by its own distinctive
principles: the route of the intellectual elite and that of the
ordinary people. There are those who say that these two cur-

---

[1] Watsuji (1886-1960), an influential philosopher and cultural historian,
published a work designed to clarify the function of climate as a factor in
human, and especially Japanese, life. There is a translation by Geoffrey Bownas:
A Climate: A Philosophical Study (Tokyo: Japanese National Commission for
UNESCO: Ministry of Education, 1961).

rents are converging rapidly in our postwar decades, but I feel that the problem is far from solved. The reason for this is to be found in the way a sudden torrent of strong and substantively different Western culture rushed into a strong and highly particular Japanese culture in which the masses of the people lived in a deep, silent world of local custom and folk life. In the final analysis, I think it stemmed from the unique position Japan was forced to occupy in world history.

To make a sweeping generalization of the kind associated with Okakura Tenshin,[2] I think we can say that the Meiji era was the most turbulent era in all of Japanese history. From the dawn of its history Japanese culture has been repeatedly washed by great waves of influence from India, China, and early modern Europe, but in each previous case that influence was stilled after a century or two, assimilated, and Japanized. The greatest of these waves was probably the wave of Chinese culture that had such an immense impact on Japan in the Nara period in the seventh and eighth centuries. But compared with the confusion that developed in the Meiji period in the latter half of the nineteenth century, that earlier influence was restricted in scope, and its impact was weak. In Meiji times the impact was not something that affected just those in power; it roused violent emotions in the middle strata of society, and its influence extended down to the lower levels as well.

Ordinary people developed a great interest in the foreign culture at that time. The people of this island country have rightly been known for their keen awareness and the quick responsiveness they always showed to superior cultures, but in the Meiji era the new culture brought with it the power of the industrial revolution and the strength of the capitalist structure of the modern nation-state. It thereby increased the Japanese sense of curiosity and emulation enormously. The terrible intensity of the Restoration activists in their struggles

[2] Okakura Tenshin (Kakuzō, 1862-1913), a leading theorist of aesthetics who wrote *Ideals of the East*, *The Book of Tea*, and other works designed to explain Japan to the West. The author has edited his writings in *Okakura Tenshin*, vol. 39 of *Nihon no meicho* (Tokyo: Chūō kōronsha, 1970).

over "opening the country" and "driving out the barbarians" was one expression of this; so, too, was the desperate struggle and hardship undergone by young men who wanted to study abroad, and the outbreaks of millenarian, *yonaoshi*[3] movements among the common people. The same is true of the civil strife that surrounded the establishment of a new political structure. That is why the Meiji period is often said to be the most dramatic in Japanese history and why Meiji Japan can be seen as a test case for the study of world cultural history.

Foreigners were inquisitive as well. Would this small, backward Asian agricultural country be able to surpass China and endure the trials of modernization? Would it be able to stand up under the burdens of those trials in the unfavorable international environment of that day? Today we know the answer. A little over a hundred years ago the American, Commodore Perry, led a small flotilla; he brought the samurai of this closed country a small model train as a present and set it in motion before their eyes. At first the Japanese watched the train fearfully from a safe distance, and when the engine began to move they uttered cries of astonishment and drew in their breath. Before long they were inspecting it closely, stroking it, and riding on it, and they kept this up throughout the day. A mere hundred years later those same Japanese, by themselves, developed and built the high-speed "Hikari" trains that travel along the Tōkaidō safely at speeds of two hundred kilometers an hour. And now they are exporting that technology to Perry's country.

The same Japanese who were shocked and fascinated by Perry's steamships that belched black smoke put their unbounded curiosity to work and became the largest shipbuilding nation in the world. This development might have been seen to germinate as early as late Tokugawa times; for the scientific aptitude of Japanese could have been predicted by the way they managed to build blast and reverberatory fur-

[3] "World renewal movements," millenarian uprisings that took place in the nineteenth-century decades that preceded the Tokugawa fall in 1868.

naces, carry out exacting measurements like those found in Inō Tadataka maps,[4] and improve methods of manufacture for everything from rifles to printing and engraving.

But if we make too much of this we will miss the forest for the trees and be prevented from painting an objective picture of modern Japan. It is no help to Japanese who are struggling for the overall reform of their country today to single out figures for the GNP or to pick out two or three leading industries that have established themselves as first rank in the world, and then to praise the marvels of Japan's feudal culture by citing it as a prerequisite for such achievements. What the Japanese need today is not a justification or rationalization of their present system in terms of that kind of historical assessment but rather an investigation of the pathology of the present system in order to reform it: they need total, basic, and structured research.

Consequently the problems with which this book is concerned are quite different from the "peculiar aspects of Japan" that have provoked the curiosity of foreign scholars. We Japanese who live in present-day Japan have to be practical if we are going to carry out our reforms. But having said that, I must also differ with the ideologues who argue that culture is just a tool of class domination. All peoples, rulers and ruled, have worked out forms of life from which they derive comfort and joy, and they have found spiritual and material value in the festivals, belief, entertainment, crafts, food, dress, shelter, and ceremony that have made their lives worth living. The culture that functioned without their realizing it in those modes of social life became a silent but powerful force in regulating their lives. Culture has always served as a latent guide for human behavior; as T. S. Eliot pointed out, the spirit of a culture is found, not in the works of individual creative humans but in "the unconscious background of all

---

[4] Inō (1745-1818), a geographer who began with the study of traditional astronomy, went on to study Western-style geography and measurement and was ordered to map Hokkaido and ultimately all Japan by the shogunate. His maps were used into the twentieth century.

our plans." (He did not, of course, mean to imply that the work of creative individuals is to be ignored.)

Minakata Kumakusu[5] provides a good example of this point in a passage describing the way that community members draw strength from a tutelary shrine. He speaks of a spiritual experience in which

> those who draw near in reverence sense, in an instant, in every part of their being, things that cannot be expressed or transmitted by word, writing, or discussion; things they will never be able to forget. . . .

He goes on to say that the worshipers, "without quite knowing which god is present, feel the tears of reverence begin to flow."

Unless culture and thought penetrate to the people's most basic level, they cannot exercise their inherent power. In modern Japan, what I term the "emperor system as spiritual structure" did in fact penetrate to that basic level, and it spread its poison there. In fact, it still does so today. Most of the riddles that foreigners might find difficult in "Meiji culture" derive from this unique ideological climate. It is all the more essential, then, that we not avoid taking up that problem of the emperor system and that I make it a basic theme in this work.

The Emperor System as a "Weight Upon the Eyes"

The "emperor system as spiritual structure" was formulated during the early part of the Meiji period, and it became a "weight upon the eyes" for the majority of Japanese in the late years of Meiji when it was fully developed. Even an intellectual like Takamura Kōtarō (1883-1956),[6] a brilliant sculp-

[5] Minakata (1867-1941), a biologist who traveled widely in the West and was a staff member of the British museum; upon his return to Japan in 1900 he became particularly known for his essays on Japanese folklore.

[6] Takamura is the subject of Hiroaki Sato, *Chieko and other Poems of Takamura Kōtarō* (Honolulu: University Press of Hawaii, 1980); the translations here and below follow, with modifications, the renditions of "Paris," p.

tor who had studied in Paris and who was also an antisocial, free-form poet, showed that he was not able to cast off this burden when he returned from France. Far from it: he was constrained to repudiate the life of rebellion and noble isolation that he had lived until the war. In the winter of 1945, after Japan's surrender, he looked back remorsefully with pangs of guilt. In *Angushoden* (A Fool's Way, 1947) he wrote as follows about the half-century through which he had passed:

> I became a man in Paris,
> First knew woman in Paris,
> First freed my soul in Paris.
> Paris showed no astonishment,
> Received all races of men. . . .
> Men can breathe in Paris;
> Modern times began in Paris
> Beauty buds and blossoms in Paris
> New brain cells form in Paris.
> France is more than France.
> In one corner of this inexhaustible world metropolis
> I sometimes forgot the country I was from.
> Japan seemed distant, insignificant, and petty.
> Seemed so irritatingly provincial.
> In Paris I first discovered sculpture
> And opened my eyes to the true beauty of poetry
> In each ordinary person
> I found the grounds for culture.
> Despite sad memories I could not help
> Feel immense differences;
> Though nostalgic for the things and patterns of Japan,
> I turned my back on them.

That is how he described himself in 1908. After his return to Japan he was determined to "live as a single, individual human being," but "in this country, which does not permit one to be fully human," this seemed "nothing short of treason."

137; "The Day of Pearl Harbor," p. 143; and "End of the War," p. 146. Used with permission.

Takamura fell into a state of decadence and sealed himself off in the middle of Tokyo, where he "struggled in a life cut off from everybody except Chieko," his wife, who shared his isolation. This abnormal "dream of an inner world" was everything to him. But Chieko, shut off from the outside world in exclusive pursuit of an inner life, was driven mad, and then she died. As empty days and months flowed in succession, Takamura's very existence began to crumble. He became "a paper screen unsupported by a frame, not knowing when it might give way." At that time, this is what he heard:

Before I heard that war had been declared,
There was word of fighting in Hawaii.
Then warfare in the Pacific
I trembled as I heard the Imperial proclamation.
At this difficult moment
My thoughts distilled.
Yesterday became long ago,
And long ago became the now.
Our Emperor endangered!
That single statement
Fixed my course.
The grandfather of my childhood,
My father, my mother, were all involved.
The mists of my childhood days
Suddenly filled my room.
My ears heard the voices of my ancestors;
"His Majesty," "His Majesty. . ."
I was dazzled by the meaning of that breathless phrase.
Clearly I must sacrifice myself.
Protect His Majesty!
Put aside those verses and write new poems!

Takamura now poured all his energy in service to the Patriotic Society of Japanese Literature and similar organizations. But Japan was defeated, and his studio was burned. He fled to the cold mountain villages of the northeast, and there he heard his own "swan song."

11

When my studio burned to the ground,
I came to Hananomaki in Ōshū,
There I heard that radio broadcast[7]
I trembled as I sat erect.
Japan stood naked
And men's spirits were in an abyss.
The Occupation army saved us from starvation
And we narrowly escaped destruction.
At that moment the Tenno came forward
And proclaimed "I am not a living god."
As day followed day,
The weight was lifted from my eyes,[8]
The burden of sixty years disappeared at once.
Grandfather, father, mother
Returned once more to their distant Nirvana, and
I breathed freely once again.
After this wondrous release,
There remains but human love.

Here we see the spiritual course of a representative intellectual in modern Japan. It may seem too pure and naive, and the conversion too extreme, but in its very intensity we can see the essence of the symbolic relationship between "emperor system" and "intellectual." At times like the Marxists' confessions in the 1930s, we find the strange phenomenon of "mass conversion" of progressive intellectuals in the history of modern Japanese thought.[9] It was not so much the case of the emperor system's overpowering them by force as it was the revelation of a sickness that had permeated those intellectuals' thought processes at their very core.

[7] That is, the August 15 noon broadcast of the Rescript announcing "extraordinary measures" to bring an end to the war by accepting the Potsdam Declaration.

[8] This is the source of the author's imagery for the emperor system as a "weight upon the eyes" adopted throughout the book.

[9] "Mass conversions" (tenkō), under conditions of psychological stress focused on obligations to family and country, are described in Richard H. Mitchell, *Thought Control in Prewar Japan* (Ithaca and London: Cornell University Press, 1976), p. 97ff.

Then we have to ask: why did such a sickness of soul permeate their inner lives? When did it form, and how did it overpower the ideas it confronted, until it came to penetrate the very soul of Japanese intellectuals and common people? Surely any interpretation of "Meiji culture" has to clarify the curses and secrets of the way this "weight upon the eyes" could, as Takamura's confession shows, suddenly emerge as the chief support of Japanese and overwhelm their entire spirit in presurrender days so that they could remember it as a "sixty years' burden" they had carried.

Takeuchi Yoshimi[10] has pointed out succinctly that "because the emperor system is a total mental and spiritual structure it is not possible to apply or borrow methods from outside Japan to overcome it. That is, we have to detach something that is part of us and treat it objectively; we have to transform something transcendental into something temporal, and thereby make the emperor system only one of a number of values. Seeing it as a part of our consciousness is the precondition for freeing ourselves from it. We have to work out the way of doing this for ourselves." That seems to me a truly instructive comment.

In my view it was only after the end of the Meiji period that the emperor system became a comprehensive system of values, or, better, "a contrivance that contravened all other values"; it was in fact a hideous miasma, enveloping and subsuming the popular mind.

The magic of the emperor system had its own troubled history; it followed a rather zigzag process of development before it came to assume holistic control over the thought processes of the masses. When we examine the mental and spiritual consciousness that gave rise to modern emperor thought, we see that the structure of the popular mind during the late Tokugawa period of change was surprisingly rich in possibilities. That structure ultimately brought forth the emperor system, but it also contained visions of things outside

[10] Takeuchi Yoshimi, "Kenryoku to geijutsu" (1958), included in *Takeuchi Yoshimi zenshū*, 17 vols. (Tokyo: Chikuma shobō, 1981), vol. 2, pp. 142-70.

that system and not related to it, visions of liberation (such as millenarian movements and *yonaoshi* utopian thought) as well as reformist strains like Nakayama Miki's (*Tenri*),[11] all of which did battle with emperor-centered thought. They might have prevailed, for the *tennō* thought was only one of several possibilities at that time, and it might well have been overcome by the others.

The fact is that it was only under the abnormal circumstances of the time in which Japan experienced the impact of world capitalism, just as the shogunal and domain system of Tokugawa feudalism was forced into self-abnegation and the powerless court was brought forth to serve as pivot for the new nation-state, that the factor of emperor thought, theretofore only one possibility among others, was reinforced by the time's pressing needs for authority and came to take a dominant position from which it could defeat the other contenders. That is why it seems necessary to work out a way of examining the basic, original thinking of the day when emperor thought was still only one of several possibilities if we are to repudiate it from within. Once we have done that, we will be able to overturn that original structure and work toward a genuine spiritual and mental revolution. If we do not use this method, and instead try to reform Japanese consciousness at the popular level with nothing more than the modern individualism that came out of Western civil society, we will end up in the despair and self-righteousness of empty modernism; bitter experience has shown this to us time and again. In this way the study of popular consciousness, unlike reliance on sterile modernism, can reveal the latent, and long-buried potential that people have for a creative revitalization by contrasting alternatives to the once-dominant strain that we now want to abolish.

Research based on this kind of awareness has convinced me that the thought and ideas of ordinary people in modern

[11] An early nineteenth-century "new religion" that remains powerful. There is a study by Henry van Straelen, *The Religion of Divine Wisdom: Japan's Most Powerful Religious Movement* (Kyoto: Veritas shoin, 1957).

Japan have followed very different routes from those of the intellectuals, and that the inability of both groups to recognize this has had tragic consequences. This probably seems a bold hypothesis, but I have substantiated it in other writings. In this book, too, I try to provide as many specific examples as possible.

The Limits and Scope of the Problem

Any attempt to treat the whole of "Meiji culture" would of course be an impossible task and beyond my capacity. Therefore I should probably begin by outlining some of the contours of the problem and the themes to which I must restrict myself.

Where does what we call "Meiji" fit in with world history and culture, and what significance does it have? To answer those questions we have to decide what qualitative change was involved in the mid-nineteenth-century response to Western influence by a Japan that had maintained the "independent culture of an island country" for over a millennium wihout being enveloped by a continental world power. In this respect Japan is too unusual for it to be taken as a model for underdeveloped countries. That is, countries like Japan and Russia, which maintained their independence when they came into contact with the modern civilization of the West, provide a contrast to countries that were colonized or dependent. They proved relatively adept at receiving and adapting and managed to develop economic and military strength, but on the other hand their appropriation of the imported culture was partial, and it brought an extended period of facile imitation and confusion. Elsewhere—in China, India, and the Arab countries—however, the imported civilization clashed head-on with national cultures; thought turned inward, and this produced fierce resistance and self-definition. Individuals like Gandhi and Nehru in India, and Sun Yat-sen and Lu Hsün in China, served to intensify the spirit of their peoples, and they were able to reevaluate positively the culture and peoples of their own countries with eyes that were free of illusions about Western "civilization."

To be sure, one cannot simply explain away all differences in national response by crediting them to the fact of a country's having been colonized or not. It is also important to note the stage of world history at which a country's people were exposed to contact. For instance, the possibilities of retaining independence were radically different for China, which had to open its doors in the early 1840s; for Japan, which was opened in the 1850s and 1860s; and for Korea, the last to open its doors in the 1870s. Of the three, only Japan was able to profit from the mutual rivalries and checks and balances of the Western powers and take advantage of the energy the Indian and Chinese masses poured into their anti-foreign civil wars in order to retain its own independence.

Then again, the cultural level and degree of national consciousness people attained when their countries experienced the impact of the West constitutes an important consideration for their ability to resist subjugation. In the case of Japan there was the maturity of early modern culture and the legacy of Dutch studies; the wide diffusion of education and the spiritual self-discipline the masses had developed were combined with the patriotic spirit that they came to share. Furthermore, all this merged with people's hopes that the new era would meet the requirements for riding out the dangers of the international situation. It will be important for us to see how the Japanese greeted the full flood of Western culture, how that culture was transformed by them, and what kind of "Meiji culture" they produced.

If it was only in the Meiji period that the Japanese were able to bring forth things that had begun to germinate in Tokugawa times, then what are these modern "elements" that we can designate in "Meiji culture"? One is a clear response to human rights. Democratic self-awareness became particularly evident during the 1880s as a popular groundswell during the Movement for People's Rights.[12] Another is probably

[12] The People's Rights movement (*jiyū minken undō*), of which much will be heard below, was the popular movement for constitutional government

an awakening individualism, a kind of self-consciousness, as we have seen in the poems of Takamura Kōtarō. This was particularly strong among those who had direct experience of the West or with the concepts of Christianity, and it was notably current among members of the former samurai class and the intelligentsia. But even among ordinary people a modern kind of individual consciousness was developing slowly, in concert with the breakdown of ideas of "village" and "household" that had characterized feudal society; to be sure, it was seldom felt as sharply as it was by Takamura. Third, elements of capitalism—materialistic values, utilitarianism, and practicality—began to replace the old values that had had a more spiritual basis. Striking aspects of this transition were to be found in the decline of Confucian ethics and of the ideals of bushido.

A fourth and final aspect of modern culture was the rapid strengthening of an ethnic and national self-consciousness that encompassed virtually all of society. This showed itself through the rediscovery of Japanese aesthetics after an infatuation with those of the West and in the reevaluation of Japanese morality, tradition, and view of life. Okakura Tenshin's new Japanese Arts movement, Kōda Rohan's movement for native literature,[13] the folklore movement of men like Yanagita Kunio,[14] and the National Essence movement of Miyake Setsurei and Kuga Katsunan[15] were all examples of this. Even

---

that was launched by samurai dissidents of the Meiji government in 1874 and became a national movement in the 1880s. In 1981, the centennial of the formation of the Jiyūtō (Liberal party), the author launched a national movement in defense of the postwar "peace" constitution.

[13] Kōda (1867-1947), a novelist, essayist, and historian, is the subject of Chieko Mulhern, *Kōda Rohan* (Boston: Twayne Publishers, 1977).

[14] Yanagita (1875-1962) was an influential folklorist who devoted his life to an accumulation of details about the agricultural life he saw rapidly changing. His influence on the author will be apparent in later pages. He is the subject of Ronald A. Morse, "The Search for Japan's National Character and Distinctiveness: Yanagita Kunio (1875-1962) and the Folklore Movement" (Ph.D. diss., Princeton University, 1974).

[15] Miyake (1860-1945) and Kuga (1856-1907) were leading figures in a literary and cultural movement reacting against the extreme Westernization of the 1880s.

so, we must not forget that this confrontation with the West lacked the kind of frontal opposition that took place in India and China, since it approved the imperialist course Japan adopted; it degenerated into eclecticism and a confused pluralistic mélange of East and West.

I think these four elements (self, democracy, capitalism, and nationalism) are the principal components that make up modernity in all countries and not in Japan alone. General theory can be developed only after definite determination of the relationship of these elements to each other in other countries, in addition to an examination of the way those relationships posed logical inconsistencies.

For instance, when self and democracy were unable to mature because of the suppression of the movement for people's rights, the growth of capitalism and of nationalism became distorted; with that, in the Meiji period, came the emergence of the "emperor system" as the focus and node of this set of contradictions. We have to understand that those special characteristics that are cited as fundamental characteristics of Meiji culture—eclecticism, "house" (*ie*) consciousness, nativism, localism, naturalism, shortcomings in civic and in public consciousness—are all ultimately elements in the "emperor system as a spiritual and mental structure."

Consequently it is of vital importance to trace the historical process in which that emperor system was hammered out and then to examine the process whereby it penetrated the minds of the Japanese. Furthermore, in order to relativize it, and to overcome it from within, to avoid regarding it as something transcendental and foreordained, we have to examine carefully the subterranean consciousness of Japan's common people from early to recent times. That task in turn requires us to employ, however modestly, the findings of specialists in related disciplines like folklore, religion, sociology, geography, and anthropology.

(Translated by Ronald A. Morse)

· I ·

THE CREATION OF A GRASS-ROOTS CULTURE

When observed across the span of a century things appear vivid and clear, just as our globe seems a beautiful blue when it is seen from the moon.

Meiji liberated the natural talents of the Japanese people and allowed the nation's military and industrial strength to develop into the most powerful in Asia. On the other hand it also gave birth to desperate farming villages, to shockingly uncivilized conditions among the urban poor, and to the "emperor system as a spiritual structure." Its poison invaded the body of the masses to form a deeply rooted slave mentality.

Nonetheless, I wish to honor the subterranean glimmer and give a just appraisal of the latent powers of Japan and the exceptional talents of its people. That is why I begin this chapter with consideration of the silent world of folklore.

THE SILENT FOLK WORLD

Tōno Monogatari is a collection of stories that Yanagita Kunio (1875-1962) heard at first hand in 1909 from Sasaki Kyōseki, a man of Tōno village in the mountainous Kitakami region of Iwate Prefecture in northeastern Japan. Yanagita wrote that the stories were "recorded just as they were told to me, without my adding or deleting a single word or phrase." The book has great symbolic importance for the light it sheds on the dark side of the mental life of the Japanese masses at that time.[1]

Some may argue that Tōno is not an appropriate place to

[1] The translation by Ronald S. Morse, *The Legends of Tōno* (Tokyo: The Japan Foundation, 1975), is the source for the quotations in the text, which can be found on pp. 52-53. Original reprinted in *Teihon Yanagita Kunio shū*, 36 vols. (Tokyo: Chikuma shobō, 1963), vol. 4, pp. 5-54.

try to learn about the basic Japanese mentality because it is too remote from the capital, located as it is in a region sometimes referred to as the "Tibet of Japan." But in fact Tōno was by no means so remote culturally. A full four decades earlier, in late Tokugawa times, there had been "European houses in nearby Kamaishi and Yamada, Christianity was practiced secretly, suspected believers had been crucified even in the village"; local people talked of having seen Western men and women kiss each other. Greek Orthodox Christianity reached the area soon after the opening of Japan.

Since Tōno was that kind of place, new types of industries also entered with the coming of the Meiji period.

> Until a few years ago there was a matchstick factory on a rich farmer's property in Hanaremori. After dark a woman would come to the doorway of the shed, look at the people, and laugh in a scary, vulgar way. The workers could not endure the loneliness, and the factory was finally moved to Yamaguchi.

Modern people might dismiss such a person lightly, labeling her insane, but to the people of that time it was not so simple a matter. Meiji people still lived in a fantasy world inhabited by mysterious divine spirits, and the coexistence of such fantasies with modern factories was one characteristic of the period. Strange hermits or gods lived deep within the mountains, the women and children were often spirited away from their homes. In old houses there were *kami* called *zashiki warashi* who carried children off to dark places. Everywhere there were woods inhabited by wolves (*oinomori*) or goblins (*tengu mori*); an incident that occurred only four or five years before the recording of *Tōno Monogatari* (around 1904-1905), in which the wife of a man named Kikuchi Kikuzō of Wano was stopped by a *tengu* as she was descending from Fuefuki Pass early in the afternoon, is told as a true story. The work contains any number of blood-chilling tales like the one in which a snow woman leads children away on piercingly cold winter nights under a full moon, or the story about the mountain hag who goes to a village, eats the girl who had been left

20

alone to watch the house, and then dresses herself in the girl's skin and impersonates her.

With the beginnings of Meiji, the call for "civilization" was heard in all parts of the country; schools were established, a new education was instituted, rails were laid, and trains began to run; nevertheless for some time the world of fantasy continued to live alongside that of modernity. It would probably be safe to say that there was not a primary school student who did not believe that *kappa* (river sprites) lived in the streams that ran through their villages. Yanagita himself wrote:

> In my own town we referred to *kappa* as *gataro*, an abbreviation for *kawataro* (river boy). Because the houses of the village were situated near the Ichikawa River and its ferry landing, we never went two summers without flood damage, and until autumn set in, *gataro* were the sole topic of our conversations at the elementary school.[2]

It is perhaps natural that until quite recent times the villagers of Tōhoku worshiped such gods as *oshirasama*, *okunaisama*, *konsesama*, *gongesama*, and *kamado no kami sama*, for they watched over their livelihood. Of course those *kami* were not the absolute God of the Christian religion. For the Japanese people, gods have an existence like that of a fragrance; they are experienced unconsciously, like ancestral spirits intimately concerned with their own lives, or like the mountains and rivers that are permeated with their own blood and sweat. People expected that such friendly and intimate *kami* would actively protect them as their descendants. (The relationship between gods and human beings was one that was confirmed repeatedly through the yearly ceremonies that accompanied the rhythmic cycles of agricultural life.)

People died and became *kami*. But the ancestral spirits of the Japanese did not fly off into eternity the way imported teachings of Buddhism would have had it. They died but did not leave their lands after death; instead they watched their

[2] Yanagita, *Yōkai dangi* (1956). Reprinted in *Teihon Yanagita Kunio shū*, vol. 4, pp. 287-438.

descendants' endeavors from a vantage point in the nearby mountains and prayed for their diligence and prosperity. Therefore, said Yanagita, "everyone expected to be worshiped after death, and in order to make sure this would be the case people unquestioningly observed ancestral rites for their ancestors during their own lives."[3]

I cannot say with certainty that such ancient beliefs lived in the minds of all Japanese of the Meiji period. But the ideas were at least accepted by the great majority of the Japanese people, and they were clearly present even in the wishes of Yanagita Kunio, himself a Meiji man, when he wrote in his later years:

> Perhaps it is because I am a Japanese that I am so pleased by the idea of remaining at my native place even after having become a spirit. If possible, I would stay in this country forever, and from some spot, perhaps from the top of a small hill, watch as a given culture unfolds a little more beautifully, and as a field of learning contributes a little more to society.[4]

Of course the two sentiments are not quite the same thing. One sees in the words of Yanagita Kunio the restraints that come to someone with an understanding of modern science, comparative history, and world religion, for he couches his wishes in expressions like "if possible" and "a field of learning." For Yanagita as an individual, the maintenance and preservation of a house (ie) line was not the problem. The central idea of his science of folklore lay in the special significance that he attached to ancestor worship (family worship in which the name of the kami is appropriated and human beings themselves worshiped); he realized that this practice

---

[3] Yanagita, Shintō to minzokugaku (1943). Reprinted in Teihon Yanagita Kunio shū, vol. 10, pp. 315-96.

[4] Yanagita, Tamashii no yukue (1949). Reprinted in Teihon Yanagita Kunio shū, vol. 15, pp. 553-61. See also Yanagita's Senzo no hanashi (1945), translated by Fanny Hagin Mayer and Ishiwara Yasuya as About Our Ancestors: The Japanese Family System (Tokyo: UNESCO Series, Ministry of Education, 1970). Original reprinted in Teihon Yanagita Kunio shū, vol. 10, pp. 1-152.

was the way the Japanese people ensured eternal life for themselves.

Japanese do not see themselves as fully self-contained individuals distinct from the flow of life. They believe that a person is a link in an unbroken flow of life that connects ancestors and descendants. That the Japanese set such an especially high value on *ie* (house) is surely because this view of an unbroken flow was deeply nurtured by the regular rhythm of agricultural life.

In order to investigate mountain villages of the Meiji period, we frequently visit villages where old families still exist, and what we have observed there is the residue of what Yanagita referred to as "a place where *kami* and people meet." Just as he said, the ancestral spirits do not reside at the homes of their descendants, but they watch over them from a graveyard on a hill above the village. Their tutelary deity (*uji-gami*) is enshrined in a sacred grove in the center of the community. The ancestral spirits come down to the village on specific occasions like *Bon* (the summer festival of the dead) and New Year's to live with their families again, and then they go back, sent off by fires to light their way. In winter they go into the mountains and become *yama no kami* (mountain deities), and in spring they enter the rice fields as paddy deities (*ta no kami*). In this way they act to protect production. Such beliefs combined to form a general set of feelings that were embodied in annual observances, and they blended with the constant change of new customs. They were transmitted, certainly to Meiji, and frequently into Taishō and Shōwa times as well.

When I was a boy in the early years of the Shōwa period, I lived in a small country town only about sixty kilometers from Tokyo; I can testify that such worship of ancestral spirits was definitely alive. Revolutionary changes in sentiment came only after the Second World War, especially after the 1960s, when the farming villages were washed away by the wave of industrialization.

Because the Japanese people of the Meiji period worshiped the spirits of their ancestors, they took great care of their graves, and they were firmly determined to preserve and maintain the *ie* no matter what should happen. I feel it was these feelings that were at the root of the resolve with which they supported their disciplined "popular morality." Their willingness to perform grinding toil under such slogans as "diligence, frugality, harmony, honesty" was indispensable if they were to preserve and maintain the house and achieve "eternal life," and their sense of fulfillment in doing so must surely have been what made their lives worth living. People today who have lost this fundamental outlook and sentiment must find it very difficult to see the mind of the Meiji populace as anything other than banal and outmoded.

I recently put together the biography of a well-known political leader from the Santama district who was active during the 1880s as leader of the radical faction of the People's Rights *jiyū minken* movement.[5] It is said that in his later years he devotedly visited his ancestors' graves, and that he repeatedly told his eldest son Ren'ichi: "I will not pass on very much material wealth to my descendants, but just enough so that you will not neglect the proper rites for your ancestors. You must never forget this!" When I heard this story I felt all the closer to Yanagita Kunio's views.

One would expect this champion of people's rights to be a liberal thinker in the Western European tradition. What, then, would his early days have been like? Let me sketch briefly, as a point of reference, the boyhood of this man, Murano Tsune'emon (1859-1927), the fifth-generation head of a wealthy farmhouse of Notsuda village (present-day Machida city), Tama county, Musashi province. Filled as it was with faith and fantasy, I think that it tells us something about the life of common people in a farming village in the southern Kantō region around the time of the Meiji Restoration. As these former scenes of everyday life and culture recede into a distant past, how rapidly present-day Japanese forget them!

[5] Murano Ren'ichi and Irokawa Daikichi, *Murano Tsune'emon den*, 2 vols. (Tokyo: Chūō kōronsha, 1969).

FIRST STIRRING

When Murano Tsune'emon was still called by his childhood name Isokichi, his home and the village of Notsuda were a joyful world of play for a boy. On New Year's Day children like Isokichi would put on new clothing and make the round of New Year's calls. On the second day came *kakizome*, the first writing of the year. On the seventh they ate *ozōni*, a kind of soup with rice cakes, cooked with the seven spring herbs, and they would trim their fingernails in water with *nazuna*, one of the seven herbs, in order to avoid illness and injury.

Isokichi's family ran a pawnshop, and on the eleventh day of January they reopened the storehouse and began the new business year in a grand manner. On the fourteenth they would roast the *dango* rice cakes. Someone would cut and drag an oak tree so that Isokichi and the other children could stick *dango* on the branches, and then they would sit in the best room admiring the display. The red and white *mayudango*, resembling silkworm cocoons, seemed to brighten up the whole house. This was done to ensure a good harvest of cocoons, and it gave the children a sense that the New Year had really arrived.

For the children happy days came one after another. On the fifteenth of January came a treat of red-bean gruel; on the twentieth, ceremonies for Ebisu, the god of wealth; and on the twenty-eighth, ceremonies for Fudō, a Buddhist deity. On the morning of the twenty-eighth they visited the Fudō shrine of Takahata. As Isokichi's mother took him by the hand, he enjoyed watching the lively crowd of people in front of the shrine who were buying talismans, *Daruma* dolls, and other good-luck charms.

With February came *mamemaki*, the bean-scattering ceremony; *Hatsuuma*, a festival day of Inari, the god of grains; and the anniversary of the death of Buddha. Such occasions were always marked by the festive steamed rice with red beans. In March, there was *Momo no sekku*, or Doll's Festival, and *Higan*, the Buddhist service of the vernal equinox; in April,

25

there was the Buddha's birthday; in May, *Tango no sekku*, the Boy's Festival. In June came the celebration of the freshly planted rice paddies; in July, *Tanabata*, or the Festival of the Weaver Star; and in August, *Obon* and the rites for the *bodhisattva* Kannon. At some times the sacred grove of the village shrine resounded with the cheerful noises of young men and women; at others the paths around the old temple and through the cemetery overflowed with lanterns and brightly colored flowers.

In September there was the autumn festival of the patron deity of the village, when relatives would gather at Isokichi's home to enjoy rice cooked with red beans, *sekihan*, and fish and vegetable stew, *nishime*. Naughty boys like Isokichi took delight in watching the sacred dances (*kagura*), and the carrying of the portable shrine (*mikoshi*); however much they might be scolded, they never returned home until late at night.

The evening of the fifteenth day of the ninth lunar month was a time for moon viewing, *o-tsukimi*. Then came the autumnal equinox and the autumn rites for Ebisu. In this manner the sound of communal ceremonies went on and on, and no one knew the meaning of boredom.

In the area around Isokichi's home December 1 had always been called *kawa-bitari*, "soaked by the river," and on that day everyone stayed at home in fear of a great flood. Isokichi's house in particular was situated on the banks of the Tsurumi River, and each time the river overflowed its banks the flood waters rose to the floors of the house and sometimes even above them. Whenever there was a great flood the entire village would turn out in force to try to protect the water wheel shack, but for children like Isokichi it was just exciting to watch the bustle and confusion.

December 8 was the long awaited *yōkazō*. People were afraid of this day because they feared that a one-eyed old woman called *mekari-baba* might come to the village and spread terrible diseases. To ward her off, they would burn the wood of silverberry trees and put bamboo cages on the rooftops.

In other words, for children like Isokichi the village "home" was still a world filled with fantasy and folk belief.

The agrarian uprisings and urban riots that broke out at the time of the Meiji Restoration shook this rhythmic pastoral life of the people to its foundations. The ripples of those events extended through the surrounding areas for a considerable distance and brought new concepts of reform to the minds of the Japanese people. A demand for "renewal" (*yonaoshi*) rose up as if in response to the slogan of "Imperial Restoration" from above. Soon after, as people were confronted with the deceptiveness of the "restoration" of the Meiji government, that demand for change was transformed into a cry for struggle against the government.

For example, I would remind you of the well-known comic entertainer who said, "Friends, listen to me! The Court is a fraud! It sounded fine on Takamagahara, but here on earth it's all a fraud."[6] But although there are examples of this sort, we have to admit that there was more usually an ominous silence on the part of the many millions of people who did not join in those uprisings.

The study of folklore was the first to provide leverage in this area. On the face of it, the silent world appeared to be asleep, as if lost in endless and monotonous repetition of agricultural life and its customs. But the careful observer can find considerable evidence that within the apparent slumber of the pastoral scene, changes toward the modern age—however quiet—were definitely taking place.

As various small events occurred one after another, an excitement developed in our villages. The rhythm of farming life, locked into the same tempo for hundreds of years, began to change—first after the coming of Perry's black ships, and again after the commencement of trade with foreign countries and the free flow of goods within the country. Especially after the establishment of the new government, village administrators were charged with carrying out numerous matters re-

[6] Takamagahara, the "High Plain of Heaven," populated by gods in traditional mythology.

27

lated to the national administration: tax laws were changed, new land values were fixed, new schools had to be established, and people were free and even encouraged to move. It had the effect of rocks successively thrown into a pond, rippling a surface that until then had been still. If one considers that the 170,000 towns and villages of the early Meiji era were consolidated into approximately 12,000 within a little over ten years, one can imagine the intensity of change.

Of course centuries-old folk customs and practices could not be completely transformed by jolts from without. Such change had to come from within, in hidden and subtle form. What facilitated and stimulated it from without was the Meiji Restoration of the village, village "civilization and enlightenment."[7]

For example, a railroad track would be laid down near a village, and then train service would begin. Soon rumors would spread that "in the middle of the night a badger races along the rails imitating the sounds of a train." Such rumors arose in all parts of the country. It may be difficult for people today to accept this, but the "sound" that the Japanese people heard then for the first time was the new and unprecedented roar of machine civilization, and this aroused in their ears all kinds of auditory hallucinations.

The same thing happened when telegrams were first delivered. People said that a badger would stand at the gates of houses and call out "Telegram!" imitating the deliveryman. When we think about it, villages of the feudal period must have been unimaginably quiet; it was a lonely and tranquil world in which one could hear a pin drop. Perhaps it is not particularly strange that people claimed to be able to hear the sound of ants wrestling under their verandas.

Nevertheless, trains that raced along, belching black smoke and making a deafening roar, provoked immense excitement among the ordinary people of Japan. They signaled the coming of the age of a spectacular steel culture and brought about

---

[7] *Bummei kaika*, "Civilization and enlightenment," was the slogan of change in Japan's metropolitan and intellectual circles in the early Meiji years.

a complete change in people's view of the landscape. For the railroads, which drew a straight and willful line of steel through the flat and monotonous countryside, encouraged people to stand up against nature and stimulated a new sort of consciousness of beauty. It may not be quite appropriate to say flatly that "railroads gave people courage." Probably one should say that the Japanese people accepted this indispensable tool of modern civilization in a most positive and creative way. There are, after all, tribes on this earth that still reject such civilization on the basis of religious taboos and emotional aversion.

The Japanese people recognized intuitively the creative direction of a modern civilization that seeks to reconstruct nature for its own purposes in the shape of these powerful trains. The locomotive was the symbol of that civilization, and it became the object of everlasting longing for Japanese children.[8] Those railroads were laid down one after another while a network of new highways was created. Such developments brought change to villages previously closed off from the world; they led to the formation of new market towns, and they became a force that freed people to seek adventure in unknown lands.

Subtle Transformations Toward Modernity

When people left the village and broadened their knowledge of different places, a revolutionary change occurred in their perception of their "native place." Pilgrimages to the Grand Shrine of Ise by millions of people during the Edo period, and especially group pilgrimages by the hundreds of religious organizations that formed during the later years of the Edo period, nurtured the people's curiosity and gave them valuable experiences. People took pleasure in comparing their own villages with other places, and they gradually abandoned

[8] Nakano Shigeharu, *Kisha no kamataki* (1937). Reprinted in *Nakano Shigeharu zenshū*, 19 vols. (Tokyo: Chikuma shobō, 1959), vol. 2, pp. 245-330. It is worth adding that these lines were written at a time when the vanishing steam locomotives were no less romantic in Japan as a symbol of the Meiji past.

the traditional view whereby their home village was ordained by heaven and could not be changed. They recognized that it could be improved. A large number of respected farmers and so-called *sekenshi* ("men of the world") holding such notions appeared in various parts of the country during the period from Tempō (1830-1844) to the early years of the Meiji era, and that proved of decisive advantage for the modernization of Japan.[9]

But it was not easy for people to abandon their native villages and go out into the world (*seken*). This is because, as Yanagita Kunio emphasized repeatedly, "From time immemorial our parents held to the belief that unless they received memorial rites from blood relatives after their death they could not find happiness in the next world," and "they prayed for the long continuation of their house because they considered it essential for peace in that world where all must someday go." Moreover, this belief was so strong that one could say "it was an unspoken promise among relatives."

According to Yanagita's aesthetic intuition, the Japanese did not by nature accept the law of the cycle of transmigration in its Indian form. They did not believe that a person would belong to another and different world immediately after death. Instead, they thought that the spirits of their ancestors, though invisible, were at rest in the mountains, rivers, and fauna of their native places, still watching longingly over life in a world in which they had once participated. From a Buddhist standpoint, they would probably be considered "wandering spirits." Consequently, the "Buddha" (*hotoke-sama*) on household altars in Japan does not refer to Sakyamuni (*oshaka-sama*). It is a general term for ancestral spirits, familiar beings who return to their former homes each year at the times of *Bon* and *Higan* and who look after their family members.

Buddhism taught that when man died he could go to heaven through the salvation of *hotoke*, or Buddha. Thus the Japanese people came to call the dead *hotoke*. But despite the teachings of the world religion, the Japanese were simply un-

---

[9] Miyamoto Tsuneichi, *Wasurerareta Nihonjin* (Tokyo: Miraisha, 1960).

able to abandon the indigenous belief in ancestral spirits that they had held from time immemorial. For that reason, Buddhist monks preached of the salvation of "wandering spirits" and introduced the images of the bodhisattva *Jizō*, the Buddha *Dainichi Nyōrai*, and the bodhisattva *Kannon* into the life of the people. Even so the monks were unable to shake the Japanese people free of their Japanized *Bon* ceremonies or of the belief that they lived together with their tutelary deity, the *ubusunagami*.

Within such a deeply rooted native belief, "many gentle heads of families felt themselves simply one link in a long chain, and they were always wavering at the crossroads of obligation and emotion." But Meiji civilization brought ever-greater pressures to bear on family heads, forcing them to set up branch families weakening the authority of the main family, and causing domestic discord; in the end the family organization was transformed into individual social units of capitalistic farming villages.

> A young man sets a goal before himself
> And leaves his ancestral home.
> Should he fail in his studies
> He will never again return, even though he die.
> How can the village graveyard be the only resting place?
> There are green hills for men everywhere.

There are probably few poems that inspired Meiji youth as much as this one by the monk Gesshō. A motif of strong defiance rings loudly in the line "How can the village graveyard be the only resting place?" This was a determined rebellion against the traditional folk practices that affirmed the supreme importance of continuing the family line. Moreover, this sentiment was a call for revolution of consciousness, not only for the former samurai (*shizoku*) and the intelligentsia, but even for ordinary people. With this willingness to "go to work wherever it may be; be prepared for any resting place," without such a revolution of consciousness, the Japanese would never have been willing to embark on great ventures to other provinces and even to foreign lands. People so motivated

31

burned with enthusiasm to leave their ancestral homes behind and set out for new frontiers, where they became the
founding fathers of new houses.

In his well-known work on social history, *Meiji-Taishō shi,
Sesō hen* (1931), Yanagita Kunio was able, without naming a
single individual, to grasp with penetrating insight the signs
of modern transformation by showing changes in food, clothing, shelter, customs, and social conditions from his study
and through miscellaneous news articles. Following his lead,
I, too, would like to sketch Japan's transformation toward the
modern age in terms of the life of the people, that is, modern
culture itself. In that way I hope to find the basis for a view
of Meiji culture that is focused not on the intellectual elite
but on a truly popular and national scale.

Let us begin with food, clothing, and shelter. During the
Edo period, with the development of cotton production and
indigo dyeing, the clothing of the common people shifted "from
hemp to cotton," and through the experience of "the fragrance of deep blue and the feel of cotton," this development
fostered in Japanese men and women a keener sensitivity to
things. The development of indigo dyeing in particular proved
beneficial in bringing to flower a sensitivity to color that was
developing among the masses. Free use of colors had been
forbidden by sumptuary regulations geared to social status
under feudalism, but when rules about "forbidden colors" were
removed at the beginning of Meiji, people's powers of imagination regarding color developed to a dazzling degree. It is
said that Wada Sanzō, a Meiji Western-style painter, used
five hundred different colors, but modern industry and the
liberalization of social status brought the possibility of a manifold increase in that number. Art historians should examine
the ways in which this change enriched and brightened the
imaginative world of the common man.

A clear change was also apparent in the culture of food.
The development of charcoal-making techniques beginning in
late Tokugawa times opened the way for wider use of charcoal
and brought a minor revolution in the life of the common
people. In the first place, the right to use the fire of the

32

sunken hearth (*irori*) and the cooking stove (*kamado*), which had been under the strict supervision of the head of the household, was now more dispersed and became apportioned to several members of the house. The sons of the house were now able to take some of the charcoal and retire to rooms where they had their own brazier (*kotatsu*). Similarly it became possible for the women to gain independence from the control of the fire by the god of the hearth (*Kōjin-sama*), and from the mistress of the house, by using small pots and casseroles for cooking.

It is often said that modern Japanese food culture was stimulated by imported European and American culture, but this is superficial and mistaken. Thanks to the increase in productivity in earlier years, small pots had become independent of the hearth, the central monopoly of fire had become dispersed, and culinary techniques had become widely shared. With the gradual collapse of control by "the house," the modernization of food culture, too, was able to progress. Various shops, from those on the major streets of the towns that sold boiled noodles (*nabeyaki udon*) to open-air food stalls, or shops specializing in buckwheat noodles (*soba*) or (*oden*) and even local delicacies, could now become part of the daily life of ordinary people, and they multiplied throughout the country. These developments brought a tremendous variety of flavors and ingredients to the Japanese diet.

Raw fish (*sashimi*), which was to become a favorite Japanese delicacy, started out as a local dish among fishermen of the Kantō region; that it later became so popular throughout the country was due to the development of the brewing industries of soy sauce and rice vinegar. The diffusion of foods like hand-rolled *sushi* would also have been impossible without a constant flow of goods to the marketplace, the production of large quantities of the necessary ingredients, and the production and refinement of polished rice. Again, within the space of only half a century following the Restoration, Japanese consumption of sugar and salt rose dramatically. This was probably due to improvements in and popular acceptance of confections and pickles. The making of European-style cakes by the Japanese, together with a variety of richly flavored Japanese confection, provides excellent evidence of the natural gift of the Japanese for the art of living. It is the same with their talent for making dozens of varieties of salted pickles out of plants ranging from vegetables and mountain greens to wild grasses or the tender buds of trees. In addition to the salted pickles, the Japanese exercised an unparalleled talent in the art of flavoring, with their pickled vegetables (*kasuzuke* and *narazuke*), their vegetables, meat and fish preserved in bean paste (*miso*), and mixed pickles (*kongōzuke*). They became the world's leading devotees of pickles.

Yanagita Kunio wrote with some pride:

> With a few exceptions, most of our traditional foods, which even in ancient times numbered in the hundreds, still preserve their original form. Several hundred new dishes were added to these in the Meiji and Taisho periods. In terms of ingredients and methods of preparation, I doubt that there is a country in the world with the variety of food and drink that Japan has.[10]

What about dwellings? It is rare to find a people as awkward as the Japanese in their manner of urban living and as unskillful in city planning. It has been the unanimous opinion of foreigners that Japanese houses were poor, flimsy structures, much like disordered storage sheds. And indeed, I too have to agree with that opinion where contemporary Japan is concerned.

People in the Edo period, however, had their own ingenious way of living and worked out a set of public moral standards for urban life. With the exception of shopkeepers and their families, for example, most city dwellers of those times lived in multifamily tenement houses, but over time they perfected a form of social training that made it possible for them to live contentedly through cooperation with their neighbors despite their cramped and flimsy dwellings. For example, they had the practice of fire watch and patrol to

[10] Yanagita, *Meiji-Taishō shi*, vol. 4: *Sesōhen* (Tokyo: Asahi, 1931), p. 16.

protect and maintain the buildings they shared. They cooperated in cleaning streets and wells, and a special etiquette
applied to the public bathhouses. In this way a code of public
morals emerged for this tenement society, which then became known as *seken dōtoku*, or social or public morality based
on mutual relations and obligation. (Urban dwellers came to
refer to their immediate environment as *seken*, "the world.")
Edo period fiction, drama, and comic stories mirror that society.

This *seken dōtoku* of the cities might have become a foundation for modern urban self-government and morality, but
with the coming of Meiji the conditions permitting such developments were destroyed. Nearly all the urban family heads
were either ruined or forced to move away, and in their place
great numbers of country people poured into the cities from
all directions to become the new residents. These newcomers
brought the energy of the countryside with them, but because they had never been taught the rules for urban social
life they lacked the requisite self-discipline. As a result the
cities developed anarchic conditions, for freedom was one-
sidedly taken to mean self-indulgence. Hence it was only natural that concepts like urban planning never took root. Yet
even if they had, geographic and historic contrasts would have
been decisive in ruling out Japanese equivalents of the kind
of civic consciousness found in the self-governing cities of
Western Europe.

The people of this island country, blessed with gentle
neighbors like Korea and China, had been able to live peaceful lives and maintain their independence for a thousand years,
during which they had no need for the social discipline that
comes from the necessity for self-defense against external
enemies. This was in decided contrast to the experience of
the peoples of Europe. The Japanese people lacked the communal necessity to defend themselves with walled cities the
way continental people did, and they had no real experience
of that kind of fighting. That resulted in clear-cut differences,
differences that were revealed in everyday life. For Western
Europeans to live in a city meant being willing to fight on

the walls in times of emergency and to accept all sorts of daily inconveniences as well as rules and regulations of collective life in anticipation of emergencies. Acceptance of such agreements was the premise on which the freedom of Europe's cities was secured, and those residents could never develop the kind of selfish indulgence that Japanese city dwellers did.

The main reasons that the morality and thought characteristic of the free cities of European civic society did not develop very far in Japan are probably related to the kind of conditioning I have mentioned. But as a more immediate cause, the actions taken by the government after the Meiji Restoration have to bear some of the blame, for these removed the foundations supporting not only the *seken dōtoku* of Edo commoners but also the customs of communal self-government that had grown up in farming villages. The stirring of modern self-government that was forming within commoner life patterns in Edo cities was frustrated and arrested. It is essential that we clarify how and by whom that was done.

When capitalism, that monster of modern times, was reinforced by the Industrial Revolution and began to show its true selfishness, Japanese cities fell into almost irrevocable confusion and disorder. They witnessed odious struggles rising out of a raw desire for power, mercenary commercialism, and naked self-interest. For newly arrived settlers the big city was a place to seek their fortunes, and those who loved the atmosphere of the old towns were driven back into narrow alleys. This was a frequent theme in works of Meiji literature. Recently Japanese citizens have begun to call for solutions to urban problems, but the underlying reason that local governance in Japan has been manipulated for such a long time by landowners, bureaucrats, and grafters without ever maturing into real local autonomy for the residents is to be found within Japanese history.[11]

And what of the farming villages? Europeans referred to Japan as "the country of paper windows (*shōji*)," but in fact it

[11] Irokawa, *Samazama na Meiji hyakunen* and *Meiji no seishin* (Tokyo: Kōka shobō, 1968).

was only after the beginning of the Meiji period that these came to be used in farmhouses. Until that time windows were covered by wooden shutters and straw matting, and the interiors of houses were completely dark. Farmers spent the greater part of the day out of doors.

The revolution in illumination, first from "shuttered windows to paper windows," and then to "plate glass," brought a profound change to the consciousness of the farming population. Paper was an expensive commodity for the farmers, and it was because of universal education that it made its appearance on the windows of their houses. From about the middle of the Meiji period, Japanese-style paper that had been used by children for lessons in writing, covered with their syllabary exercises *i ro ha ni ho he to*, came to be seen on sliding panels and windows everywhere. The brighter interior of the home stimulated the desire to remodel it and heightened people's aesthetic awareness of household furniture and other fixtures of everyday life. In particular, the delicate softness of the light that passed through Japanese paper influenced people's psychological makeup to no small degree.

"Large buildings like farmhouses grew brighter from corner to corner, and that suggested the possibility of creating partitions within the house." These, in turn, provided young people with a space where they could read quietly, off by themselves; before long "they came to know and think about things that the heads of their families did not know. The little rooms that were their minds came to be subdivided in the same way."[12]

The change in windows and the general acceptance of them accompanied the development of modern industrial production. Simultaneously, the illumination industry grew, progressing rapidly from paper-covered lamps using rape seed oil to oil lamps, and on to electric lamps. These changes pushed back the boundaries of peoples' mental world, accelerated the breakup of the household (*ie*), and assisted in the birth of a modern individual consciousness in everyday life.

[12] Yanagita, *Sesōhen*, p. 88.

Roof design was liberated as well. The Tokugawa feudal system had imposed status limitations on the use of roof tiles. Ordinary people could use tiles only on the ridge and a portion of the eaves of their roof, and almost all private houses were either shingled or thatched with straw. Lifting these restrictions in Meiji changed the shape of private houses completely. Tiles not only made it possible to design windows that got more light through a gentle roof slope, but they also brought a feeling of liberation from the weight of nature. The development of reddish tiles (*shioyakigawara*, tiles with a shiny salt glaze) in particular brought a new and cheerful look to houses, even in the forlorn and somber greenery along the Japan Sea Coast. That in itself is surely one of the marks of Meiji culture.

By the Meiji period, a traveler looking out the window of a local train could see a rich variety of color in the plantings around the farmhouses. There were flowering trees like peach and apricot, and flowers like sweet oleander, hibiscus, hydrangea, and crepe myrtle. Added to these in the spring were strongly accented and brilliant colors like the purple of Chinese milk vetch that blanketed entire fields, or the golden yellow of fields of rape blossoms, or the dazzling green of the mulberry bushes. These scenes symbolized the agricultural commodities of Meiji and even became the theme of an elementary school song, "The Spring Brook Gurgles On."

Once farmers were free to plant what they wished after the Meiji Restoration and commodities could be distributed rapidly all over the country, flowering plants also spread; before long the whole country overflowed with European flowers like tulips, gladioli, carnations, and pansies, and farm villages brightened more and more. After Meiji, Japanese villages were patterned with a variety of colors so rich as to be almost unrecognizable. Without this chromatic change in the life of the people, it would be hard to explain Meiji romantic and naturalistic literature with its frequent reference to color.

The coloring in the nature poems of Shimazaki Tōson and Kunikida Doppo, or in the romantic "new style" poetry with its awakened consciousness of self, would probably have been inconceivable without the unconscious premises of Meiji popular culture. This relationship is obvious, of course, in "Sketches of the Chikuma River," but it extends to the internal features of landscape paintings by members of groups like the Meiji Fine Arts Association and the White Horse Association. When we look at paintings such as Asai Chū's "Harvest" or "Rice Paddy Ridges in Spring," we can sense the reflection of light that prevailed in farming villages in the early Meiji decades. The only difference is that in Tōson's "Sketches" there is a strong tone of sentimentality that is absent in Asai's "Paddy Ridges." Is it then possible that differences in the sense of color in Meiji literary and artistic works were related to the intensity of the artist's ego?[13]

The change in Japanese views of landscape in the Meiji period was surely brought about by more than a heightened knowledge of natural science and the influence of Shiga Shigetaka's famous *On Landscape* (*Nihon fūkei ron*, 1894). The traditional, restricted focus on standard scenic spots and the aesthetics based on Japan's "three scenic places" gradually fell victim to the liberation of color in everyday life and the changes in productive labor we have examined. It was the intellectuals who first noticed this and articulated it.

The hunger of the people for beauty in the Meiji period is apparent not only in their curiosity about things Western but also in their interest in parks and places of historic importance. Even fortified castles, the strongholds of domination of feudal lords who had held the power of life and death until recently, were suddenly made public or private property, and they became objects of sightseeing for people who were now declared equal. People devised enjoyable occasions like cherry-blossom viewing in the spring, dancing in the summer, and moon viewing in the autumn, in the gardens of the castles of lords whose samurai might well have decapitated their forebears for trespassing.

In these pages I have tried to grasp the underlying tone of

[13] Shimazaki Tōson (1872-1943) was a poet and novelist who established new forms of verse and pioneered the naturalist novel in Japan.

the people's transformation toward modern life. In my haste, I may have painted too rosy a picture, and I may have taken up some aspects too abstractly. For the people, "modern" cannot have been so simple and pleasant, or so pastoral. Far from it; seen differently, their steps toward the "modern" meant change to a new form of slavery, one accompanied by previously unimaginable pain and anxiety of isolation. Especially during the last half of the Meiji period—after the suppression of the early democratic movement and after the firmly established control of the emperor system, the bourgeoisie, and the landlord class—"modernity" was something that hemmed in the people with greater oppression and suffering than ever.

We should now reexamine popular culture from a historical standpoint and ask whether or not the sufferings and the creativity of intellectuals at the top of society derived from changes in the lives of ordinary people below them.

A SICKNESS OF SOUL

The Meiji intellectual who was probably the most keenly aware of this problem was, once again, Yanagita Kunio. His *Tōno Monogatari*, written in 1910, can be interpreted as implied criticism of naturalism, the school of literature that was then fashionable among the intelligentsia. Similarly, I think that his "Life in the Mountains" (*Yama no jinsei*), published in 1926, with its depiction of the Japanese people alienated from and crushed by modernization, can be seen as a methodological criticism of the Marxism that was so popular at that time. In other words, the people whose image Yanagita portrayed had to shoulder problems that neither Japanese naturalism nor communism could resolve.

In one story, a construction worker lost his way in the vicinity of Obanazawa in Yamagata Prefecture and found himself deep in the mountains, where he unexpectedly discovered a family of three—a couple and their child—at the bottom of a ravine, which seemed a very unlikely place for anyone to live. The family was living in a shabby cabin they had built, but all three of them were completely naked. The woman felt

40

a painful yearning for human beings and asked the construction worker all sorts of things about her village. The husband "seemed to feel great resentment against existing society, and had gone into the mountains determined never to return to the plains below." It is said that when the construction worker visited the cabin again sometime later, he found the woman had been tied up and beaten.[14]

The next story is one that Yanagita heard from Nitobe Inazō,[15] and it has the ring of truth. A man had gone to hunt in a remote mountain area of Ninoe-gun in Iwate Prefecture and was camping there when another man suddenly came out of the woods. Shortly the first man recognized the other as a teacher from the village elementary school who had disappeared several years before. The teacher gave the following account: he had felt the desire to go into the mountains for no particular reason and had run away from his home. Living in an utterly different manner from the people in the valley below, he was on his way to becoming a complete hermit when one day he came upon a hunter's lunch. After eating the lunch, he was suddenly filled with a longing for the taste of grain. From then on life in the mountains became increasingly unpleasant for him, and he yearned for the company of people; finally he had come out of the back country.

Why did Yanagita collect so many stories of this nature? He insisted that the quest for new knowledge alone is not true learning, and he asserted: "It is wrong if we do not observe, record, and study the deeds, thoughts, and experiences of the majority of our fellow countrymen over the past several thousand years. Such an undertaking is *extremely* necessary as preparation for future *social reconstruction*. I think I have shown this by the examples obtained through field work." But the examples he obtained through his field work were not accepted by the archivists who were working

[14] Yanagita, *Yama no jinsei*, Pt. 3 (1926). Reprinted in *Teihon Yanagita Kunio shū*, vol. 4, pp. 55-186; Pt. 3, 63-65.

[15] Nitobe (1862-1933), agronomist, educator, and moralist, with a graduate education in America, was widely known as an interpreter of Japan to the non-Japanese world.

for social liberation in the Shōwa period, simply because they seemed to lack theory and method. This is most unfortunate.

Yanagita's *Yama no jinsei* nevertheless sounded a warning about the fact that millions of people were in a state of mental and spiritual confusion, unable to cope with the violent changes occurring in Meiji society and in their daily lives. Put in today's terms, it was a matter of people "running away and vanishing into thin air." Even in the late Edo and early Meiji years there were many people who fell into a state of neurosis. Because people were often regarded as possessed by a fox (*kitsune-tsuki*) it is said that a new profession came into existence—that of *Inari-kyōshi*—the purpose of which was to exorcise the spirit that had taken possession of the people.

Even Deguchi Onisaburō (born Ueda Kisaburō, 1871-1948), who is sometimes called one of the giants of modern Japan, was an *Inari-kyōshi*. Born the son of a poor farmer, he tried his hand at various jobs, from substitute teacher to farm servant, assistant to a veterinarian, herdsman, and even vigilante before he became a doctor of people's souls (*Inari-kyōshi*) and met Deguchi Nao, the founder of the Ōmotokyō cult.[16]

Onisaburō once composed a poem in the manner of Takuboku[17] that gives a good feel for the culture of the impoverished farming population:

A farmer's houseboy,
Driven from morning to evening—
How like an ox I am!

Had he not been born in Meiji he might have ended his days as some kind of swashbuckler, but it is unlikely that he would have had the chance to become a leader of the people. The story goes that when Onisaburō was fourteen years old, he

[16] Deguchi (1871-1948) was the organizer of the Ōmotokyō cult that had been founded by Nao in the years after World War I. He was arrested and imprisoned for *lèse-majesté* and made his peace with Japanese expansion for a time thereafter, only to predict defeat and disaster for Japan. He was a charismatic, unpredictable, and popular figure.

[17] Ishikawa Takuboku (1886-1912), despite a short life, had a major impact on poetry through use of modern language and development of social themes.

thrust a bamboo spear smeared with human feces at his despotic home room teacher, thereby driving the teacher to resign; he was then invited to be the substitute teacher. Such an event would probably have been inconceivable had it not taken place during the period of the People's Rights movement. In that respect, the benefits of Meiji civilization accrued wonderfully, even to children of poor farmers. Deguchi Nao, the founder of Ōmotokyō and the one who discovered this great man Onisaburō, had survived the depths of poverty during the upheaval of the early years of Meiji.

Deguchi Nao (1837-1918) was the daughter born to a hard-drinking carpenter of Fukuchiyama Basin in western Japan. At the age of eleven she left home to become an indentured servant and later married a carpenter, but he was a lazy alcoholic, and as a result she suffered a great deal. In the end her husband became paralyzed and was bedridden for three years before his death. Surviving him were eight children; counting those who died, Nao mothered eleven children. Working as a rag picker, she endured the terrible depression of the 1880s. Her daily life was one to make her sweat blood; as if that were not enough, her two eldest daughters ran away from home; her eldest son attempted suicide and then disappeared; and the second son, on whom she most relied, died in battle. Most people confronted by such a series of disasters would have given up, but Nao not only endured but also remained honest and sincere and did nothing to degrade herself. Such a person is truly worthy of being revered as a leader of the people and has the qualifications to be a physician of people's souls.

At times of upheaval, history simultaneously produces people who are ailing in spirit as well as men and women who can heal them. The people who rose up in revolt, those who were possessed by foxes, and those who "ran away and vanished into thin air" were the same ordinary people who normally lived next door to each other, men and women whose personalities contained remarkable, and often contradictory, potentialities.

THE IMPACT OF THE RESTORATION
ON MOUNTAIN VILLAGES

In the summer of 1968, I went with the students under my supervision on a field trip to a certain mountain village in Nishi Tama county, approximately sixty kilometers from the center of Tokyo. To get to the village one has to transfer at Tachikawa to the Musashi-Itsukaichi line, get off at the last stop, and then walk about two and a half miles along a road that follows a stream into the mountains. It is a remote village of approximately twenty houses, and it was once called Fukasawa-mura in Tama-gun, Musashi-no-kuni. The village, whose livelihood is forestry, is exactly as its name connotes, a "deep gorge" (*sawa*). It is said that in the Meiji period it took nearly an entire day to reach Tokyo from there.

I had been engaged in historical study of the farming and mountain villages of eastern Japan for more than ten years, but I had never come upon historical materials as important as those I discovered in the storehouse of the Fukasawa family in this Fukasawa village (now a part of Itsukaichi-machi). The place is now almost in ruins; there is no trace of either the main house or the outer buildings, and all that remains is the small storehouse, a gate, and a graveplot. Moreover, the storehouse itself was in terrible condition and on the verge of collapse; a part of the roof had fallen, the walls were crumbling, and the door was broken. For that reason, many of the documents had disintegrated to the point where they were almost trash. Yet from among them we were able to dig out, one by one, bundles of documents arranged in proper sequence dating back to the mid-Edo period, with particularly startling records from the period of the People's Rights movement.

For example, we discovered in this long-forgotten storehouse a draft of a people's constitution consisting of 204 articles. We discovered a petition urging the early establishment of a national assembly; only two or three other such examples exist today in Japan. Furthermore, we found several hundred

44

The Fukasawa storehouse in Itsukaichi, where documents
relating to the events described were found.

books that showed how excited the people there were about
learning and politics, as well as more than ten memoranda,
bylaws, and so forth relating to liberal political associations.
Through these materials we learned that the village leaders
and the men who drafted that constitution, hitherto unknown
to history, were without exception family men: farmers, merchants, and school teachers—in other words, "commoners"
with deep ties to the life of the people.

The draft of the people's constitution was based on the discussions of thirty members of two associations composed of
public-minded men living in towns and villages of the area:

45

the Itsukaichi Gakujutsu Tōronkai (The Itsukaichi Learning and Study Discussion Society) and the Gakugei Kōdankai (The Lecture-Discussion Society for Arts and Science). The man who wrote the draft was a Chiba Takusaburō, who was an associate teacher at Itsukaichi Kannō Gakkō (Itsukaichi School for the Encouragement of Talents), an elementary school of the area. This man's eventful life is fascinating, and I will discuss him in detail in Chapter III as "a Japanese Faust."

What first surprised me in the course of this field work were two discoveries: that the impact of the Meiji Restoration had reached even such a remote mountain village (for the village is located far from the main highway; houses stand only here and there along a mountain path inaccessible even to a horsedrawn coach, and even that path ends at the wall of the overwhelming mass of Oku Tama mountains), and that the shock caused by the coming of Perry's black ships had aroused a profound sense of nationalism not only among the national leaders and patriots but even among ordinary people at the lower levels of society.

For example, there was Fukasawa Naomaru, who was the head of the household at that time. The eldest son of Saemon, a village head, he was born in 1811. From as early as 1854, he had carefully copied down in notebooks not only the complete text of the Treaty of Friendship and Amity between Japan and the United States but also texts of similar treaties, as well as the commercial treaties, that Japan had signed with Holland, Russia, Great Britain, Germany, and France. This should surely inspire in us feelings of reverence, especially when we compare it with the attitude of today's intellectuals and students, who shout "Smash the Security Pact!" without even having read it, to say nothing of copying out the entire text.

Naomaru's father, according to the records, was a *gōshi* ("rustic samurai"), until the 1850s, and one of a group known as *sennin dōshi* (one thousand like-minded men). According to a record of the Edo period, he went by the name Shimizu, but the family register of the early Meiji years gives his name as Fukasawa and notes his status as *heimin* (commoner) and his occupation as "farmer." Nevertheless, he was just one inhabitant of a small village under the jurisdiction of the *daikan* of Musashi province. At that time it was a serious crime for inhabitants of a domain to discuss matters relating to the affairs of government. That in such times these people resolutely copied various international agreements article by article surely indicates the great degree to which concern about national affairs had spread among them. We can probably say that the path taken by someone like Fukasawa Naomaru, from the copying of entire texts of treaties through the final touches on a draft of a people's constitution, was of a single consistency and devotion. What moves us in our investigation of such historical records in farming villages is the knowledge that we are actually touching the hidden passions of these men, and our conviction that this passion was a driving force behind the evolution of Japanese society and the creation of a new culture.

Another surprise in this investigation was the empirical confirmation of the fact that the movement toward a modern consciousness and thought in Japan was advancing steadily, deep within mud-mired traditions at the lower levels of society. This took place through people's original and independent reinterpretations of ruling class thought, through a radical regeneration of tradition based on the experiences of ordinary people. Western thought merely provided the catalyst for that reconsideration. This conclusion differs from the assumption of our sagacious intellectuals, whose thought patterns, of course, derive from very different bases that condition their assumptions. They fail to see this because the steps people took toward modernization were obliterated midway by the collapse of the People's Rights movement, and thereafter that movement was reduced to a tremor beneath the surface. Nevertheless, this plunge from the main current of history to an undercurrent does not negate the importance of popular progress toward modernity or justify our ignoring it. I think that we have demonstrated this through our present investigations.[18]

[18] This point has already been developed by Ichii Saburō in *Dentōteki Kakushin shisōron josetsu* 1 (October 1969).

When he was young, Fukasawa Naomaru held the additional post of Shintō priest at a small shrine in his community called Anazawa Tenjin. Therefore it was natural that he should have had an interest in both Japanese and Chinese studies. His eldest son, Gompachi, also seems to have been familiar with the works of classical Chinese literature. Of course, at this time the study of Chinese literature and poetry was still a normal undertaking for young men in the farm village; during the first two decades of Meiji, Chinese poetry was extremely popular in farming villages. Gompachi had a special love of Chinese poetry, and during his short life of twenty-nine years he composed close to seven hundred poems, leaving behind seventeen hand-sewn volumes of them.

Why did this father and son make two copies of *Sakura Sōgorō shōden* (A Brief Biography of Sakura Shōden)? Why did they open with the line: "Is it really true that the concept of popular rights is a recent import from the West and there was not even a seed of it in our country before this?" Why did Gompachi copy out *Ōshio Heihachirō no gekibun* (The Manifesto of Ōshio Heihachirō) on the back of his notebook? Why did he copy the entire text of *Rukonroku* (A Record of My Soul), the last testament of Yoshida Shōin? And why was he attracted by Kumoi Tatsuo's *Zetsumei no shi* (My Last Poem)?[19]

What was the reason that this same father and son avidly read Fukuzawa Yukichi's *Sekai kunizukushi* (Countries of the World) and *Gakumon no susume* (The Encouragement of Learning); that they underscored in red ink *Minyaku yakkai*, Nakae Chōmin's translation of Rousseau's *Social Contract*; and, finally, why did they come to participate in the movement

[19] Each reference is to a voice of protest in Tokugawa Japan. Sakura Sōgorō was executed in the seventeenth century for speaking to the needs of the farmers in the village he ruled as headman; Ōshio Heihachirō resigned office, gave away his possessions, and finally organized a putsch to relieve suffering in Osaka in 1837; Yoshida Shōin was executed for opposing the shogunate's indifference to the emperor's wishes and organizing an assassination plan in 1859; and Kumoi Tatsuo, who will appear again below, led a rebellion against the early Meiji government in 1870.

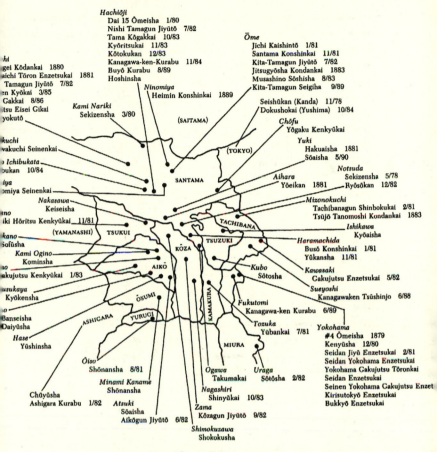

FIGURE 1
Distribution of Minken Organizations
in Kanagawa Prefecture

for the establishment of a national assembly and in the drafting of a people's constitution? It is probably necessary that
we clarify the internal relationship of this combination of
Western and traditional reformist thought.

These historical documents of the Itsukaichi area, which

49

took us more than one year from the summer of 1968 to analyze, are only the tip of an iceberg. Just within the small area
of the three counties of Tama, we discovered similar data at
more than a dozen places. We also found numerous similar
examples of the enthusiasm for classical Chinese poetry, for
the study of government, and for the establishment of political associations, as well as for a radical regeneration of traditional thought. Figure 1 shows the locations of associations
for people's rights that existed in former Kanagawa Prefecture
and the Musashi and Sagami areas during the first half of
Meiji. The number of associations definitely located already
exceeds sixty, and each of those has numerous unique events
and a concealed history of its own.

Surely, it is not an overstatement to say that discovery of
a carefully arranged sequence of documents like those of Fukusawa village is extraordinary. Each time we recover the
historical image of splendid people buried away at the grass
roots of society we can feel more and more confident about
the convictions I have stated. We possess abundant data that
testify to the prevalence of such developments not only in
the Musashi-Sagami area but also in many parts of eastern
Japan and, in fact, throughout the country. For this we are
indebted to our colleagues in local history who have published many excellent reports and papers.

Before I go into this subject, however, I would like to examine the main current of thought that was held by the enlightened bureaucrats who assumed hegemony with the
emergence of the Meiji state and their efforts toward the
modernization of Japan. Unless we do that, our "theory of
Meiji culture" will be quite biased and subjective.

(Translated by Nobuu Hiraga)

· II ·

THE IMPACT OF WESTERN CULTURE

THE APPROACH OF REFORM BUREAUCRATS

The influence of European and American civilization on Japan during the 1860s and 1870s was traumatic and disruptive to a degree that is rarely found in the history of cultural intercourse. We were engulfed both by capitalist culture that proudly brandished enormous industrial and military power, and by science and technology.

The situation bore no similarity to the introduction of Sui and T'ang civilization from China in early times, the permeation of Sung and Yuan culture in medieval times, or the influence of Iberian Catholic culture in early modern Japan. Since Japan somehow managed, however, to abolish its feudal system unaided and to maintain its sovereignty as a united country, in the meantime struggling against the pressure of the Western powers, it can be understood that the major concern of its leaders was not so much one of protecting traditional culture as mastering the secrets of their (Western) enemies' wealth and power quickly—in other words, the utilization of Western civilization to strengthen Japan.

This concern was shared by almost everyone, including of course late Tokugawa thinkers like Sakuma Shōzan, Yokoi Shōnan, and Yoshida Shōin, as well as those who held power in the new Meiji government, their subordinate officials, and public-spirited men in private life. Any thought of "protecting traditional culture" was scorned as an idle diversion from the critical need to respond to the urgent situation that faced the country. What had to be done was to penetrate the enemies' camp, grasp their weapons of civilization for use against them, and then turn to use them in the national interest. These men were driven by a deep, strong sense of national crisis and independence that kept them from falling into blind

51

worship of the West. Even so, they divided on the most basic issues: What kind of culture was Japan to have? How were they to build it, what was to be its center, and to what purpose?

Out of these internal disputes the "reform" or "enlightened" bureaucrats—a faction led by men like Ōkubo Toshimichi, Kido Takayoshi, and Itō Hirobumi—came to dominate. It was they who held the reins of government under the emperor system. In a series of civil wars they first defeated and eliminated the "Invade Korea" faction led by Saigō Takamori and Etō Shimpei, and then went on to destroy the nationwide opposition known as the "People's Rights" (*jiyū minken*) movement in a struggle that took more than ten years. Their methods of suppression were highly authoritarian, but for a period of two decades constant disputes centered on the vision of what modernized Japan should be like. In the summer of 1881 the government was so hard pressed that it seemed on the verge of collapse. It extricated itself once again by bringing out the emperor and using him to destroy and discredit the opposition.

What we need to know is this: What kind of perception of the Western threat formed in the mind of the "key figures" who took the helm in Japan's history; how did they intend to confront that threat, and how did they envisage Japan's grand plan—its blueprint for modernization—for the century to come? Let us take the case of Kido Takayoshi, a Councilor of State and the most powerful Chōshū figure in the new government, as our model "key figure" and examine his diary and other documents for the period 1871-1873.[1]

Kido toured America and Europe for the first time in a mission that extended from the autumn of 1871 to the summer of 1873. In November 1871, shortly after the great reform that abolished the domains and established prefectures,

---

[1] Kido (1833-1877), leader of the Chōshū group of Restoration leaders, is usually bracketed with Ōkubo Toshimichi and Saigō Takamori as key leaders of the first decade of Meiji. His diary, translated by Sidney Brown and Akiko Hirota, is being published by the University of Tokyo Press. Volume 1, *The Diary of Kido Takayoshi*, covering the years 1868-1871, appeared in 1983.

the government dispatched a large embassy of forty-six men to America and Europe with Iwakura Tomomi, Foreign Minister, as Ambassador Plenipotentiary; Kido Takayoshi (Councilor of State), Ōkubo Toshimichi (Finance Minister), Itō Hirobumi (Assistant Minister of Industry and Communications), and Yamaguchi Naoyoshi (Assistant Minister of Foreign Affairs) were deputy ambassadors.

One purpose of the mission was to conduct preliminary negotiations for treaty revision; the other was to work out a vision for the future of Japan through firsthand observation of the advanced civilizations of the West. Almost all the people included in the embassy were men who would later play leading roles in their fields: Sasaki Takayuki, Higashikuse Michitomi, Yamada Akiyoshi, Tanaka Mitsuaki, Tanaka Fujimaro, Tanabe Taichi, Watanabe Kōki, Fukuchi Genichirō, Nomura Yasushi, Yasuba Yasukazu, and Kume Kunitake.[2] You could say the mission included nearly half of the leaders in the Meiji government, and it can be imagined how keenly they looked forward to their travels. Since Kido, with Ōkubo, was second only to Iwakura in authority, his diary and letters, together with the official account of the mission by Kume, *Tokumei zenken taishi Bei-Ō kairan jikki*, provide the best information about the circumstances surrounding this great journey.[3]

On January 24, 1872 (Japanese 12/15/1871) Kido visited three elementary schools in San Francisco and made the following entry in his diary:

[2] On the mission, see Marlene J. Mayo, "Rationality in the Restoration: The Iwakura Embassy," in Bernard S. Silberman and Harry D. Harootunian, *Modern Japanese Leadership* (Tucson: University of Arizona Press, 1966), and Marius B. Jansen, *Japan and its World: Two Centuries of Change* (Princeton: Princeton University Press, 1980), chap. 2.

[3] The Kume account is discussed by Marlene J. Mayo, "The Western Education of Kume Kunitake," *Monumenta Nipponica* 27 (1973): 1-67, and Eugene Soviak, "On the Nature of Western Progress: The Journal of the Iwakura Embassy," in Donald H. Shively, ed., *Tradition and Modernization in Japanese Culture* (Princeton: Princeton University Press, 1971), pp. 7-34, and Tanaka Akira, *Iwakura shisetsudan* (Tokyo: Kōdansha, 1977). It has recently been reissued in five volumes with notes by Tanaka Akira (Tokyo: Iwanami shoten, 1977).

We visited three elementary schools. The largest one had 1,300-1,400 children. The regulations were something to see. Some schools are restricted to one sex, others have both boys and girls. We clearly must have schools if we are to encourage our country's development as a civilized country, improve ordinary people's knowledge, establish the power of the state, and maintain our independence and sovereignty. It is not enough to have a few able men make good; nothing is more important than schools.[4]

In those days universal public school education was already established in the United States. Kido wrote that in 1872 there were as many as 141,700 schools, 221,400 teachers, and 7,210,000 students. We can easily imagine Kido's surprise, since he had known nothing beyond a few feudal domain (hankō) and village schools (terakoya). Civilization required men of talent first of all, and Kido realized that the only way to produce them was through state-sponsored national education. Two days later, on January 26, he wrote to Sugiyama Takatoshi that the towns and cities he had seen were not so different from what he had imagined, but

when it comes to things like schools and factories, it is impossible to tell you everything, for it defies description. From now on, unless we pay a great deal of attention to the children, the preservation of order in our country in the future will be impossible. . . . The maintenance of a stable state will be difficult unless we take social conditions into consideration and pay attention to social evils. Nothing is more important than schools for improving social conditions and uprooting social evils. The civilization we have in our country today is not a true civilization, and our enlightenment (kaika) is not true enlightenment. To prevent trouble ten years from now,

[4] *Kido Takayoshi nikki* (Tokyo: Nihon shiseki kyōkai, 1933), vol. 2, pp. 126-27. (Kido gives dates on the Japanese calendar, which was abandoned in 1873.)

THE IMPACT OF WESTERN CULTURE

there is only one thing to do, and that is to establish schools worthy of the name. A long-range program for the stability of our country will never be attained if we have only a small number of able people; we have to develop universal adherence to the moral principles of loyalty, justice, humanity, and decorum. Unless we establish an unshakable national foundation, we will not be able to elevate our country's prestige in a thousand years. The creation of such public morals and the establishment of such a national foundation depends entirely on people. And the supply of such people in endless numbers over a long period of time clearly depends on education, and on education alone. Our people are no different from the Americans or Europeans of today: it is all a matter of education or lack of education.[5]

It is not necessary for me to repeat that Kido's goals were first and foremost "the preservation of order in the country," "a stable government," and "a long-range program for stability in our country." But is it not also true that under feudal rule people were deliberately kept in a state of ignorance, and kept from education for the same reasons of "order" and "stability"? Now we see a 180-degree change. What Kido is saying here is that the Meiji government's ability to uproot social evils, create a true civilization, and enhance the glory of the country all depend on whether or not the Japanese people are educated. This great change in his values would probably not have been very easy if he had not seen with his own eyes, by direct experience, the vitality of those 140,000 modern schools with their 7,200,000 students. Kido's strong resolve on this matter was immediately transmitted to the government's Ministry of Education.

On February 1, 1872 (Japanese 12/23/71) the Ministry of Education announced the "establishment of public elementary schools and schools for Western studies in the Tokyo metropolitan prefecture," and permission was granted for school administrators to accept applications from commoners. Then

[5] *Kido Takayoshi monjo* (Tokyo: Nihon shiseki kyōkai, 1930), vol. 4, p. 320.

on September 4, 1872 (8/2/72) the government issued decree No. 214 that proclaimed a universal education system to ensure that "henceforth there shall be no community with an illiterate family nor a family with an illiterate person." This was an astonishingly resolute step.

Kido's amazement grew as he saw the prosperous factories, iron mills, and shipyards; grand maneuvers by a modern army of several tens of thousands; and railroads, communication facilities, marketplaces, and the like in the United States and in Europe. This seems to have awakened him to the realization of the role of "the modern nation-state," itself the beneficiary of this sort of "civilization," in leading and controlling it. In a diary entry for March 1, 1872 (1/22/72) he wrote as follows:

> From this day on, I will devote myself entirely to military and educational matters. I will have Secretary Ga [Noriyuki] attached to me. In the first year of the Restoration, we worked out the five-article Charter Oath hastily and had it accepted by the leaders, daimyo, and court nobles, setting out the direction for the people's future. But now it is time for us to have an unshakable fundamental law. Therefore, from now on I want to concentrate my attention on matters such as the basic laws and governmental structures of other countries.[6]

Kido was saying that from then on he wanted to study the basic charters—the constitutions and government systems of other countries—and their governmental institutions and operations. As he proceeded with his observation of the United States and a number of European countries, he discovered that the modern constitutional form of government was the norm in advanced countries, great or small, and he realized that without adopting this system, a small country would be unable to hold its own with big countries and would find it difficult to build wealth and power. Sooner or later Japan, like Belgium, Prussia, Italy, Switzerland, Denmark, and Sar-

[6] *Kido Takayoshi nikki*, vol. 2, p. 142.

dinia, would have to adopt a constitutional form of government. That realization was accompanied by a new concern that weighed on the minds of Kido and his associates.

The official chronicle of the mission, Kume's *Bei-Ō kairan jikki*, reveals this point clearly:

> Under the influence of the French Revolution, the countries of Europe increased the freedom of their peoples and *adopted constitutional forms of government.* Eighty years have passed since then. Austria, though it remained a monarchy, also *changed to a constitutional form of government* twenty years ago, and even the autocratic state of Russia has been working for the past ten years to grant its people more freedoms. *Contemporary European civilization takes its point of origin from the degree to which those reforms have been carried out* and its products blossomed in the form of industrial arts. Today the profits come pouring out. (Emphasis added)[7]

For men like Kido and Ōkubo the main concern was how to harmonize the contradictions between the liberal Western system and a despotic emperor system, which they saw as Japan's "national character," and how to work out a strategy for "civilization" that would not harm the "national polity." This was not easy. The Meiji government they led rested on absolute power centered on the charisma of the emperor, and there was no way of avoiding the basic incompatibility this posed for modern constitutionalism. In March 1873, however, the last year of their long journey, they visited Prussia, where they were deeply impressed by the power of German militarism, which had defeated a culturally more advanced France in the Franco-Prussian War; by the way Bismarck was able to manipulate the Reichstag; and by the brilliance of the autocratic government of the Kaiser. "This is our solution," they thought.

If we grant that they returned home with definite ideas in

---

[7] Kume Kunitake, *Tokumei zenken taishi Bei-Ō kairan jikki*, 5 vols. (Tokyo, 1878), vol. 5, p. 12.

mind, their later actions show that those consisted of the rapid adoption of Anglo-American civili.ation and the institution-alization of a sham constitution like the one they lad admired in Prussia as support for an empe.or system. Upon their return they put first priority on internal affairs and quashed the projected invasion of Korea. Their steps to strengthen the despotic administrative machinery headed by Ōkubo pro-gressed in tandem with the preparation of memorials propos-ing constitutional government, as a result of which they had the emperor issue a rescript promising gradual movement to-ward constitutionalism. It was all part of their long-range plan, and not in any sense contradictory.

Gotō Yasushi has pointed out that the experience gained by members of the Iwakura Mission in the West was the one factor in determining positions on government programs that had been advanced up to this time, both for those who trav-eled abroad and those who advocated invading Korea. He analyzes it in the following way:

> The travelers came to understand that not just in the major powers but also in the smaller countries of Eu-rope, national education, large-scale mechanized facto-ries, a constitutional form of government, and a modern military system were the things that supported the polit-ical, economic, and social forces.[8]

That understanding became the basis for the policies of the government, leading to enactment of the decrees on the school system and education, the encouragement of manufacturing, the organization of the Ministry of Home Affairs, the prepa-ration for constitutional government through the establish-ment of the Genrōin,[9] and the implementation of a conscrip-tion system and the build-up of modern military power.

[8] Gotō Yasushi, *Shizoku hanran no kenkyū* (Tokyo: Aoki shoten, 1967), p. 20.

[9] The Genrōin, sometimes misleadingly translated as "Senate," was an ap-pointive body set up in 1875 as a first effort to deal with demands for greater representation. Its powers were few, but its members produced a number of draft proposals for a constitution. It was formally abolished upon the in-stitution of the Imperial Diet in 1890.

In this way, the key figures of the day came to hold to a vision of modernized Japan that would be in tune with the laws of world capitalism. That perception took form in a long-lived ideology that was to dominate the entire nation until 1945.

ADVOCATES OF ENLIGHTENMENT AND THE PEOPLE

It was Fukuzawa Yukichi who said a civilization begins with "doubts generated from within oneself." The value of his book, *Gakumon no susume* (The Encouragement of Learning), surpasses his own greatness. He thought about the problem of what it is that creates civilization and arrived at an earlier and more profound understanding than that of Kido Takayoshi. More than that, Fukuzawa put his ideas into action. As he put it, "*Gakumon no susume* was prepared primarily as popular reading or as a textbook for elementary school children. Therefore, in the first two or three essays I used as many colloquial expressions as possible and I wrote in a way that would be easily understood." From this it is clear that he gave a good deal of attention to the problem of producing individuals who were prepared to be agents of the turn toward civilization, and that on a national scale.

Why did this book become such a tremendous best seller in the early years of the Meiji period, and how was it able to give such inspiration and stimulation to the Japanese people, who were then searching for a way of living appropriate to a new age? Let us examine *Gakumon no susume* again, not to understand Fukuzawa's thought, but to discover what there was in it that was so fascinating for the nation.

First of all, the people were astonished by the book's first line: "It is said that Heaven does not create one man above another man, nor does it create one man below another." In the whirlpool of the Restoration, the people were gradually coming to the realization that all men should be equal, that "whether daimyo or laborer, the importance of a life is the same"; even so, they were surprised that a book should appear that pronounced the idea so clearly and that, moreover, justified that idea with the traditional concept of "heaven" and utilized the Western idea of "social contract" to make rational arguments.

The feudal order had comprised two distinct classes, sam-urai and commoners, which were further subdivided into sev-eral hundred smaller status divisions. The Meiji Restoration had been envisioned by the people as a revolution that would negate all those divisions; it would be the harbinger of a new world order (yonaoshi) portending the "equality of four classes" and "all people under one ruler." What actually took place under the Meiji government after the collapse of the shogun-ate, however, was so far from living up to the cry for "equality of all classes" that the people came to feel that in the end the "renewal" would have to be attained by their own hands. This passionate book appeared in March (2/1872) just as they were beginning to take action.

Of the seventeen essays that make up *Gakumon no su-sume*, the first three, published between March 1872 (2/72) and December 1873 (those in plain and simple language), are the most elegant in tone and the most piercing in terms of ideas, and these were in fact the most widely read. What was it in these three sections that would have appealed most to the people? It was Fukuzawa's confirmation that men are equal in their fundamental rights; moreover, that same equality ex-ists between countries, and even though there may be differ-ences in "outward appearances" of poor and rich, weak and powerful, the "fundamental rights" of all countries should be equal.

> In general, the countries of Europe and America are rich and strong, whereas the countries of Asia are poor and weak. Nevertheless, the wealth and strength of nations are outward appearances, and it is natural that they are all different. But if the strong and wealthy powers op-press the poor and weak nations. . . . By reason of the inherent rights of nations this cannot be allowed.[10]

[10] *Gakumon no susume* has been translated by David A. Dilworth and Umeyo Hirano as *An Encouragement of Learning* (Tokyo: Sophia University, 1969), and that translation is drawn on for excerpts cited in the text.

He goes on to say, however, that "wealth and power are not irrevocably fixed by Heaven. They can be changed by the diligent efforts of men." Therefore, "If we Japanese begin to pursue learning with spirit and energy, so as to achieve personal independence and thereby enrich and strengthen the nation, why should we fear the power of the Westerners?" In other words, Fukuzawa perceived reality as a changeable entity; he held up goals for the people's striving, and he inspired their dedication to learning. This constituted an incalculable contribution toward the liberation of the energy of the people.

"Independent individuals make for an independent country." In this way Fukuzawa expressed the fundamental principle of the modern age in simple terms easily understandable to the people. How could men lacking in the spirit of self-reliance and independence assert their right to independence of foreigners? "Japan must be filled with the spirit of independence if we are to defend our country against foreign threats. *Every citizen must take the responsibility of the nation upon himself, regardless of personal status or prestige.*"[11] For that goal of patriotism as well, people were first to study practical subjects, nurture a spirit of independence and self-respect, and establish for themselves a position of independent livelihood. In short, Fukuzawa's writing criticized and attacked the servile mentality of the Japanese people.

Before long hundreds of thousands, in fact millions, of people who were inspired by reading this book silently accepted its arguments and rose up to take part in the People's Rights movement, wanting to "spread the spirit of liberty and independence throughout the land." Ueki Emori and Baba Tatsui, the outstanding advocates of people's rights from Tosa, and the Tama farmers Nakamura Jū'emon and Fukasawa Gompachi were representative of those hundreds of thousands. In fact, there were elements in Fukuzawa's early arguments that might, had he pushed them to their logical con-

[11] *An Encouragement of Learning*, p. 17.

clusion, have led directly to a linkup with the nationalism of the advocates of the people's rights. What kept that from happening was something within Fukuzawa Yukichi himself. He certainly had no grounds for finding fault with readers of *Gakumon no susume* who rushed to join the *jiyū minken* movement. But why did men who started out from the same point divide into two clearly defined groups? Some, like Ueki and the early Fukasawa (Gompachi), moved on to join the movement for people's rights, whereas others, with Fukuzawa himself, later followed the path of compromise with the government. The explanation for this is to be found partly in the historical conditions of the early Meiji years, but also within *Gakumon no susume* itself, especially in Fukuzawa's logic about "the contract between government and people," which shocked his readers.

This happened as Fukuzawa attempted to apply the idea of modern natural law in the form of a theory of social contract to existing conditions in Japan. Of course, he was not the first to make such an attempt. Katō Hiroyuki had already stressed the theory of social contract in his books, *Rikken seitai ryaku* (An Outline of Constitutional Forn s of Government) and *Kokutai shinron* (A New Discourse on the National Polity).[12] Katō's naive arguments inevitably led to the repudiation of the emperor system and the autocratic Meiji government; contrary to his intentions, they encouraged the liberal movement. This so dismayed him that he announced that no more copies of two of his books would be printed. As proof of his conversion he published *Jinken shinsetsu* (A New View of Human Rights) in 1882. Whether or not Fukuzawa discerned this kind of danger, by the sixth and seventh essays of *Gakumon no susume* (published in 1874), he surreptitiously tried to substitute theory for reality.

[12] Katō Hiroyuki (1836-1916), first president of Tokyo Imperial University, began as a scholar of Dutch Learning in Tokugawa times, served in the shogunate's Institute for Western Studies, mastered German, and became a leading transmitter of German political thought and of Social Darwinism. He was appointed to the House of Peers in the Imperial Diet and is usually described as the archetypically establishment scholar.

Fukuzawa's argument for a theory of social contract goes as follows: What is a government? What does it mean to say that people should obey the laws of their government? To explain it in figurative terms, it is as though "the entire population of a country agreed to form an organization called a country, and then established and enacted bylaws and regulations." Since a government has been created by a social contract of the people, that "government is a proxy of the people, and therefore, it should act according to their wishes." The government's authority to declare war and conclude treaties with foreign nations and to tax its own citizens "ultimately derives from a covenant with those citizens. Hence, people not connected with government administration should not comment on its affairs." "For people to obey the government does not mean to obey laws someone else made, but to obey laws that they themselves made." Therefore, Fukuzawa argues, "people . . . should not violate their contract, even to the slightest degree, by disobeying the law."

The idea that a government was created by the people's contract was itself revolutionary because it had as requisite the assumption that sovereign power resided with the people. Moreover such a government could be revamped, changed, or repudiated at any time. Seen in this light, Chu Hsi Confucianism's view of the social and political order as something transcendental would be flatly denied; so too, of course, would the Tokugawa shogunate, and equally so, the Satsuma and Chōshū clique government, which had been organized without a word of consultation with or consent from the people.

It is out of the question that a man like Fukuzawa could have believed for a moment that the existing Meiji government was one "created by the people's contract." He knew only too well that it had been set up by the might of the Satsuma and Chōshū forces after they had crushed the resistance of Tokugawa retainers (like Fukuzawa himself) and the pro-Tokugawa domains. In spite of this, he argued his case as though the existing government had really been established "as proxy of the people" and was now a "contractual government" exercising power with the confidence and trust of the people. So, in his seventh essay, "On the Duties of Citizens of the Nation," while saying that "the people are both the household head and the master" he raises the question: "What should people do when the government oversteps its bounds and rules in an oppressive manner?" He replies as follows:

Number one: Do we bend our honor and principles to obey the government? No, that would be subservience. Number two: Do we resist the government by force? No, that would be "nothing but substituting violence for violence, or stupidity for stupidity," and "improper." Number three: Should we be willing to protect reason at the sacrifice of our lives? Yes, for no matter what kind of tyranny and harshness we are subject to, the true way is to endure pain, and to bring pressure to bear on the government by advocating just principles, neither taking up arms nor applying any pressure at all.[13]

If one reads this section purely as an exercise in appearance or "theory" (*tatemae*) it is all well enough. But when we take into consideration the context of the situation at the time this essay was written and published—that is, 1874, when the first memorial calling for establishment of a representative assembly was sent to the government, just as the movement for people's rights was getting underway—and then distinguish between Fukuzawa's "theory" (*tatemae*) and "actuality" (*honne*), then Fukuzawa seems to be engaged in some sort of intellectual deception or ideological ploy. That this must be so can be seen from the fact that he does not even touch on the question of where (i.e. the national assembly) the state or government should receive the people's trust and delegation of power, or on the question of whether the control should be mutually binding (i.e. a constitution agreed on by the nation). Instead, he stresses only the logic of duty: people should submit to the laws of the state and should even tolerate governmental tyranny, restricting themselves to calls for reason and justice.

[13] *An Encouragement of Learning*, p. 45. Argument summarized in the text.

It was shortly after this that Ueki Emori, the first victim of the suppression of thought, was imprisoned for writing the articles, "Enjin seifu" (Monkey Government) and "Jiyū wa senketsu o motte kawazaru bekarazaru ron" (Freedom Must be Purchased at the Price of Blood). Of course the People's Rights movement had already diverged greatly from the path taken by Fukuzawa. Once readers of the first sections of *Gakumon no susume* learned the road the Japanese people should follow in the new era, grasped revolutionary concepts like "natural rights" and "social contract," and then went on to carry those ideals to their logical conclusion, what other course of action was open to them than the course chosen by the People's Rights movement, which confronted the existing autocratic government and demanded the establishment of a national assembly?

There was no possibility for compromise between the two, for the existing government was not the kind conceptualized by Fukuzawa; its alternative to the doctrines of natural rights and social contract was to insist on an emperor system instituted by the gods, one that was inviolable and that represented a ruling line "unbroken through the ages eternal." Not even the genius of Fukuzawa could have devised a line of reasoning that could reconcile such theory and fact. No wonder that thereafter he maintained silence on theories of statehood.

Instead, this question was taken up by Katō Hiroyuki, the president of Tokyo University, who resorted to social Darwinism. Katō, who was a staunch friend of Fukuzawa's, launched the most heated ideological controversy of the first half of the Meiji when he challenged the *jiyū minken* faction. The so-called debate over the natural rights of man came in 1881-1882, when former followers of Fukuzawa like Baba Tatsui and Ueki Emori sharpened their pens to attack Katō's espousal of an organic theory of state and the survival of the fittest. This controversy was not confined to the highest intellectual circles; it spread to the local activists of the liberal movement and on down to long-forgotten young men in the countryside, who took it as the main topic for their lecture

65

meetings and other forums. In 1884 Kitamura Tōkoku, who was only sixteen years old, was so stirred by this that he wrote, "I shall become a great statesman and restore the declining fortunes of East Asia"; he had "decided on the basis of earnest consideration, to do great things for all people." But first, "in order to achieve this I must become a great philosopher and crush advocates of the new theory of the survival of the fittest that is so popular in Europe."[14]

Be that as it may, the impact of Western civilization, first crystallized as the blueprint drafted by high-ranking bureaucrats who toured the United States and Europe, was not limited to them. Thanks to the efforts of enlightenment intellectuals like Fukuzawa, it soon penetrated to the very base of society.

The extent of Fukuzawa's influence in this respect is clear to all who have carried out fieldwork in agricultural villages. Nothing is as frequently encountered in old storehouses as his early works. There are also striking instances, like the request of 23,555 residents in the nine counties of Sagami province (today's Kanagawa Prefecture) for "Fukuzawa Sensei" to draft their petition for the establishment of a national assembly. So many private academies and primary schools competed to adopt as textbooks the works of men like Fukuzawa that the government began to censor, and in some cases to ban, his books.

Then there is the case of Ogasawara Tōyō (Tesshirō), a former samurai of Himeji, who opened a village school called Kōyojuku in the village of Hattori near the Fujisawa station on the Tōkaidō in 1872. It was said that every time he held his class he would take the children to the Sagaminada beach and make them chant Fukuzawa's book *Sekai kunizukushi* (The Countries of the World) facing the open sea. The villagers were pleased by this and would say, "Ah, Tōyō Sensei has

<hr/>

[14] Kitamura's letter to Ishizuka Mina dated August 18, 1887, is included in Katsumoto Sei'ichirō, ed., *Tōkoku zenshi*, vol. 3 (Tokyo, 1955). The author includes a detailed study of Tōkoku in his *Shimpen Meiji seishinshi* (Tokyo: Chūō Kōronsha, 1973), pp. 440-530.

them chanting the sutra again."[15] Does this scene not some-how symbolize the dawn of modern Japan?

Fukuzawa was probably not aware of this, but a good num-ber of core leaders of the *jiyū minken* movement in the Kantō region came out of this village school of Master Tōyō. Men like Murano Tsune'emon, Hirano Tomosuke, Ōshima Masa-yoshi, and Kaneko Kakunosuke, whose names appear in this book, all received this kind of education.[16]

Fukuzawa Yukichi, who once said civilization starts with "doubt generated from within," taught the Japanese people a broad, world-encompassing outlook, freed from their insular-ity and their slave mentality. But he also taught many other things: that human desire was respectable and that one should not despise money and pleasure, that one should adopt a spirit of skepticism toward all authority, and that one should main-tain a rationalistic attitude in everyday life. There was an ide-ological pitfall of partisanship in his thought when he seemed to justify the Meiji state, but even so we must never forget that of all the men of Meiji, his was the loudest call for na-tional independence, self-reliance, and self-respect, for lib-eration of human nature and desire from oppressive moral restraints, abolition of the feudal system, and rejection of an ethos that exalted government at the expense of the people. This spirit of Fukuzawa's was embraced by countless num-bers of ordinary people, who believed that it represented the most hopeful and most advanced thought.

And yet, it must remain a matter of regret that Fukuzawa's "modernism," because it developed in accordance with the laws of capitalism, came to stand against the movement that expressed the real desire of the people in the 1880s for pro-tection of their rights to livelihood and people's rights. Fu-

[15] Carmen Blacker, *The Japanese Enlightenment: A Study of the Writings of Fukuzawa Yukichi* (Cambridge: Cambridge University Press, 1964), notes that the book in question "describes the different continents and countries of the world in the easily memorized 'seven-five' metre in which much of the information in the old temple-school textbooks had been set out" (p. 8).

[16] See Irokawa Daikichi, *Meiji jin: sono seishun gunzō* (Tokyo: Chikuma shobō, 1965), pp. 27-36, for personality sketch and observations.

kuzawa was against the early establishment of a national assembly and opposed any overthrow of the autocratic government by the *minken* faction. He regarded the Meiji regime as a "progressive government" and advocated harmony between government and people. He proposed that Japan cut its ties with Asia, pressed for the build-up of a navy and army designed for continental expansion, and urged a quick increase of national wealth by favoring the privileged capitalists. These things surely must have perplexed many of the masses who respected him.

I think it is because of this that today, a century later, we still have not been able to work out a conclusive appraisal of Fukuzawa. At the very time that the government, during the political crisis of 1881, kept a watchful eye on him as "a truly formidable enemy of the Meiji state," he himself, better than anyone else, must have known how mistaken that was. He took no part in government throughout his life, but very few others contributed so much to the establishment of Japanese capitalism and to the strengthening of the Meiji state. In this sense, Fukuzawa truly deserves the name "champion of civilization."

THE CULTURAL GULF BETWEEN JAPAN AND THE WEST

The period from the second half of the nineteenth century to the beginning of the twentieth century, during which Meiji culture took shape, coincided with the period in which the Industrial Revolution reached the end of a crucial stage in the West; science, technology, and productivity made remarkable progress.

One might select some epoch-making events that took place during this period in the history of science: the world's first international exposition was held in London in 1851, and in 1859 Darwin's *Origin of the Species*, a book that drastically changed mankind's view of things, was published. Both were introduced to Japan within about twenty years. Ōkubo Toshimichi utilized expositions to accelerate and show the advantages and products of his policies of industrialization, and

Darwinism was popularized as an organic theory of social evolution and did its part to overwhelm political liberalism.

In 1863, the world's first subway was opened in London, J. S. Mill's *Utilitarianism* was published, and the emancipation of slaves was proclaimed in the United States. In 1866, Dostoevski's *Crime and Punishment* and Tolstoi's *War and Peace* were published. Mill entered Japan very early, and by the 1880s his writings, along with those of Spencer and Rousseau, were among the most widely read. *Crime and Punishment* was not translated by Uchida Roan from the English until after 1892, but Kitamura Tōkoku demonstrated an essential understanding of the work very early.

The year 1867 brought many inventions and discoveries that made lasting impressions on the modern history of Japan. For example, dynamite was invented by Nobel (Sweden), ferroconcrete by Monnier (France), the use of carbolic acid as an antiseptic was discovered by Lister (England), and the first volume of Marx's *Das Kapital* was published. During the 1880s, dynamite was used by the radical faction of the *jiyū minken* in their bombs and became so well known that it was sung about in an activist's ballad, "Dynamite, Boom!"

> For our more than forty million countrymen,
> We're not afraid of wearing convict red;
> Promote the national interest and the people's welfare,
> Foster the people's strength!
> And if we can't,
> Dynamite, Boom!

Nobel cannot have dreamed that his discovery would be used to embolden extremists in the Orient. Lister's discovery was utilized in place of charms when epidemics swept through Japan in the 1880s and 1890s. It is said that people believed they could ward off the evil gods of sickness if they put carbolic acid in little bags and carried it with them. *Das Kapital* did not begin to pose a threat to government authority until much later in the last years of Meiji and, in real sense, only in the 1920s.

In 1869 a transcontinental railroad began operation in the

United States; within two years high Japanese government officials, who rode one of its trains to the east coast, were thoroughly impressed by the greatness of railroads. (By 1889 Japanese railroad trackage exceeded a thousand miles.) In 1876 the American, Alexander Graham Bell, invented the telephone, and within a few years a Japanese government agency had imported it. Following the invention of the phonograph (1877), Thomas Edison (United States) perfected the incandescent electric lamp in 1879. This raised the curtain on the age of the electric lamp at a time when people in Japan were still gazing wide-eyed at the brightness of kerosene lamps.

In 1882, Koch (Germany) discovered the tuberculosis bacteria and in the following year, the cholera bacteria. From then on bacteria of communicable diseases were discovered one after another, and the causes of those diseases became clear. For Japan, where tens to hundreds of thousands of people died from communicable diseases every year, these discoveries were indeed heaven-sent blessings. In 1892 Kitazato Shibasaburō, after diligent study under Dr. Koch, founded the Institute for Communicable Diseases in Tokyo with the support of private sources, not long after the National Research Institute of Communicable Diseases had been set up in Germany with Koch as head in 1891.

The revolution in transportation made rapid progress in the West from the 1880s on. In 1882 Daimler (Germany) invented the automobile, in 1884 Persons (England) invented the steam turbine, and in the following year, 1885, Benz of Germany developed an automobile powered by a gasoline engine, which made it practical. In 1893 ships powered by steam turbines were equipped with diesel engines, and in 1895 radium was discovered, which ultimately led to the age of atomic energy a half century later. The Wright brothers' first flight in an airplane was in 1903. Japan used almost all these inventions and discoveries for military purposes, however, and among civilians widespread use of the automobile and airplanes was delayed for a half century. It was the Imperial navy and army that were the most enthusiastic about diesel engines and gasoline cars. Japan's technology in those areas reached world standards by the 1920s, when the main fleet was built and a mechanized army consolidated.

When we contrast the dates of these nineteenth- and twentieth-century inventions and discoveries in science and technology with the speed with which the Japanese adopted them, we have to be astonished by the alert and sensitive reaction of the Japanese to more advanced civilizations. On closer examination, however, it turns out that almost none of this technology, with the exception of the Institute for Communicable Diseases, was imported to satisfy the needs that the people themselves had voiced. On the contrary, each of these technological advances was to a great extent seen as an instrument of national policy with political, commercial, and class implications, and thus caused gaps between the life style of the masses and technological civilization. The most extreme expression of this was a Japan that built a first-rank military power through the sacrifices of workers and farmers, so that, contrary to the official slogan, the program could be described as one to "impoverish the country and strengthen the army." This resembles the contrast in present-day America between the country's capacity to launch spaceships and the misery of black ghettos. We must refuse to evaluate the development of modern science and technology in Meiji culture by two or three of its peaks because of the problem created by this contradictory structure.

Basil Hall Chamberlain, a British scholar who lived in Japan for thirty years, commented on this flurry of change in Japan by saying "To have lived through the transition stage of modern Japan makes a man feel that preternaturally old; for here he is in modern times, with the air full of talk about bicycles and bacilli and 'spheres of influence,' and yet he can himself distinctly remember the Middle Ages. . . . Old things pass away between a night and a morning."[17]

Dr. Raphael von Koeber was a German philosopher whose eighteen-year residence in Japan was shorter than Chamber-

[17] Basil Hall Chamberlain, *Things Japanese* (London: John Murray, 1905), p. 1.

71

lain's. Nishida Kitarō, who audited his lectures in the Department of Philosophy at Tokyo Imperial University, described von Koeber's position in 1893 as follows:

> Japan's attitude in adopting European culture was prob-
> lematic in every respect. The Japanese did not try to
> transplant the roots of the plant, but simply cut off eye-
> catching flowers. As a result the people who brought the
> flowers were respected enormously, but the plants that
> could have produced such blossoms did not come to grow
> in our country. Despite this, Japanese scholars and prod-
> igies strutted about displaying their knowledge of West-
> ern things noisily and proudly. Dr. Koeber seemed to
> feel that that kind of pose and pretension was utterly
> revolting. Takayama Chogyū was representative of that
> type of man. Thereupon Koeber *sensei* strove quietly to
> follow the correct path of transplanting the plant by the
> roots and discarding the blossoms, and as a result, a sense
> of the "real thing" gradually developed among those
> around him.[18]

Sun Yat-sen's comment was much more severe. In 1924 he
gave Japan a friendly warning, that now that it had become
strong by modernization, it would have to choose between
becoming "the hawk of Western-style Might or the tower of
Eastern Right."[19] But it is impossible to turn back the wheel
of history. Japan had clearly entered the road to imperialism
after the Russo-Japanese War; and by 1924, when Sun Yat-
sen delivered his warning, a national policy of agression in
China had already been adopted.

In the field of literature and the arts, the period between
1868 and 1912 called Meiji marked the maturity of bourgeois
culture in the West. Baudelaire, the decadent poet of *Les
fleurs du mal*, died in 1867, and Jean Arthur Rimbaud had
already abandoned his poetry in 1880 and had gone to sea as

[18] Watsuji Tetsurō, *Koeber sensei* (Tokyo: Kyōbundo, 1948).

[19] Marius B. Jansen, *The Japanese and Sun Yat-sen* (Cambridge: Harvard
University Press, 1954), pp. 210ff.

a trader. Nietzsche, a rebel against bourgeois culture, completed his *Zarathustra* during 1883-1885. In Japan, however, a few modern European novels were just then being introduced in the form of political novels. In the United States this era coincided with the setting depicted in John Ford's masterly Western, *Duel in the Sun*.

In 1890, the painter van Gogh died, and in the following year Gauguin fled bourgeois civilization for Tahiti. In 1892 the Russian writer Chekhov published his *Ward No. 6*. But in Japan, modern literature had yet to appear in a real sense; only a few men like Tōkoku and Futabatei were carrying on pioneer struggles with their uncompleted works.[20] Far from reaching the maturity or decadence of bourgeois culture in the West, in Japan individual consciousness was just beginning to be liberated from the yoke of feudal culture, and the composition of modern Romantic poetry was just getting underway. Shimazaki Tōson's *Wakanashū* was published in 1897, a time when in Western literary circles the age of Romanticism was already long past, and even the era of Naturalism was approaching its end.

Thus there was a big gulf between Japan and the West in terms of "spiritual culture," and that gulf was far more difficult to bridge than the technological gap. But in fact there was no need to hurry things. The history of Meiji literature shows that during the 1880s and 1890s writers like Shakespeare, Goethe, Wordsworth, Byron, and Heine were just being introduced to Japan while works like *Crime and Punishment* were appreciated simply as detective stories.

In the past studies of Japan's modern cultural history have treated this contrast with the West as something fateful and serious, and writers have spent a great deal of time on descriptions of the various tragicomedies that were encountered in the process of reducing this gap. Japan's modernization has been depicted as fraught with restless impatience and uneas-

[20] Futabatei Shimei (1864-1909) was a translator of Gogol and Turgenev and was himself a novelist. See Marleigh Grayer Ryan, *Japan's First Modern Novel: Ukigumo of Futabatei Shimei* (New York: Columbia University Press, 1967).

iness, and writers have focused on people who were constantly tormented by an inferiority complex arising from feelings of being behind. But is such an approach really justified?[21]

Why should Meiji Japan—which experienced a different international environment, had a distinctive indigenous tradition, and underwent modernization at a totally different point in its historical development—have been expected to show rapid assimilation and covergence with the West? Was it really necessary for these men to suffer from irritation and uneasiness and to fall into an inferiority complex so profound that they lost sight of themselves as conscious agents of modernization and instead became controlled by it? This cannot be explained away by citing their intense determination to build a "rich country, strong army" or to "achieve independence," for that consciousness of inferiority and compulsive desire to follow the West continued even after Japan had become a major military and imperialist power. Let us remember the lamentation of Natsume Sōseki at the end of the Meiji era. I doubt that it would be possible to find a lament of this sort coming from the intellectuals of China, India, or Korea:

> Until recently we generated our development on our own terms from within, but now we have suddenly lost the ability to be our own master. We are being forced by others to do exactly as we are told, whether we want to or not. . . . The condition of survival for Japan-as-Japan will probably involve responding to pressure in this way from now on, and there is probably nothing we can do about it. What it comes down to is the conclusion that the enlightenment of modern Japan is still superficial and shallow. . . . Still, I'm not saying we should stop this or that it is bad. We are in fact unable to stop; we just have to swallow our pride and go on being shallow and superficial.[22]

[21] Iwai Tadakuma, ed., *Kōza Nihon bunka shi*, vol. 7 (Tokyo, 1962), and Nakamura Mitsuo, *Meiji bungaku shi* (Tokyo, 1963).

[22] Natsume Sōseki, *Gendai Nihon no kaika* (November 1911). Reprinted in *Sōseki zenshū*, 16 vols. (Tokyo: Iwanami, 1966), vol. 11, p. 334.

We have become accustomed to viewing modern Japanese history, especially cultural and intellectual history, with intellectuals at the center. Natsume Sōseki's theme in *Gendai Nihon no kaika* (The Enlightenment of Modern Japan) was exactly like that: cultural and intellectual history were at the center of his attention. To say, however, that modern Japan suffered to an abnormal degree from an inferiority complex or anxiety about the West does not necessarily imply that those feelings were shared by the entire nation. Can we conclude that this was the case with the ordinary people as well? Was it not rather a psychological phenomenon that was seen especially among Japan's ruling and intellectual classes who were determined to achieve imperialist power? And have not most histories of Japanese thought and cultural history been written by intellectuals who were subject to such a mentality and who accepted the standards of the Meiji elite?

I would like to reconsider the question of Japan's modernization by posing such questions. My basic project involves giving special attention to two areas that have been dealt with only abstractly in the past: the culture of the people's everyday life, and the intellectual and cultural creativity at the grassroots level of society. Of course I do not mean to say that the cultural endeavors of all members of the nameless masses were more significant than, or should be substituted for, those of Kido Takayoshi, Fukuzawa Yukichi, Nakae Chōmin, Futabatei Shimei, or Natsume Sōseki. But I do think that if we do not clarify those areas we will not be able to understand adequately the meaning of the lives and work of men like Chōmin, Shimei, and Sōseki.

(Translated by Noburu Hiraga)

· III ·

WANDERING PILGRIMS

RESTORATION YOUTH

Near the border of Miyagi and Iwate Prefectures on the main
Tōhoku line there is a small station called Ishikoshi. Five miles
west of Ishikoshi, on the Hazama River, is the town of Shi-
wahime; it was created as Shirahata by the merger of Izuno
hamlet with two adjacent settlements in 1878. The name of
the new village came from the names of the tutelary deities
of two local Shintō shrines. Shirahata was the birthplace of
Chiba Takusaburō, the young man whose life's journey we
will follow.

The Hazama River has its source in Mt. Kurikoma. Its waters
irrigate the paddy fields in the rice-growing districts through
which it flows before it merges with the Kitakami River and
continues its journey to the sea. The climate there is cold;
the first frost comes in the middle of October, and freezing
temperatures last well into May when lotus plants bloom. In
the Tokugawa period bailiffs of Sendai domain administered
the district and levied heavy taxes on the people; their hardship aroused the wrath of Yasui Sokken (1799-1876), an Edo
poet who frequently visited this part of the country. Sokken
was a Confucian scholar of the Ancient Studies School under
Matsuzaki Kōdō (1771-1844). In 1853, Sokken wrote *Kaibō
shigi* (Treatise on Naval Defense), which greatly impressed
Tokugawa Nariaki.[1] He was subsequently promoted to the
faculty of the Shōheikō, the shogunate's most prestigious
academy. A poet and a great patriot, he transmitted his spirit
of fierce independence to his pupils, among them Kumoi Tatsuo.[2] Enraged by what he saw of the savage exploitation of

[1] Nariaki (1800-1860), daimyo of the Mito domain, was a leading advocate
of stronger national defense and a major political figure in the 1850s.
[2] Kumoi Tatsuo (1844-1870), a Yonezawa samurai who organized a group
of discontented former samurai with the intention of assassinating Meiji government officials, appears again below.

76

the Sendai peasantry, Sokken wrote the following lament titled "Wailing Voices From the Fields":

> Taxes and taxes; nothing to eat
> and penniless peasants steal away.
> Hunger and starvation riot in the valleys
> The people are skin and bones.
> Do you know, You in the palace, that the
> timbre of the shamisen is only
> wailing voices from the fields?

In a letter to one of his disciples, Sokken wrote of the poem,
"After twenty years of scholarship, this is what my learning
amounts to. I will have to wait another twenty years before
passing judgment on its impact on government. I smile bitterly."

Those "wailing voices from the fields" had been heard from
in an uprising of 20,000 destitute farmers in Kurihara county
in 1866. At that time Chiba, our subject, was a young adult
of fifteen. Born into a rural samurai (*gōshi*) family in Shirahata
village of Kurihara county, he can hardly have been indifferent to this state of affairs as "somebody else's business." In
the census survey of 1872 he is listed simply as "commoner,
farmer, twenty-one years old, residence 134, Shirahata village." By then his father Takunojō was no longer living.

From an 1872 document found in the Fukasawa storehouse
in Itsukaichi we learn that Takusaburō had left home alone in
June of that year, leaving behind his older brother Rihachi
and his foster mother Sada, who was to die in his absence
four months later. Neither one was a blood relative. A Chiba
family history[3] shows that the father, Takunojō, had no children by either of his two wives. After consulting Sada, the
second wife, he took a concubine named Chikano who eventually bore Takusaburō. Takunojō, however, became gravely
ill in the middle of Chikano's pregnancy, and fearing that he
would die without leaving an heir, decided to adopt a son to

---

[3] *Chiba-ke kindai no shikō*; manuscript in the private collection of Chiba
Toshio.

make sure that the family name would be carried on. The child he adopted was Shimizu Hikoemon, the foster child of his first wife. Hikoemon was renamed Chiba Rihachi, and it was he and not Takusaburō who inherited the headship of the Chiba family and later, after the Restoration, was granted the status of *shizoku*, reserved for former samurai. It seems that the Chiba family bought its samurai status from Sendai *han*; the family traced its lineage to a rural military clan in the medieval period and had strong local roots. Takusaburō, the son of his father's concubine, was born on 6/17/1852, in Izuno, Kurihara. At three he was separated from his real mother and reared by Sada, his foster mother. At twelve he became a student of Ōtsuki Bankei, and he remained under his tutelage until he went off to take part in the Restoration wars of 1868-1869.[4]

Ōtsuki Bankei's father, Gentaku (1757-1827), was a nationally prominent, progressive student of Dutch learning, and Bankei followed in his father's footsteps as an advocate of opening the country. He traveled widely throughout Japan, visiting Edo, Kyoto, and Nagasaki, and he associated with people like Rai San'yō and Sakuma Shōzan,[5] under whom he studied Confucian prose and poetry and Western artillery. With the arrival of Perry's "black ships" in 1853, Bankei took a leading role in advocating an end to national seclusion. His unusually sophisticated grasp of international power politics was evident in his advocacy of an alliance with Imperial Russia to balance the Anglo-American threat. In 1862 he was appointed assistant director of the official domain school in Sendai, the Yōkendō. During the Restoration war he played

---

[4] *Chiba Takusaburō jihitsu rirekisho.* Unless otherwise noted, documents relating to Chiba Takusaburō and the Itsukaichi group are now in two collections; the Fukasawa family papers (*Fukasawa-ke monjo*) at Tokyo Keizai Daigaku Library, and *Santama jiyū minken shiryō shū*, in the Irokawa Kenkyūshitsu, Tokyo Keizai Daigaku (i.e. in the author's institution).

[5] Rai San'yō (1780-1832), an influential poet and historian whose *Unofficial History of Japan* was centered on the imperial court. Sakuma Shōzan (1811-1864), a leading student of Western military science and advocate of opening Japan, was assassinated by an antiforeign zealot.

an important role in forging the alliance of northeastern domains that resisted the Satsuma-Chōshū forces.[6] After those
forces triumphed Bankei was arrested and imprisoned; for a
while his very life was in peril.

Chiba Takusaburō, seventeen, left his old teacher to join
in the fighting of the Restoration war of 1868. In his own
words, "I answered the call for men to enlist and became a
foot soldier. I was sent to Shirakawaguchi and I saw action
twice." But his unit was defeated, and he fled. Naganuma
Orinojō (1836-1916), the headmaster of a small academy located near the lower reaches of the Kitakami River in Nabu-
rihama, Momou district, also fought in the same battle as
commander of a detachment of farmers that had been recruited to resist the "imperial" forces. He was subsequently
arrested and imprisoned. There is no way of knowing whether
the thirty-one-year-old Orinojō and the seventeen-year-old
Takusaburō met on the battlefield, but we do know that they
were to meet seven or eight years later in Itsukaichi, Musashi
district.[7] Branded a rebel, Chiba Takusaburō stole back to his
home town only to find that his old teacher, Bankei, was in
prison and that the domain government had collapsed. With
nowhere to turn, he began his life anew as a "wanderer seeking truth."

Much of the fascination of the Meiji era lies in the appearance of an extraordinary number of men like Chiba Takusaburō. What was it about that era that created young men like
Chiba, who some years later, in a moment of sheer exuberance, was to call himself "Professor of Japanese Law, Resident of Freedom Prefecture, Independence District, Righteous Spirit Village"? This young man's life will provide an
example.

In the late fall of 1868, a month after the name of the era
had been changed to Meiji, Takusaburō began to study med-

---

[6] The northeastern domains, led by Sendai, organized less to support the
Tokugawa cause than to resist what seemed like a grab for power by Satsuma
and Chōshū.

[7] As will be seen below, Takusaburō later found employment as a teacher
in the Itsukaichi school that Naganuma Orinojō headed.

icine under Ishikawa Ōsho (1824-1882) in Matsushima near Sendai. He studied under Ōsho for nine months, and although we do not know what led Takusaburō to him, it is clear that Ōsho was more than an ordinary doctor. He was one of the "new intellectuals" who, during the latter years of the Tokugawa period, studied Western medicine under Itō Genboku (1800-1871) and under Dutch doctors in Nagasaki. During the Restoration upheaval he followed the Tokugawa shogun and traveled constantly between Osaka, Edo, and Mito. Ōsho was greatly admired by Ōtsuki's students, and it is probable that Takusaburō was looking to Ōsho to find what he had earlier sought from his old teacher. His studies were cut short the following summer, however, when Ōsho was arrested and jailed by the Meiji government for the crime of "aiding and abetting the shogun."[8] Thus, several months later in the fall of 1868 Takusaburō left Matsushima and went to Kesennuma where he began to study National Learning (*Kokugaku*) under Nabeshima Ichirō.

Nabeshima was an eccentric. He was obsessed by the special mystique of the Japanese language, and he was known to be a "habitual drinker and an uninhibited individualist." He had been in the Kesennuma area for a long time and had numerous students whom he instructed in arithmetic and classical Japanese literature. We can surmise that Takusaburō's intent was to find out what lay at the heart of the new Meiji government, since leaders like Iwakura Tomomi (1825-1883) and Sanjō Sanetomi (1837-1891) were trying to find ideological foundations for state authority in Shintō and *Kokugaku* as expounded by Hirata Atsutane (1776-1843) and Ōkuni Takamasa (1792-1871). But theories legitimating the new imperial system were not the stuff to salve the wounds of people who had fought on the losing side in the Restoration.

How was Takusaburō to support himself? The world he faced was dominated by the Satsuma-Chōshū clique, and all doors to political offices were closed to "traitors" who had sided with the *bakufu*. Aizu samurai were certainly not the only

[8] In later years, however, Ōsho became an officer in the new government's Military Medical Bureau.

ones to find the road to the future blocked.[9] For example, Watari *han* near Sendai, which was rated at 30,000 *koku*,[10] supported 1,362 retainers and their dependents, or a total of over 8,000 persons. After the Restoration, the Meiji government first reduced the *han*'s holdings to a mere 65 *koku* and subsequently assumed direct control of the domain, leaving Watari samurai unemployed and homeless. The former daimyo, Date Kunishige (1841-1904), who led a large migration of former Watari housemen to settle in Hokkaido in 1870, was one of the many displaced men grasping for a lifeline.

His future blighted by his role in the Restoration war, young Takusaburō must have thought that his life had come to an agonizing impasse. In 1872 he placed himself under the tutelage of Sakurai Kyōhaku, a Pure Land sect Buddhist priest, but perhaps because of some new perplexity he left again after only five months. About that time Takusaburō began to hear people talk about a Russian Orthodox monk, Father Nikolai (1836-1912), and not long after he turned to Christianity and the Russian Orthodox Church. To explain how the Orthodox Church penetrated northeastern Japan at a time when Christianity was still proscribed requires a closer look at Father Nikolai's special relationship to Sendai *han*.

Father Nikolai, who was born in 1836 as Ivan Dimitriyevitch Kasatkin, first began to dream of going to Japan when, as a seminary student in St. Petersburg, he read Captain Vasilii Golovnin's *Memoirs of A Captivity in Japan*.[11] After finishing his studies, he was ordained in 1860 and immediately

[9] The imperial armies made a special target of the Aizu castle town of Wakamatsu, and Aizu losses (2,847 samurai) were the highest in the Restoration wars. The domain was kept as prefecture. The daimyo family was given an infertile and harsh territory about one tenth of Aizu's productivity, and the 17,000 samurai and dependents who moved there were soon so destitute that they petitioned the government for help to bury their dead. See Harold Bolitho, "Aizu 1853-1868" in *Proceedings* (London: British Association for Japanese Studies, 1977), vol. 2.

[10] Tokugawa domains were rated according to estimated productivity calculated in *koku* (approximately five bushels) of rice.

[11] Vasilii Golovnin (1776-1831), who commanded a Russian surveying expedition that was seized in 1811, wrote these memoirs of his two years' captivity.

requested and received permission to proceed to the new Russian consulate in Hakodate, Hokkaido. After crossing Siberia with a single buggy, he sailed down the Amur River, passed the winter, and set sail for Japan the following spring. Arriving in Hakodate in the late spring of 1861, he immediately took up his duties as priest at the Russian consulate.

Father Nikolai was then twenty-five years old. He had fulfilled his first ambition in coming to Japan but could not preach publicly because of the anti-Christian proscriptions that were still enforced by the Japanese government. He therefore devoted the next seven years to the study of Japan. He began with the Japanese language, and his interests soon grew to include Japanese history, Confucianism, Buddhism, Shintō, and Japanese art history. He was particularly fascinated by Buddhism and studied both Mahayana and Hinayana doctrines. Preserved in the Ecclesiastical Library in Hakodate are copies of such books as the *Lotus Sutra*, histories like Rai San'yō's *Nihon gaishi*, the Mito classic *Dai Nihon shi* (Great History of Japan), and even popular books like Jippensha Ikku's *Dōchū hizakurige*. All these books contain detailed marginalia written in Father Nikolai's hand.[12]

Father Nikolai baptized his first Japanese converts in 1868 as the clouds of the final battle of the Restoration war gathered over Hakodate. His first convert was Sawabe Takuma[13] who had married into the family of a Hakodate Shintō priest three years earlier. Sawabe had been persuaded by Father Nikolai's forceful arguments and converted to Christianity. The next two converts were Sakai Atsunori, a Sendai doctor, and Urano Taizō of the Nambu domain. Needless to say, the baptisms were performed secretly in Father Nikolai's private chambers. Soon after, the remnants of the bakufu's navy un-

---

[12] *Daishūkyō Nikorai shi jiseki*, archives of the Nikolai chapel. See also George Alexander Lensen, *The Russian Push Toward Japan* (Princeton: Princeton University Press, 1959).

[13] Sawabe Takuma (1835-1913) was a Tosa participant in the Restoration movement who had made his way to Hokkaido after compromising himself with his comrades. At the end of his life he was head of the Orthodox community in Japan. *Kōchi ken jimmei jiten* (Kōchi: Kōchi shimin toshokan, 1971).

der Admiral Enomoto Takeaki (1836-1908) put into port. Volunteers from northeastern Japan and infantry units under Hijikata Toshizō and other bakufu retainers began arriving in Hakodate, and the city became the last center of resistance to the Restoration government.

Early in 1869 Father Nikolai returned to Russia, not because he feared for his safety but because he wanted to organize a Japan mission society. Fighting erupted a month later, and Father Nikolai's three converts slipped out of Hakodate. Sakai Atsunori secretly made his way to Kannari village in the Kurihari district only a few miles from Chiba Takusaburō's home. The first converts there had been Kannari Zenbei and his son Zensaemon. Zenbei and Zensaemon had been too proud to surrender following the capitulation of Sendai *han* to the imperial army. Leading a militia unit, they joined up with the bakufu fleet and entered Hakodate fortress. There they heard about Sawabe Takuma, Father Nikolai's first convert, and after visiting him, they eventually converted to Christianity. The third convert was also from Sendai, a young soldier named Arai Tsunenoshin. Father Nikolai returned to Japan in February 1871, and baptized the Sendai samurai whom Sawabe had won to the faith. Father Nikolai then dispatched Ono Sōgorō and other converts to Sendai. In fact, the year before Father Nikolai's return there had been frequent contacts between Hakodate and Sendai as part of a special effort to win converts.

This is how the tenets of the Russian Orthodox Church first reached Sendai and Chiba Takusaburō, who was then twenty-one years old and a follower of Pure Land Buddhism. In Sendai, Father Nikolai's converts held secret meetings to spread the faith. They argued against continuing armed resistance, and they asserted that Father Nikolai's teachings were "superior to Confucianism and Buddhism: it is the eternal truth of the Holy Kingdom, the one and only road to national salvation." It was a very persuasive appeal. By 1871 there were over one hundred converts, most of them from Sendai. Earlier, Ōtsuki Bankei had advocated the policy of rapprochement with Imperial Russia to stave off Anglo-American aggression; this may have been one factor that explains why so many Sendai samurai flocked to Father Nikolai.

A SPIRITUAL JOURNEY

In the *curriculum vitae* that Takusaburō wrote several years later, he stated that he followed Father Nikolai to Tokyo in June of 1871. He appears to have been mistaken, however, for Father Nikolai first went to Tokyo in early 1872 and opened the theological academy at Surugadai in September of that year. The academy was both a boarding school and a Russian language school. Takusaburō did not leave a record of his experiences at the academy, but we have an account written by someone else that probably describes the conditions Takusaburō found there.

> I had neither friends nor acquaintances, and sat forlornly in my Tokyo room not knowing where to turn, while the small sum of money that I brought with me trickled away . . . but a native of my home in the north, Hoshina Tamotsu, helped me enroll at the Russian Orthodox seminary that Father Nikolai had established in Surugadai. As a Confucianist I had to reject the dogmas of this religion completely, but every night I was summoned by senior students of the school who pressured me. I never gave in; instead, I became increasingly angry and argued so violently that people would stare at me with astonishment. This went on for about three months until one night Andō Kenzō, Yoshii Tatsutarō, and Kumaya Tatsujirō met with me in secret. They spoke with great compassion and said that if I was indeed so stubborn and had no intention of becoming a convert, there was no reason for me to stay. I replied that it troubled me deeply to stay such a long time at the seminary, but that since I was penniless and had nowhere else to go I had no choice but to stay and suffer this daily humiliation.[14]

[14] The paragraph is by Amada Gorō (Guan, 1854-1904), the son of an Iwakitaira *han* samurai who spent twenty years searching for his parents and

Many youths, similarly scarred, arrived at Father Nikolai's, and Takusaburō no doubt looked with sympathetic eyes upon these young men who had experienced similar hardships. Takusaburō stayed there for four years, until April of 1875. What must he have thought and done there?

The seminary's baptismal records begin in September 1872; they mention someone named Alexander Chiba Bunji, but the name Takusaburō does not appear. Destitute youths were allowed to board at the seminary without charge for up to three months. There was also a provision that permitted students who showed great promise to stay on indefinitely. Takusaburō must have been one of these youths, considering the length of his stay, although it is also possible that he served as a lay preacher and proselytized in the countryside.[15]

It can be suggested that one of the reasons for Father Nikolai's popularity among "ruined samurai" from northeastern Japan was that the Russian Orthodox Church offered a new set of spiritual ideals tempered by just enough of the comforting conservatism that was inherent in its status as the national religion of imperial Russia. An incident that occurred late in 1872 lends credence to this view. Confronted by the Japanese government with what were apparently false accusations that he advocated disloyalty and disparaged the Meiji emperor in his sermons, Father Nikolai responded that the Russian Orthodox Church emphasized submission to state authority, and he assured the government that if any of his followers "spoke even one disrespectful word against the Emperor" he would immediately expel him. This stands in sharp contrast to the combative attitude that was shown by Roman Catholics and Protestants. Nikolai went on to equate disloyalty to the Emperor with unfaithfulness to God, explaining that

younger sister who had disappeared after the fall of the Iwakitaira castle in the Restoration war. Amada, who was nineteen when he arrived at the Nikolai seminary, is the author of *Tōkai yūkyō den* (Life of a Chivalrous Man from the Eastern Sea). From *Nihon zankoku monogatari*, vol. 4 (Tokyo, 1960).

[15] Proselytizing Regulations (*Denkyō kisoku*), Articles 7 and 9, Nikolai Chapel Archives.

There is nothing at all in our religious teachings that preaches disrespect toward His Majesty the Emperor. The religion that I preach is not my privately held belief; it is the Holy Word of God. The Scriptures command us as follows: "people should be obedient to their ruler"; and "without God's ordinance no ruler may occupy his throne"; "anyone who opposes his ruler thereby opposes God's ordinance, and that constitutes a sin"; "thou shalt obey the commands of thy sovereign and those who rule over the common people"; "be respectful and obedient to your ruler" and so on. Similar injunctions are too numerous to repeat. If I encouraged disloyalty, would I not betray God's commandments? I entreat Your Excellencies to render a just verdict.

It is clear that this kind of thinking was easy for samurai to assimilate in the early Meiji period.

When Father Nikolai purchased the plot of land of 2,300 *tsubo* (c. one-third of an acre) for his theological academy at Surugadai in September 1872, Soejima Taneomi (1828-1905), then State Minister for Foreign Affairs in the Meiji government, advanced him the money and went to great lengths to lend assistance. In February 1873 the government, which was then concerned about Western public opinion while Ōkubo, Kido, and the others were in America and Europe with the Iwakura Mission, revoked Tokugawa proscriptions against the practice of Christianity. Japanese Christians who had been imprisoned in Hakodate, Nagasaki, and Sendai were released from jail.[16] From this moment the fortunes of the Russian Orthodox Church began to rise. Six lecture halls were established in Kanda and other sites in Tokyo, and missionaries were sent to every corner of the land. In 1876 the first evangelical efforts were carried out in the area around Hachiōji,

[16] In 1865, after completion of a Catholic church by the French in Nagasaki, Japanese Christians, underground since the initiation of persecution in the seventeenth century, came to worship. They were arrested, separated, and imprisoned at several points in the country.

near Takusaburō's future school. But by that time Takusaburō was no longer connected with Father Nikolai's mission.

Takusaburō suffered a major spiritual crisis in the spring of 1875, for he left Father Nikolai for the Ichigaya academy of Yasui Sokken (1799-1876). At least on the surface this was a radical shift and conversion, for Sokken was the author of *Benmō* and perhaps the most renowned anti-Christian intellectual in early Meiji Japan. Ten or more anti-Christian polemics dating from earlier days, the so-called *Haja shomoku*, were republished in the early Meiji period, but Christians considered Sokken—who represented the thinking of educated, ascetic, and skeptical Japanese—their most formidable adversary. Fukasawa Naomaru (1841-1892) and his son Gompachi (1861-1890), who were to become Takusaburō's closest friends, possessed the entire corpus of Sokken's works. Gompachi wrote the following critique of *Benmō*:

> This is the work of the great Confucian scholar of our days, Yasui Sokken. Its superlative logic and exhilarating prose make it something every man of spirit (*shishi*) should read.

Why did Takusaburō leave the church to study under Yasui Sokken? Was it because of doubts that he could not resolve, or did he see himself as a Christian soldier striding boldly into the enemy camp armed with the Holy Scriptures? It is difficult to say, because it is impossible to follow his footsteps. We will have more to say about his beliefs later. If we look more closely at Sokken himself, however, we may find some clues.

Sokken was seventy-six years old when Takusaburō went to study under him. He was still widely recognized as a major Confucian scholar, but his best students had died, leaving him to face his last years alone. His beloved disciple Kumoi Tatsuo (1844-1870) wrote the following poem just before he was beheaded by the Meiji government in 1870. Kumoi was executed for planning an insurrection to reestablish feudal rule, and ten years later his poem would inspire supporters of the People's Rights movement, for whom it provided a compelling image of resolute revolutionary resistance to authoritarianism.[17] Kitamura Tōkoku (1868-1894), when a young activist, lauded and memorized this poem.

Sokken My Teacher
What a drifting thing life is,
Drifting here and there, beyond control.
Feeling and reflecting on my situation I look down;
My heart is heavy, my body wasted.
This insignificant form I offer you, my teacher;
But I will not be able to nurture you in your old age.
I shed tears as I set out from your gate
And my prison cart moves down the distant, solitary road.
I do not fear the pain that awaits me
My beliefs are deep within me
What if my bones are crushed?
My principles will not bend
My life is something I alone control
And I will not beg heaven or earth

Did Takusaburō know that Sokken, who had once traveled through Sendai, considered that his own poem, "Wailing Voices from the Fields," summed up his twenty years of scholarship?[18] This was the other side of Sokken's strong appeal. Takusaburō was probably more attracted by Sokken's spiritual intensity than by his reputation as an anti-Christian polemicist. But fate was not kind to Takusaburō: Sokken died ten months after he began to study with him. First Bankei, then Ōsho; now Sokken. Takusaburō had lost a master a third time. Once again he shouldered his pack and set out alone.

That same fall the young men who called themselves "League of the Divine Wind" (*Shimpūren*) erupted in revolt in Kumamoto in western Japan. This was one of the largest of a series of risings by former samurai. The Kumamoto Prefectural governor and the military commander were wounded and nearly killed. Kinoshita Junji's excellent drama *Furō*

[17] Irokawa, "Jiyū minken no chikasui o kumu mono," *Meiji seishin shi* (Tokyo: Kōka shobō, 1968), pp. 51-116.
[18] See above, p. 77.

(Wandering) describes the mental agony suffered by Restoration youth that led them into rebellion. One of the protagonists starts out as a member of the Shimpūren band; then joins an eclectic, "practical learning" (jitsugaku) group; next seeks fulfillment in a group of Christians (the "Kumamoto Band" fellowship); and then, failing once again to find what he has been searching for, eventually dies in battle in the Satsuma Rebellion.[19] There were men like Miyazaki Hachirō, who started out by joining the fiercely democratic Kumamoto Minkentō (People's Rights party) but ended his life fighting against the Meiji government in the Satsuma Rebellion; there were also others, like Matsuyama Shuzen, who started out in the Shimpūren and went on to join the People's Rights movement. The extraordinary flux that characterized life in the Meiji period is well illustrated by the life of Miyazaki Tōten, Hachirō's younger brother. After the Satsuma Rebellion, Tōten entered Tokutomi Sohō's (1863-1957) academy, Ōe Gijuku. There he was first attracted to "practical studies" and then to liberalism. He became disillusioned with Sohō, turned to Christianity, and finally decided to devote his life to the Chinese revolution as a *tairiku rōnin*, or China activist.[20] After tracking down several hundred such Meiji youths I find that despite the sincerity and order they displayed, most of them ended in obscurity and defeat, buried and lost to history. The spirit of Chiba Takusaburō, one such youth, was shared by hundreds, if not thousands and even tens of thousands of Meiji youths.

In April 1876 Takusaburō went to study under the well-known French Catholic priest Father Vigroux; he stayed with him until the beginning of the Satsuma Rebellion in February 1877. Father Vigroux, who was associated with the Paris

[19] The *Shimpūren* uprising of 1876 provided the ideal for military radicals in the 1900s, as Mishima Yukio's novel *Runaway Horses* shows (trans. Michael Gallagher. New York: Knopf, 1973). In 1877 the Satsuma Restoration leader Saigō Takamori led a rebellion of Satsuma samurai that was the most severe test of strength the Meiji government faced.

[20] See Etō Shinkichi and Marius B. Jansen, trans., *My Thirty-Three Years' Dream: The Autobiography of Miyazaki Tōten* (Princeton: Princeton University Press, 1982).

Overseas Mission, was known as the "walking" priest. Like his successor Father Testevuide, he had close ties with the Tama region, and it is likely that Takusaburō accompanied him on the proselytizing walking tours that he began in the Hachiōji area in 1875 or 1876.

In Moto Hachiōji of Tama county there was a Shimo Ichibugata village with a ghetto hamlet[21] called Fukuoka. A young man from there named Yamagami Takuju, while accompanying his father on his rounds as a peddler in the metropolitan area, made the acquaintance of Nakamura Masanao[22] of the Meirokusha (Meiji Six Society) and managed to enter Nakamura's *Dōjinsha* academy: he met Father Testevuide in Yokohama. In 1876 he was converted to Catholicism, and in the same year he built the St. Mary Chapel in his native village with the help of some fellow outcasts. As outcasts who had endured inhuman discrimination, these men turned first to Christianity and then to the People's Rights movement in their search for equality. In the course of their work for the People's Rights movement, they frequented Itsukaichi village and there became friends with Takusaburō and Fukasawa.

Why did Takusaburō, who fled the Orthodox Church to study under an anti-Christian Confucianist, now turn to Catholicism? The sources we have do not tell us, but what is important to our story is that by evangelizing with Father Vigroux, Takusaburō became acquainted with the people of Itsukaichi, where he would soon take up residence as a teacher at the local school and thereby end his wandering. Just when he first settled in Itsukaichi is not entirely clear. After his death in December 1883, friends of Takusaburō's sent a letter to Hiroda Takatomo, his closest living relative, which included the lines, "Mr. Chiba spent about eight or nine years teaching at the Kannō Elementary School in our village. Because he lived a frugal life, he left only a few possessions. He was a man who held dearly to the principles of freedom and

---

[21] The discriminated underclass, *eta* (later *tokushu burakumin*). See George deVos and Hiroshi Wagatsuma, *Japan's Hidden Race* (Berkeley: University of California Press, 1966).

[22] Nakamura (1832-1891), educator, translator of Samuel Smiles's *Self-Help*, and leading member of the Enlightenment Intellectuals of early Meiji.

equality. . . ." Yet this statement that Takusaburō began to teach at the Kannō Elementary School in 1875 and 1876 contradicts information contained in his personal statement, which says that he studied with the mathematician Fukuda Riken from February to June 1876; then studied with the Reverend R. S. Maclay, a Methodist minister in Yokohama, until November 1879; and failed in a business venture in March 1880 before he took his position at the Itsukaichi Kannō school in April of that year.

It is probable that the facts of the matter will elude us. But it is important to remember that Takusaburō's own account was prepared in October 1881, when he was nominated principal of the Kannō school, and since his appointment had to be approved by the prefectural authorities it would have been difficult to avoid some falsification; it was imperative for him to conceal his activities in the Restoration war and the People's Rights movement. The mayor and school officials who had to transmit that account were his confederates in the People's Rights movement and not likely to reveal information that could be used against him. He probably did go to Tokyo occasionally while he was serving as an instructor at the Kannō school, and he probably did make contact with Father Vigroux and the Reverend Maclay at such times. But why would he have switched again, this time from Catholicism to Protestantism? We have no way of knowing. But it is unlikely that he studied as long as two years with the Reverend Maclay. I think it is more probable that he spent most of that time as an instructor in Itsukaichi, or that he worked with liberals in the Tama area to advance the People's Rights movement; analysis of documents we have recently come upon seems to support that likelihood.

On April 17, 1880, when Kataoka Kenkichi and Kōno Hironaka,[23] representing the Society of Patriots (*Aikokusha*), addressed a petition for an elective assembly to the government on behalf of "100,000 petitioners from twenty-two prefectures and two metropolitan centers," Takusaburō had no expecta-

[23] Kataoka (1843-1903), from Tosa, and Kōno (1849-1923), from Iwaki, were leading liberal politicians.

tion of results because, as he put it in his correspondence, the people had no right of appeal; he went on to assail the autocratic government harshly. In that same letter he noted that "this is the year my wanderings brought me to the Tama area," thus indicating a prior period of drift. The Fukasawa family papers also show that Takusaburō attended a gathering of a poetry club in Fukusawa in December 1879. Nevertheless, Maclay, the Protestant missionary he came to know, had been sent to Japan in 1873 by the Methodist Episcopal Church, which was known, even among Protestant sects, for its fervent social activism. Many of its members went on to join the People's Rights, peace, and social reform movements. Antigovernment in tone, it certainly contrasted with the Orthodox Church that Takusaburō had known. When Takusaburō visited the Reverend Maclay in August of 1877, Methodist mission stations had been established in Shizuoka, Nagasaki, Mikawa, Nishio, Hakodate, Tsukiji, Numazu, Shinshū, and Kanda, but not yet in Yokohama, although a Methodist seminary had been started there. Later Ishizaka Kōreki, Tōkoku's younger brother-in-law, trained at this seminary, and when he went on to California in 1886 he and others received shelter at Methodist churches there. It seems certain that this step into Methodism was closely related to Takusaburō's leap into political activism for liberalism. It was but a step from Methodism to the movement for People's Rights, and it was not uncommon for enthusiasts for political liberties to turn to Methodism at that time.

And so Chiba's spiritual quest that led him from Western Studies to national studies, to Shintō, to Buddhism, to Greek Orthodoxy, and to anti-Christian thought, then to Catholicism and on to Protestantism, finally came to an end about 1879. Now Chiba Takusaburō, of the People's Rights movement, was born.

GRASS-ROOTS SELF-GOVERNMENT

When Takusaburō came to the Tama region with Father Vigroux, a familiar name came to his attention. It was that of

Naganuma Orinojō, who had opened a private academy near Takusaburō's native village in the Sendai domain about three decades before the Meiji Restoration. Naganuma's school had become well known because he taught ordinary farmers reading, writing, and the martial arts. During the Restoration war, Naganuma had led a detachment on the losing side, and performed with valor, but thereafter no one knew what had become of him. Now Chiba heard that he was serving as principal of the Kannō School, a public school in Itsukaichi, Nishi Tama District. On hearing that several Sendai men were teaching there, Chiba headed for the school. It must have been his desire to see them that led Chiba to this remote mountain village. Naganuma had been placed under modified house arrest by the new government. In 1872 he had closed his Sendai academy and headed for Tokyo. While studying there with Fujino Kainan and Oka Rokumon he happened to fall in with Sunagawa Gengoemon, a member of a prominent Musashino family who was also opposed to the Satsuma-Chōshū government, and by this ironic chain of events he was invited to head the new elementary school in Itsukaichi. The records of the Kannō School show that Naganuma took up his position in November 1873; he was thirty-eight years old then.

Looking at the map, we see that the Nishi Tama district of Musashi, though close to Tokyo, is actually cut off from the Kantō plain by rugged mountains. The limpid waters that run down from the Chichibu-Okutama mountains feed the Aki River that flows by Hinohara and into the valley where Itsukaichi is located. Surrounded on three sides by mountains, the settlement at Itsukaichi grew up along both sides of the road that runs parallel to the cliff above the Aki River. The village was called Itsukaichi or "fifth-day market" because by custom a market for villagers from the surrounding area was held on the fifth, fifteenth, and twenty-fifth days of the month. Under provision of a new ordinance established for towns, Itsukaichi with its Kannō School was chosen as the site for a new government elementary school for the town and four neighboring villages in 1876.

The Kannō Elementary School was a more modest affair

Imagined reconstruction of the Itsukaichi Kannō School,
drawn from a Meiji photograph with the help
of the recollections of a contemporary, around the time
that Chiba Takusaburō served as teacher. Building
was a refurbished temple. (Nihon kindaishi
kenkyūkai, ed. *Kindai Nihonshi*,
Vol. 3: *Jiyū minken
undō*. Tokyo: Kokubunsha, 1966.)

than its official status might imply. It met in the local temple,
as had the old parish school (*terakoya*). In addition to the
"Great Teacher" (*Dai Sensei*), as the villagers called Naganuma, there were at most two or three assistants who rarely
stayed at the school very long. Though "in the center of town,"

the temple was situated on the edge of the bluff that over-looked the Aki River. At dusk apparitions like will o' the wisps and occasionally white foxes could be seen at the edge of the property. At first there were about forty or fifty pupils, and the teachers either lodged at the temple or boarded at the homes of well-to-do residents such as the Uchiyama, Baba, and Tsuchiya families. Still, the school made an immediate impact on at least some of its pupils. Fukasawa Gompachi, the son of the headman of a neighboring hamlet, enrolled as soon as the school opened and is credited with racing through the curriculum, advancing one grade a month. He completed his studies very rapidly, and after graduating in 1882 he became an overseer of the school. He was now in a position to assist the teachers from whom he had received his basic education a year or two earlier.

Fukasawa Gompachi's close friend Uchiyama Yasubei, the son and heir of Itsukaichi's hereditary headman, also enrolled at the Kannō Elementary School. In 1878, however, he left to go to Tokyo where he enrolled in Nakamura's Dōjinsha and imbibed the heady spirit of the People's Rights movement. When he returned home the next year, the movement had begun to sweep through the Musashi region, and it soon engulfed Itsukaichi and its environs.

Beginning in 1879, the People's Rights movement in Nishi Tama steadily gathered momentum, and early in 1880 there were numerous public lectures, study groups, and informal meetings. On January 17, the fifteenth branch of the Ōmei Society was established in Hachiōji, and Numa Morikazu (1843-1890), its Tokyo head, attended gala ceremonies celebrating its founding.[24] In early 1880 Itsukaichi was the scene of meetings that were attended by intellectuals from the metropolitan area, among them Numa Morikazu and Okumiya Kenshi (1856-1911). A newspaper correspondent who visited Itsukai-

---

[24] Numa Morikazu (1843-1890), son of a Tokugawa retainer, political leader, and newspaperman, founded the Ōmeisha, a political society, in 1873 as a discussion center for law and politics. The organization became increasingly active as the People's Rights movement rose in the 1880s, but the authorities ordered it dissolved in 1882.

chi at this time reported that there were public reading stalls heavily patronized by the villagers where, "Newspapers and periodicals from all over the country are piled as high as a mountain."[25] In other words, this village, where Chiba had his first opportunity to work out his ideas, was "on the crest" of the People's Rights movement. There is also the testimony of Hatano Denzaburō, the renowned orator of the Ōmei Society. Invited to appear before the Itsukaichi "Learning and Debating Society" (Gakujutsu tōron kai) in December 1881, he was startled by the high quality of the speeches and debates. Incredulous, he inquired further and was told that "We have held lectures and discussions three times a month for the last two years to improve our debating skills." He was tremendously impressed: "Their oratory was passionate and the points were eloquent and incisive. Even the most indifferent bystander would have been moved."[26] This Itsukaichi "Learning and Debating Society" came into being through the initiative of mountain villagers inspired by a new sense of freedom, and it became the breeding ground for local People's Rights activists. The society's charter begins as follows:

> We seek to stimulate and promote intellectual exchange among all members by holding lectures, speeches, and public debates on a wide range of subjects. . . . To this end the society shall from time to time invite distinguished visitors to give talks and lectures. . . . Society members shall read the books and periodicals that are provided by the society in order to increase their knowledge.

Here we see that the society's members sought to gain new knowledge and invited People's Rights activists from Tokyo in order to raise their own level of political discussion. Before long there was a significant change as the society ceased to be a mere receiver of outside ideology and became increasingly creative and independent. In the process it produced

[25] *Tokyo-Yokohama Mainichi shimbun*, April 20, 1880.
[26] Ibid., December 4, 1880.

self-trained farmer-orators like Tsuchiya Kambei and Tsune-shichi, and Fukasawa Naomaru and his son Gompachi, all of whom developed into fine public speakers. And we must not forget to add to this list the name of Chiba Takusaburō, who soon became a key member of the group.

By 1880 Takusaburō had already obtained a sophisticated grasp of natural rights theory. In a letter addressed to Fukasawa Naomaru, probably written in May of that year, he lashed out at the leaders of the Meiji government, who, behind a veneer of reformist and progressive policies, "surreptitiously deprive us of our most precious freedoms." He strongly believed that Japan's territory belonged to the people as a whole, or to the "nation" (*kokka*); it was not the private possession of the government. Nevertheless, the Meiji government had concluded the Karafuto-Chishima Exchange Treaty and launched the punitive expedition against Taiwan without even pretending to consult the people.[27] It was the same with Ōkubo Toshimichi's subsequent negotiations with the Ch'ing government; for Takusaburō this had been tantamount to cheating the people. Small wonder that one group after another had taken up arms against a tyrannical government that did as it pleased. The government had been able to maintain order only at enormous cost; "was that cost not the product of our brothers' blood, sweat, and toil?" Moreover, the government had flooded the country with paper money that triggered rampant inflation, which added to the hardships of the people day by day.

But there was an even greater problem. "Liberty and the rights of the people must be protected now and transmitted to our descendants for all eternity." Yet in spite of the Emperor's edict to that effect, the government had not yet adopted a constitution or opened a national assembly; to the contrary, it had promulgated the Newspaper and Public Assembly Laws

[27] In May 1875, an agreement with Russia fixed Japan's northern boundary by granting Russia Sakhalin while Russia recognized Japan's claim to the Kuriles. In 1874 Japan sent an expedition to Taiwan using an incident in which aborigines had attacked Okinawans as justification.

to suppress freedom of speech and people's rights.[28] The Council of State was reported to have rejected the petition for the early establishment of a constitution that had been presented by Kataoka Kenkichi on behalf of the Society of Patriots (Aikokusha) with the contemptuous response that "the people have no rights," despite the fact that Kataoka and the others represented people from "twenty-two prefectures and two metropolitan areas." Regarding this rejection, he wrote,

> What kind of government corruption is this? If public-spirited men hear of this, they will rage, speak bitterly, gnash their teeth and clench their fists in defiant lamentation. Those who grieve for their country and love their people must become the eyes and ears, the body and soul of the nation and dedicate themselves whole-heartedly to the task of establishing a national assembly to consider carefully what will prosper or harm the country in the days to come. They must debate whether or not a constitution will serve the people's interests. They must guarantee the people's rights, uphold justice, preserve freedom, and ensure happiness.

To achieve this end, Takusaburō argued that people should form associations for the critical exchange of opinions through study and discussion.

Here we find Takusaburō's personal convictions overflowing: He and his group must become "the eyes and ears, the body and the soul of the nation"; they must "debate whether or not a constitution will serve the people's interests" and ensure their "rights . . . justice . . . freedom . . . and happiness." This determination led him to debate after debate in the Itsukaichi "Learning and Debating Society" and to draft a national constitution in his own hand. This spirit of self-reliance—his refusal to seek help from other individuals or organizations—was already apparent in the letter he wrote to

[28] Article 7 of the Public Meetings Law of 1880 forbade teachers, students, and public officials from belonging to political associations and attending political meetings.

Fukasawa Naomaru in 1880, which said that "this was the year my wanderings brought me to the Tama area." In the same letter he expressed his great admiration for men in the Tama area; "they have a superb ability to see through current events." He clearly had Naomaru and his friends in mind. Chiba had made up his mind to work together with them.[29]

I think that Fukasawa Naomaru (1848-1892) and his son Gompachi (1861-1890) lived up to Takusaburō's hopes. At times they were more perceptive than he was. Nor were they the only men in the Itsukaichi "Learning and Debating Society" (there were four other groups with similar names) who lent assistance to Takusaburō. We should add the names of Baba Kanzaemon (forty-five in 1871), at that time the mayor of Itsukaichi; Tsuchiya Tsuneshichi (forty-three) and Uchino Shōbei (thirty-eight), the overseers of the Kannō Elementary School; and Tsuchiya Kambei (forty-nine), the former mayor. These men gave considerable aid and psychological support to Takusaburō. Tsuchiya Kambei, a delegate to the Prefectural Assembly, was the channel for a borrowed copy of the draft constitution prepared by the Ōmei Society that helped Chiba to write his own draft constitution.[30] Known affectionately as "Tsuchikan," "Tsuchitsune," and "Bakan," these men were the leaders of the "Learning and Debating Society"; they joined the Liberal party (Jiyūtō) in 1882. When that party disbanded in November 1884, they did not give up their struggle for popular government but submitted their own petition to the Genrōin urging the early establishment of a national assembly.

Many pundits in Japan today mistakenly think that the vast majority of People's Rights activists were youths and students, but this is only because the Meiji government tried to downgrade the movement by calling its supporters "mere youngsters and students." A look at rural People's Rights supporters shows that there were more men in their thirties than in their twenties. We hear that many of the left-wing activists

[29] See note 4 above.
[30] The Ōmei Society draft was the earliest of the popular drafts.

of the early Shōwa period were young intellectuals who had left their homes, villages, and towns, but the People's Rights movement was not like that. One must never overlook the fact that these were men with firm local roots. In the case of the People's Rights movement of the three Tama districts, for instance, we see that mature men in their middle years provided the leadership while younger men did the leg work and carried out the plans. A large number of those who participated were either heads of households or eldest sons. They were responsible men with high social standing in their communities. A "Learning and Debating Society" circular dated 25 August, 1881 shows that the society had thirty members, about half of whom were men in their thirties and forties. The elected executives consisted of Baba Kanzaemon of Itsukaichi, the chairman, and villagers Ōbuku Seibei, Ōueda Hikozaemon, and Fukasawa Gompachi. The secretaries of the society were Naganuma Orinojō, the headmaster of the Kannō Elementary School, and Tajima Shintarō. The same circular listed three topics scheduled to be discussed at the meeting, two of which focused on constitutional issues: "A monocameral legislature, pro and con," "Should there be capital punishment?" and "Is it advantageous or disadvantageous to export rice?" Of those three, two relate to the problem of a constitution. In addition to this short list, we are fortunate to have a comprehensive list of discussion topics drawn up by Fukasawa Gompachi, who was probably the society's most energetic member. Here there are a total of sixty-three titles that, when analyzed, provide considerable insight into the character of the Itsukaichi "Learning and Debating Society."

The largest category consists of fifteen topics that relate directly to the drafting of a national constitution. Nine topics are concerned with the legal system and six with people's rights; together these three categories cover almost half of the sixty-three titles. In addition, there are thirteen topics devoted to economic problems. The remainder range from politics, foreign policy, and military affairs to a variety of everyday problems. The society discussed, for example, "the pros and cons of allowing the people to bear arms" and the pros and cons of "organizing local militia units in the case of war or rebellion." One topic touched on extraterritoriality: "Is a sovereign state obliged to extradite foreign nationals who have committed crimes?" There were even some humorous topics, for example: "What should be the punishment for a man who encounters another man's wife on the road and kisses her?"

Nor did the society shy away from discussion relating to the emperor. "Should the Imperial Palace be located in the capital or not?" "Should the aristocracy be abolished?" and "What are the advantages and disadvantages of giving the Emperor exclusive power to conclude treaties?" In the draft constitution that Takusaburō wrote, the emperor is given that power, but this power is severely restricted. "Treaties that affect the security of the people, their welfare (trade and commerce), treaties that require government expenditure, treaties that surrender or in any way alter national boundaries, and revisions of such treaties shall be null and void unless approved by the national assembly."[31] He also gave the assembly power to "pass judgment on and revise proposals emanating from the bureaucracy and from the Emperor,"[32] and "the assembly will be required to approve treaties with other countries."[33]

The draft constitution of the Ōmei Society that Takusaburō had in front of him contained no comparable restraints on the power of the emperor. It would be of the greatest interest to analyze the way these local discussions were incorporated into the draft constitution, but that would require another study with a detailed, section-by-section exposition, not only of the memoranda of the debating societies' officers but also of the notebooks of Chiba Takusaburō. His notations are so numerous that entire pages of his books about law and constitutions (almost one hundred remain) are filled with red markings and marginal comments that reflect his study. Such a study would

[31] Section 3, Article 35 of the Itsukaichi draft. See Irokawa, "Meiji zenki no jinmin kempō," *Kaishi* (Tokyo: Tokyo Keizai Daigaku, 1969), no. 61.

[32] Section 1, Article 9, Itsukaichi Draft.

[33] Section 3, Article 57, Itsukaichi Draft.

101

certainly demonstrate the concern and intensity of the People's Rights enthusiasts in that mountain village.

SUBSTITUTION AND RESTATEMENT

In the autumn of 1968 we announced to the Tokyo press the discovery of an astounding document we had found among an immense cache of historical materials, dating from the time of the Meiji Restoration, that had been buried eighty-six years in a storehouse in Fukasawa village in the mountains of Nishi Tama. This was the "Itsukaichi Draft Constitution." Painstakingly brushed on traditional Japanese paper (*washi*), Chiba Takusaburō's constitution is one of more than thirty extant draft constitutions that were written by private citizens, study groups, and political societies.

With the exception of the constitution Ueki Emori (1857-1892) prepared for the Risshisha,[34] Takusaburō's 204-article constitution contains more articles than any other draft constitution, three times as many as the Meiji Constitution, and twice as many as the present Japanese constitution.

When we compare Takusaburō's draft with the 180-article draft of the Ōmei Society, which he used as a model, we see that there is little difference in the number of articles that deal with the emperor in Chapter I. But in Chapter II, which concerns public law (people's rights), Takusaburō's constitution contains 36 articles compared with the Ōmei Society's 10, and in Chapter III, the legislature, Takusaburō has 79 articles, 31 more than the other draft. Both drafts have 13 for Chapter IV, the cabinet. From this we can see how strongly Takusaburō was concerned with the rights of the people and the powers of the elected assembly.[35] Equally impressive is the care he lavished on the chapter devoted to the judiciary, which contains 35 articles compared with only 8 in the Ōmei Society's draft. This is not only because law was Takusaburō's forte; more important, we find here evidence of his convic-

---

[34] The *Risshisha*, a Tosa samurai organization, was the earliest of the organizations championing constitutional government. Ueki Emori was one of its intellectual leaders.

[35] Ei Hideo, "Ōmeisha kempō sōan ni tsuite no kōshō," *Kaishi*, no. 61.

tion that basic human rights should be doubly guaranteed and receive protection from both the legislature and the judicial branches of government. The constitution stipulates, for example, that the national assembly has the power to veto any action of the administration that violates the freedoms guaranteed by the constitution, and individual citizens are to be protected by legal rights built into the judicial process. Most of the draft constitutions that came out of the People's Rights movement followed either the English model of a constitutional monarchy with a Parliament (emperor, elected lower house, and upper chamber) and a cabinet based on the lower house, or the American constitution with a tripartite division of powers, but in none does one find the detailed enumeration of people's rights found in the 151 clauses devoted to them in Takusaburō's draft constitution. Of course, compared with the "Declaration of the Rights of Man and Revolution" in the Jacobin Constitution of 1793, or to the constitution drafted by Ueki Emori, which called for a single-house legislature and sanctioned popular resistance, Takusaburō's constitution may seem compromising and overly moderate. But in terms of what was feasible at the time, it probably came closest to embodying the hopes and aspirations of most Japanese who advocated democratic government.[36]

We cannot assume that the "Itsukaichi Draft Constitution" is a precise reflection of Takusaburō's personal political beliefs, because in addition to the constitution we also have a memorandum Takusaburō wrote that contains an explicit rejection of the principles of monarchical sovereignty. The occasion for this was the publication by the Genrōin in 1878 of a translation of Peter Brougham's *Institutional Maxims*. Under the title *Hōritsu kakugen* as a guide to the preparation of a constitution. Takusaburō wrote a humorous countercommentary that he titled "The Institutional Maxims of Chiba Takusaburō, Distinguished Professor of Japanese Law." In his critique we can see how a teaching assistant at a remote public elementary school playfully challenged the legal precepts

[36] Ienaga Saburō and Emura Eichi, *Meiji zenki no kempō kōzō* (Tokyo: Fukumura shuppansha, 1967).

103

of Brougham (1778-1868), a distinguished English jurist and political theorist. For example, Takusaburō substituted "The king may die but the people never die" for the maxim "The king never dies." Again, he added to the statement "The King is not under the authority of man, but only under that of God and the Law" to make it read, "The King is not under the authority of men, but only under that of Heaven; the people too are not under the authority of men, but only under that of Heaven." This kind of substitution and restatement by Takusaburō of Brougham's ponderous *Institutional Maxims* illustrates how Japanese in the Meiji period freely created their own political thought.

Genrōin Translation of Institutional Maxims
1. The King never dies.
2. The law is the supreme inheritance of the King.
3. The throne is established by justice.
4. The spirit of the sovereign is presumed to be the same as that of the law; in cases of doubt, the presumption is always in favor of the King.
5. When the right of the sovereign and the right of the subject conflict, the right of the sovereign takes precedence.
6. The sovereign is the source of justice.
7. The King cannot deceive the People, nor be deceived by them.
8. The sovereign's privileges do not depend on written records.
9. The sovereign's sanction shall be absolute.
10. Lapse of time does not impair the rights of the King.
11. Differences of time and place do not impair sovereign authority.
12. The Senate is part of the body of the King.
13. The right to mint coin is among those rights of the crown that are never relinquished.

Takusaburō's "Restatements"
1. The King may die, but the People never die.
2. The law is the People's supreme inheritance.

3. The throne is established by justice and so are the People.

4. The spirit of the People is presumed to be the same as that of the law; in cases of doubt, the presumption is always in favor of the People.

5. When the right of the People and the right of the sovereign conflict, the right of the People takes precedence.

6. The sovereign is the source of justice and so, equally, are the People.

7. The King cannot deceive the People, nor can the People deceive the People.

8. The sovereign is never to be granted special privileges.

9. The People's sanction shall be absolute.

10. Lapse of time does not impair the rights of the People.

11. Differences of time and place (within Japan) do not impair the People's authority.

12. The Senate is part of the body of the People.

13. The right to mint coin is among the rights that are never relinquished by the People.

This kind of restatement was common with Meiji people, and it was applied to traditional Confucian writings and even to imperial proclamations as well as to Western thought. It was a method of free interpretation and transportation that could reverse the thrust of the original. In this case we see the principles of monarchical absolutism transformed into liberal sentiments with the retention of an almost identical formulation and vocabulary, and we can learn a good deal from this witty stroke by an ordinary Japanese.

Takusaburō perfected this technique in an unpublished essay, "Treatise on the Way of the Ruler" (*Ōdō ron*), which he wrote in the late autumn of 1882. Drawing astutely on the *Shu Ching* and other Chinese Classics, he used Confucian concepts to advocate English-style constitutional monarchy. He also seized upon the Charter Oath of 1868 and the 1875

Imperial Proclamation that promised an eventual constitution, to charge the Meiji government with "disobedience" of
an imperial decree: "Anyone who rejects a constitutional system of government—who opposes a popularly drafted constitution and the establishment of a popular assembly—is guilty
of disobeying an Imperial Decree."

In 1880 Matsusawa Kyūsaku (1855-1887) of Shinano (Nagano Prefecture) used a petition signed by over 21,000 people
as the cornerstone of a fifty-day campaign that he single-handedly carried out in the capital for an elected assembly and a
constitution. A passage from that petition reveals the same
popular rhetoric and argument that we detected in Takusaburō's writing:

> Can the Emperor be unaware? Is the trend of the times
> changing? Are people indignant? Last summer, all across
> Japan people were to memorize the Charter Oath and
> the Imperial Proclamation of 1875 that promised a na-
> tional assembly. All classes, all ages, have joined to-
> gether to demand a national assembly. Heedless of the
> costs to themselves, the people are devoting themselves
> to the movement, giving speeches, rallying supporters,
> and organizing local societies and political parties. Each
> group tries to outdo the other and to make the other
> struggle to keep up. Enthusiasm is so high that it can be
> compared with the spirit of the loyalist activists who re-
> stored the Emperor and overthrew the *bakufu* at the
> time of the Restoration-Revolution. Starting in Fukuoka
> and Okayama, we have presented over fifty petitions,
> and we are now drafting scores of constitutions. This alone
> is proof that over half of the more than seven million
> households in Japan support the opening of a national
> assembly. It is no exaggeration to say that it is the "pub-
> lic opinion" of the nation.[37]

This logic of "restatement" (*yomigae*—lit. "read and substitute") was not adopted by progressive intellectuals or social-

---

[37] Irokawa Daikichi, *Kindai Nihon no shuppatsu* (Tokyo: Chūō kōronsha,
History of Japan Series, 1966), vol. 21, pp. 109-40.

ists in the post-Meiji period, but rightists and cultural nationalists like Gondō Seikyō and Kita Ikki did carry on this
tradition.[38]

We can surmise that it was in November 1880 that the
Itsukaichi "Learning and Debating Society" and its "Distinguished Professor of Japanese Law" became infected by the
rising tide of constitutionalist sentiment that was sweeping
the nation. This was the same month that the Alliance for
Establishing a National Assembly (Kokkai kisei dōmei) held
its second meeting in Tokyo and resolved that affiliated organizations should prepare a prospectus for a properly drafted
constitution within the year. This decision ignited a nationwide movement that eventually produced scores of draft constitutions, and it seems that our friends in Itsukaichi were
also responsive to this appeal and began to work on a constitution.

During the last ten or fifteen years I have perused massive
quantities of historical documents, but in no period of Japanese history have I encountered evidence of the same kind
of enthusiasm for study and learning that existed in mountain
farming villages in the 1880s. This enthusiasm was not limited
to the southern Kantō region where I have done my field
work; the same phenomenon can undoubtedly be found
throughout eastern Japan and, in fact, from Tsugaru in the
north to Hizen, Hyūga, and even Okinawa in the south. If
we immerse ourselves in contemporary grass-roots opinion
and documents, we find this enthusiasm almost everywhere.
We should not be surprised, then, to come across a mountain
village in Musashi where there was a local study society
founded by the mayor, who was himself a People's Rights
activist, and that it included many prominent citizens—the
headmaster and supervisors of the local school, Shintō and
Buddhist priests, the doctor, landlords, and even peasant

---

[38] Gondō (1868-1937), twentieth-century agrarianist and anticapitalist, and
Kita (1883-1937) were major voices of discontent in the ultranationalist move-
ment of the interwar years. See Thomas R. H. Havens, *Farm and Nation in
Modern Japan: Agrarian Nationalism, 1870-1940* (Princeton: Princeton Uni-
versity Press, 1974), and George M. Wilson, *Radical Nationalist in Japan:
Kita Ikki, 1883-1937* (Cambridge: Harvard University Press, 1969).

farmers. This was a unique period in our history, and Takusaburō himself began to display his remarkable talents only
after becoming part of a community of this kind.

Creating A People's Constitution

Chiba Takusaburō wandered for ten years before finding happiness in a sympathetic and receptive environment. In his
own words:

> The members of this study group ("The Learning and
> Debating Society") have firmly resolved to devote them-
> selves to furthering freedom and to reforming society.
> Sharing an inflexible determination to overcome all ob-
> stacles, we are united by a spirit of affection, esteem,
> and harmony. It is almost as if we were of the same flesh
> and blood, or brothers in one large family.

Moreover, these men were in firm control of local political
power, which made them a kind of commune—though not,
of course, in the strict sense of the word. During the long
winter of 1880 they discussed deep into the night and to the
sound of a crackling fire the matter of drafting a national constitution. This was the first real happiness that Takusaburō
had known. The letter he addressed to Fukasawa in December of 1880 shows an almost delirious joy.

Further evidence of the ardor and seriousness with which
local People's Rights societies dedicated themselves to the
drafting of constitutions can be seen in the case of the Kumamoto Sōai (Mutual Love) Society in Kyushu. Members held
all-night sessions for ten consecutive days before they were
able to reach a consensus. They finally delegated the drafting
assignment to Yano Hayao, a Tokyo People's Rights activist.[39]
It is a matter of the most profound regret that modern Japan
was not able to adopt a constitution that emanated from the
spirit of the people and embodied their enthusiasm and wisdom. In the process of preparing his draft constitution, Taku-

[39] "Matsuyama Shuzen jijoden," unpublished manuscript.

saburō, along with Fukasawa Naomaru and Gompachi, read all the pertinent books that were in the Fukasawa collection. We cannot help being astonished by the tremendous drive of this man who pursued such a long spiritual and intellectual pilgrimage, and who changed directions three or four times, without once losing his determination to find the truth.

Among the books of Takusaburō that were found in the Fukasawa storehouse were eight translations of the sets of lectures by Gustave Emile Boissonade (1825-1910), a French legal scholar who went to Japan in 1873 at the invitation of the Japanese government. It should be noted that almost all these papers were government documents used by official planners. In addition, he read Tanaka Kōzō, *Kakoku kempō* (Every Country's Constitution); translations of John Stuart Mill, *Considerations on Representative Government*; Joseph Story, *Commentaries on the Constitution of the United States*; A. M. Chambers, *A Constitutional History of England*; Albert Beine, *Lectures on French Constitutional Law*; George de Bousquet, *Lectures on French Commercial Law*; Jeremy Bentham, *On Laws in General and Theory of Legislation*; Simon Greenleaf, *Treatise on the Law of Evidence*; Francis Lieber, *On Civil Liberty and Self-Government*; Bernhard Windscheid, *Introduction to German Civil Law*; and six or seven books and manuals published by the government. Some of the books had been stamped with Takusaburō's seal and were filled with marginalia that he wrote in red ink. When discovered in the Fukasawa storehouse, they were already half worm-eaten. That they survived to come into our hands at all is nothing less than a miracle.

On 5 December 1880, while Takusaburō was hard at work preparing his draft constitution, a regional People's Rights meeting, the Bushū konshin kai (Musashi Friendship Society) was held at the Kōanji temple in northern Tama as a preparatory step for the convening of a regional association of People's Rights supporters from Musashi and Sagami. Koizuka Ryū (1851-1920), of the Tokyo Ōmei Society, was invited, and Ishizaka Masataka, the first chairman of the Kanagawa Prefectural Assembly, Nakamura Kokushō, Yoshino Taizō, and

Satō Teikan addressed the meeting as directors of the organization. In addition there were many present from the Tama districts and other areas, many of them members of the Prefectural Assembly. Itsukaichi was represented by Tsuchiya Kambei and Chiba Takusaburō. Chiba's excitement seemed to know no bounds, as can be seen from a letter:

> Oh, to meet in person four distinguished leaders of our Prefectural Assembly! The first preparatory meeting for the prefectural Liberal party meets here in Fuchū! Despite my humble status, I was allowed to participate in the meeting and witness its success. . . . My enthusiasm and joy were boundless. If I could wish for anything more, it would be that under the guidance (of these men) we may advance step by step, and taking hold of the ideas of the people of England and America, build a democratic future for Japan.

A joint meeting of the Musashi and Sagami People's Rights groups was held 2 January 1881, in Minami Tama district. Three days later the Jichi kaishin tō (Self-Government Progressive party) was established at the Kōanji temple with Sunagawa Gengoemon as chairman and Yoshino Taizō and Nakamura Katsuaki among the officers. The tide of the People's Rights movement was spreading ever faster. It was at this time that Takusaburō first obtained a copy of the Ōmei Society draft constitution; it had been given by Nomura Motonosuke to Tsuchiya Kambei and then passed on to Takusaburō by Fukasawa Gompachi. With the Ōmei Society draft in hand, Takusaburō redoubled his own efforts to draft a constitution. At meetings of the Itsukaichi "Learning and Debating Society" he worked out the fine points of the articles that delineated the rights of the people and the powers of the national assembly. He also needed specialized reference books, and as the above list shows, Fukasawa Naomaru did not stint on efforts to get whatever was available. In addition, Takusaburō had at his disposal reference materials that had been specifically prepared for the use of government officials in the

Genrōin and Law Ministry, thanks to Nakajima Nobuyuki, who lent them to Fukasawa Naomaru.

The constitution that Takusaburō wrote was not without defects. The first chapter, which dealt with the constitutional position of the emperor, was copied directly from the Ōmei Society's draft; consequently the powers delegated to the emperor negated or were at variance with successive chapters that gave the rights of the people and powers of national assembly. Also, a number of articles lacked legal sophistication. For example, Article 35 read:

> If the government transgresses the constitutional principles of religion, morality, freedom of belief, and individual freedom, or if it does not respect the principle of the equality of all people and the right to property as written in the constitution, or if it impairs the defenses of the country, the national assembly shall have the power to argue resolutely against, remand, and prohibit the promulgation of such acts.

In addition, certain articles took up inappropriately mundane topics such as public sanitation.

In certain articles of Takusaburō's constitution we can see ideas that had been discussed at the Itsukaichi "Learning and Debating Society." One topic debated by the society was the merits of a two-house legislature. Takusaburō's constitution provided for a nonelected upper house, as did the Ōmei Society's constitution, but he reversed its criteria for membership by listing in order, (1) the speaker of the elected house, (2) third-term members of the elected house, (3) ministers of state, and (4) councilors, leaving (5) royal family and aristocracy last instead of first. The question of capital punishment, another subject discussed by the Itsukaichi society, was handled by Takusaburō's constitution clearly: "Persons convicted of crimes against the state shall not be subject to capital punishment. Moreover, guilt or innocence in such trials shall be determined by trial by jury." Thus his constitution did not duplicate either Western models or the Ōmei Society's draft constitution. In my estimation, it was the product of the Itsukaichi People's Rights "commune," and it was a document that spoke with the voices of the people of Nishi Tama. This is why I call it the "Itsukaichi Draft Constitution."[40]

It is not clear when Takusaburō finished working on his constitution, but it was probably well before August 1881, when Ueki Emori and Naitō Roichi wrote their constitution, which has received so much praise. Takusaburō does not seem to have referred to the well-known constitution of the Kōjun-sha that was drafted in May and June of 1881 and published in the *Yubin Hōchi* daily, probably because he had already left Itsukaichi by July 1881. There is a post card dated July 13, 1881, which he sent to Fukasawa Naomaru and Gompa-chi, posted from Narabashi in Kita Tama district, in which he complained that the government was now extending to school teachers the same strict controls it had on government administrators. He announced that he had "firmly decided to resign" his position at the Kannō Elementary School, and he asked for advice about alternative employment.

In this we see Takusaburō's reaction to a decree issued by the Kanagawa prefectural governor on 6 July 1881 prohibiting elementary school teachers from engaging in political activity. Soon after the decree became law Takusaburō resigned. In September 1881 he wrote to Naomaru to express his gratitude formally: "During the period of my employment I benefited from your benevolence constantly, even to the extent of money for a vacation . . . remembering all this brings tears to my eyes." By this time he had taken up residence in Sayama. He wrote, "I am staying at the Enjōin Temple in the mountain village of Sayama; on the 25th of this month we will hold a People's Rights rally here to which we have invited members of the Ōmei Society."[41] He extended an invitation to Gompachi to speak at the meeting. Research shows that a rally was in fact held there on September 25, with Akabane Manjirō as speaker.

[40] Irokawa Daikichi, Ei Hideo, and Arai Katsuhiro, *Minshū kempō no sōzō* (Tokyo: Hyōronsha, 1970), is entirely devoted to the Itsukaichi Draft Constitution.

[41] Letter dated September 15, 1881.

Of course, government repression was not the only reason for Takusaburō's resignation from the Kannō Elementary School. It seems that he was not getting along well with Naganuma Orinojō, the school principal, and he was also suffering from pulmonary tuberculosis, a disease that was later to take his life. Leaving Itsukaichi was a wrenching experience for Takusaburō, and living in Sayama seems to have produced extreme depression. But his friendship with Fukasawa Naomaru and Gompachi did not fade away; on the contrary it deepened. The very act of separation from the Itsukaichi "commune" made him all the more aware that it was his spiritual home.

In October 1881, there was a major crisis within the ruling oligarchy of the Meiji government[42] and at the same time the People's Rights movement reached its apogee. Takusaburō had obtained copies of the newly founded Liberal party's covenant and membership list, and since he stamped his seal on both documents, he had apparently decided to join. His stay in Sayama, however, was interrupted by an unexpected turn of events. Naganuma resigned from the Kannō Elementary School; he had decided to return to Tokyo after his nine years' absence from the capital. The people of Itsukaichi gave their "Great Teacher" a gala farewell dinner, after which they invited Takusaburō to become the school's new principal. Now twenty-nine years old, Takusaburō returned "home."

SWAN SONG

One can see how liberal Takusaburō must have been as principal from the very critical report that was filed by his successor at the Kannō Elementary School. He charged that for all intents and purposes the school had become a bastion of the People's Rights movement, and that under Takusaburō's directorship teachers assigned to the school by the prefec-

---

[42] The crisis centered on revelations of corruption in the disposal of government-initiated enterprises; its two major political effects were the ouster of Ōkuma Shigenobu from government and a promise from the throne that a constitution would be prepared within the decade.

tural education authorities had been pressured to leave. What made this possible was that the mayor of Itsukaichi, Baba Kanzaemon, had joined the Liberal party (Jiyūtō) in 1882, and the school's overseers, Fukasawa Gompachi and Uchino Shōbei, were also Liberal party members. Clearly Takusaburō had been given free rein. But just as his hands were freed, his health began to fail. At the urging of his friends, he went to the Kusatsu hot spring in June 1882, to recuperate for sixty days. From his sickbed he sent letter after letter expressing his anger at recent government moves to suppress freedom of speech and public assembly. But willpower was not enough, and his health failed to improve.

> Around eleven o'clock on the evening of June 20, I was stricken by excruciating pains in my intestines that caused me to writhe uncontrollably and flail about. The next day my bowels stopped moving, a condition which remains unchanged. The pain is indescribable. I haven't eaten in two days, and feel as if I might as well be dead.[43]

The tuberculosis had probably spread to his intestines, causing ilius.

Between exhausting bouts with pain Takusaburō wrote a heart-rending letter to Gompachi, which he meant as a last will and testament. It shows that the future of the Itsukaichi group of comrades was his chief concern. He advised Gompachi that "you and the Tsuchiya brothers will be the only lecturers left." He warned Gompachi against people who simply pay attention to a speaker's personality and oratory, who "do not stick to principles but just follow a leader and not a principle." Such people were to be attacked relentlessly. He encouraged Naomaru and Gompachi to "take initiative in siding with justice, set the agenda for discussion topics, and lead the followers away from error." He also warned that the liberal society must not become a social club for wealthy farmers and prominent citizens, "a hand-out for dilettante poets and painters."

[43] Message to Fukasawa Gompachi.

Takusaburō's health did not improve in 1882 or the following year. Although there were ups and downs in his condition, it gradually became apparent that his disease was incurable. But nothing in his journal indicates that he was praying to a "god"; what we see instead is his indignation at the government's ruthless suppression of his friends in the People's Rights movement. His journal makes note of the government's arrest of "subversives" and the verdict of the high court that followed the mass arrests of People's Rights activists in Fukushima.[44] The only indications of a spiritual life are occasional references to Buddhist or Shintō religious texts; the reader may well wonder what became of Takusaburō's earlier faith in Christianity.

I too am unclear on this point. There is no direct evidence in his letters, notes, or journals that he was still a believer, and on occasion he went out of his way to mock individual Christians. For example, at one point in his journal he poked fun at Naganuma Orinojō who, like himself, was a convert to the Orthodox Church. Referring to a meeting held in the summer of 1882, Takusaburō wrote: "There was a meeting at a Christian evangelical center at Nishikichō, and Naganuma persuaded that Christian Ōi Kentarō[45] to address the gathering. Speaking directly to Matsui, Ōgoshi, Nizuma, and other new converts, he gave a lecture on Christian ethics. As he expounded his ideas I was impressed by how terribly corrupt Naganuma's purpose seemed." This suggests that he had lost his faith.

This post card was written to Fukasawa Naomaru and Gompachi from the spa at Kusatsu. In Itsukaichi, where there were many converts to the Russian Orthodox Church, Naomaru and Gompachi were conspicuous for their hostility to Christianity. Naomaru had once served as the priest of the

---

[44] The Fukushima incident, which was concluded by the arrest of Kōno Hironaka and five other People's Rights leaders in 1882, is described in Roger Bowen, *Rebellion and Democracy in Meiji Japan* (Berkeley: University of California Press, 1980), pp. 8ff.

[45] Ōi (1843-1922) was a People's Rights leader from Ōita, student of French law and political thought, and activist in Asian causes.

local Shintō shrine, and Gompachi studied and made notes on a nine-volume anti-Christian collection, the *Jakyō sho-moku*.[46] These men were Takusaburō's closest friends. We can also find in his journal a reference to the left-wing Jiyūtō leader Ōi Kentarō as "that Christian," a choice of words that reinforces the suspicion that he no longer identified with the Christian faith. In all the letters and in the journal he kept during his agonizing illness of the year and three months that remained to him, there is not a single sentence asking for forgiveness for his sins.

"*Ōdō* (The Kingly Way) is to administer the Great Way of Governance; it is not the Way of a prince. Even in countries where there is no prince, there must be *Ōdō*." These are the opening lines of the "Treatise on the Kingly Way" (*Ōdō ron*), which Takusaburō wrote to systematize and give coherence to his political thought, despite his critical illness.[47] It was written in the late autumn of 1882. The original text has survived, written by brush on thirty-two sheets of Japanese-style paper with an average of two hundred characters per page. It can be credited to his last months by the epilogue written by the Liberal party member Akiyama Fumikazu.

The treatise used the vocabulary of the ancient Chinese classics and Confucian thought to express concepts on which to build a Meiji constitutional order. For example, he tried to explain the concept of natural rights by drawing on phrases from the *Shih Ching* (Classic of Poetry), which was widely known among the people. In another case Takusaburō used the phrase, "Heaven embraces the people and Heaven shall heed the wishes of the people," which appears in the *Shu Ching* (Book of History) to argue that "*Ōdō* stresses restraint." As in his draft constitution, Takusaburō adopted the realistic position that Japan's constitutional system would have

[46] Ichii Saburō, "Dochaku shisō no saikentō," *Shisō no kagaku* (January 1970).
[47] Translated by Richard Devine as "The Way of the King" in *Monumenta Nipponica* 34, no. 1 (Spring 1979): 62-72.

to accommodate itself to sovereignty shared by ruler and people.

"Nothing weakens the Kingly Way more than a ruler who despises his people or a people that observes no restraint on its liberties." *Ōdō* was a Kingly Way that recognized the importance of people's rights, but Takusaburō also argued that "Those who think only of increasing people's rights without exercising restraints on their liberties are ignorant of *Ōdō*" as well. At the same time, since limits had to be placed on the authority of the ruler ("restraints on Imperial prerogatives") the polity could be kept in balance only by maintaining the two sets of "restraints" in a "Great Harmony." If the power of the ruler became excessive and violated this principle, the doctrine of revolution found in the *Shu Ching* ("the people will overthrow their government") could justly be invoked.

> Thus the True Kingly Way consists of establishing two sets of "restraints" that are voluntarily observed by sovereign and people alike in a Great Harmony. These restraints are established by means of a constitution, and the Great Harmony is mutually observed by means of the national assembly. A "constitutional form of government" consists of creating a constitution and a national assembly.[48]

Moreover, Chiba cited "The Charter Oath" and imperial pronouncements of 1875 and 1881 to assert that the creation of "this constitutional form of government, which establishes restraints on Imperial prerogatives and popular liberties, has been a long-embraced desire of His Majesty," and that therefore "Anyone who refuses to implement a constitutional system of government, that is, who opposes a popularly drafted constitution and the establishment of a popular assembly, is guilty of disobeying an Imperial decree."

The political thought of Takusaburō's "Treatise on the Kingly

---

[48] In his "Draft Constitution," Chiba Takusaburō defined "National Assembly" as the "Great Harmony" between "popularly elected assembly, upper house, and Emperor."

Way" was widely shared among nonofficeholding People's Rights enthusiasts, as we saw earlier in Matsusawa Kyūsaku's rhetoric. Taking into consideration the level of consciousness of the common people and the relative strength of the anti-government forces within the emperor-centered polity of the early Meiji period, and remembering that at this time the Emperor was still in some ways a symbol of progressive government, Chiba's was a realistic and viable route of attack. We should not disparage it. As Ichii Saburō writes, "We see here the creative struggle of a Meiji People's Rights youth who, faced with his own imminent death, tried to breathe new life into a long-suppressed tradition."[49] Nevertheless, the argument also contained the potential for degenerating into narrowminded and obscurantist "direct action" nationalism. Writing from the standpoint of Protestant Christianity in 1886, Kozaki Hiromichi (1856-1938) made the following critique in *Seikyō shinron*, which he published in 1886:

> Ōdō is limited to a single country and a single government, but God's Heaven encompasses the entire world. Ōdō sets apart those who are superiors from inferiors, the noble from the servile, and the esteemed from the despised, and seeks to maintain this strict social hierarchy. In Heaven, on the other hand, nobody is superior or inferior, noble or servile, esteemed or despised; all stand equal before God. By eradicating these social distinctions, all the people of the realm become comrades, brothers, and sisters, and dedicate themselves to loving their fellow man. Ōdō is propagated from above, from the country down to the individual in a descending hierarchy. This is not so with God's Heaven, which extends from the bottom up, starting with the individual and finally encompassing the entire nation.

This critique starts with the conviction that "all humans are equal in the sight of God." It posits the Western European conception of the individual in civil society and builds a world

---

[49] See note 46 above.

order that begins with him and then goes on to consider state, globe, and universe. It is a powerful conception. Contemporary People's Rights activists in Japan, however, were not receptive to Kozaki's arguments, since such modern concepts were foreign to the traditions of the Japanese people. People's Rights supporters who struggled steadfastly at the local level were better able to assimilate the traditional concepts of revolution that one finds in Takusaburō's "Treatise on the Kingly Way." Kozaki's systematic, modern theories never took hold among the people. If they were absorbed at all, it was among the elite.

This may appear to be one of history's ironies, but it is not. Is it not what one would expect of ideas that are the product of one cultural and intellectual environment and find themselves utilized by the people of another land? It is a tortuous process; like Takusaburō's own quest, the road will twist and turn and sometimes backtrack before reaching its destination.

And yet, I do not feel that Takusaburō's "Treatise on the Kingly Way" is a mature intellectual work; it contains potential, but that is all. If he was trying to develop his ideas into something that would liberate the Japanese people, he probably should have honed them more carefully, as he did in his earlier "Institutional Maxims of Takuron Chiba." In sum, he should surely have laid bare in critical fashion the essence of his "Great Harmony" between "restraints on Imperial prerogatives" and "restraints on popular liberties." As it stands, his thinking lacks the dynamism needed to break through and to transcend compromises with traditional ideas such as communal conformity and indigenous, family-centered orientation.

Early in the summer of 1883 it became evident that Takusaburō did not have long to live. In desperation his friends raised enough money to send him to a Tokyo hospital, but it was apparently already too late; death moved relentlessly closer. Sensing that his days were numbered, Takusaburō summoned his remaining strength to write a lengthy essay titled "On the Futility of Book Learning" (*Dokusho mueki ron*). The preface to this essay is strikingly similar in part to

119

Kitamura Tōkoku's essay, "The Poet and the Voice of the Universe" (*Banbutsu no koe to shijin*).

> Man is a microcosm of the great universe. His body exists in this living universe, and must be a living chapter in the giant volume of the universe. What is this chapter? The universe is a great school of learning. Established at creation, the world around us is an encyclopedia written by creation, and the sun and moon are lamps hung by the creation.

Takusaburō's simile of the world as a great book of learning was meant to show that real knowledge could be gained only by "reading" the everyday world. Mere book learning, no matter how many volumes, is insufficient; but by opening our eyes and ears we can pursue the truth in the streets, in factories, behind the plow: "Even the tumult of a crowd or the bustle of the marketplace can be the laboratory in which man attains wisdom." The message is clear: learn from direct experience, and do not forget to seek after the truth in daily toil. Takusaburō called for an end to the ideal of the versatile Renaissance man and urged the mastering of a single skill or art: "The goal of manifold accomplishments and a life devoted to reading are the greatest extravagance." Severely critical of himself, Takusaburō wrote:

> What is meant by versatile abilities? I say that it is to begin Chinese studies and after a few days, take up Western studies, then to turn to law, to medicine, to mining, to astronomy and so on in endless succession. Everything is left half done, abandoning first this and then that without mastering anything. . . . To be incapable of finding self-repose and of alleviating the burden of one's family—that is the fruit of "versatility."

Forced to take stock of his short life, Takusaburō wrenched forth his painful confession, for was he not describing his own course? Fighting on the losing side in the Meiji Restoration, losing one teacher after another and moving from one religion to another in his desperate youthful quest for a new life, he had finally found his way to the Itsukaichi People's Rights "commune," where he developed a vision of a liberal and free Japan. Then, with Takusaburō beaten back, dying a lonely death at the very moment that the People's Rights movement was collapsing, do we not encounter here the deep regret and pain of Meiji men? Listen to this poem of his:

Mountain barrier in snow and river rain
Ten years of search, with all gone wrong,
Half a life spent traveling in vain, a dream reflected in a window,
The cuckoo from the grove, calls
"Better retreat than continue on."

Takusaburō, who had once referred to himself with unrestrained exuberance as "Mr. Takusaburō Chiba, Distinguished Professor of Japanese Law, resident of Freedom Prefecture, Independence District, Righteous Spirit Village," now succumbed to homesickness—feelings that, one must regretfully admit, show that he was very Japanese.

After a life of wandering, Goethe's Faust cried, "O for a kingdom of freedom on earth, to be celebrated by ten million men!" But our Meiji "Dr. Faust" lamented, "Half a life spent in vain travel, a dream reflected in a window!" Here we see a deep gulf between the historical experience of Japan and that of the West.

Nonetheless, there was light in the early Meiji years. The call for freedom continued to be heard in the mountain village of Nishi Tama, and those who joined the funeral procession for their departed friend were numerous. And how had Japan changed by the time the Meiji period had entered its later years? Metaphorically, Takusaburō's swan song was transformed in the famous poem of Kunikida Doppo (1871-1908):

Yearning and pursuing vanity
Ten years have left me a handful of dust
Looking back, I see that village of freedom
Has receded beyond these misty mountains.

Ah, but freedom lives in mountain forests
Reciting this poem, my blood revives again.
Ah, freedom lives in mountain forests
Come what may, I shall not leave them.

When Kunikida Doppo wrote this poem in 1897, he was forced to admit Japan's "freedom village" had already "receded far beyond these misty mountains." Therefore, when he voiced again his lonely plaint that "freedom lives in mountain forests," what he meant was that it could still exist in nature: in mountain forests, but not possibly in mountain villages.

Takusaburō's short life came to a close on 12 November 1883, when he was barely thirty-one years and five months of age. His friend Fukasawa Gompachi was deeply distressed by Takusaburō's death; in an effort to lift himself from the depression into which he had sunk, he wrote this farewell salute to his friend's spirit, titled "Lament for Chiba Takusaburō":

Your spirit envelops the swirling billows
You tower above my country friends

In oratory, you rank with Patrick Henry
In argument, you seem worthy of Rousseau.

In a single sentence you expressed it all
A sword that served its country in one hundred battles

With your death a valiant spirit will rise no more
Incense wafts in hopeless coils against the willow swamp.

(Translated by Stephen Vlastos)

· IV ·

POETRY IN CHINESE
AND REVOLUTIONARY THOUGHT

Ōnuma Chinzan and Mori Shuntō—Two
Contrasting Undercurrents

When this book of mine is compared with conventional studies of Meiji cultural history that deal with the development of enlightenment thought, romanticism, and naturalism or that describe the works of great Meiji artists and writers, it may seem a bit unusual. To begin with, although I do take up "The Impact of Western Culture," I seldom, if ever, use the periodizations that are usual in literary history. Then again, I devote considerable space and attention to chapters that bear titles such as "The Silent Folk World," "Creating Culture from the Grass Roots," or "Wanderers Seeking Truth." All this may make the reader wonder whether I have really written about Meiji *culture*. But those are the ideas with which I set out to write this book. In this chapter I address a problem—"poetry in Chinese and revolutionary thought"—that has not been discussed very much in conventional histories of Meiji culture in the past. I do so by focusing on the life of an obscure farmer whom I recently discovered and restored to the light of day.

This man was a true sympathizer, close friend, and staunch supporter of "Takuron Chiba." Unfortunately, however, he died at the early age of twenty-nine, and the two friends were buried next to each other. Undoubtedly they would have remained unknown if we had not, seventy-eight years later, opened the door to that one small storehouse in Fukasawa that had somehow managed to remain intact. Its interior was so rotted away, and the documents left behind by those two youths were so worm-eaten, that they would not have been readable much longer.

With the passing of time the names of many, in fact most,

great men are lost, especially if they belong to the masses. In the vast sweep of history, this heartless process of selection may be inexorable, and who will be remembered and who forgotten is largely a matter of chance. Nietzsche once derided historians as "men who exhume the graves of the past," but anyone who succeeds in exhuming the real grave of a great man must count himself fortunate, for such success is a matter of chance. Without a keen awareness of this cruel fact, no one—least of all myself—may presume to speak of history.

Fukasawa Gompachi is such a great man, and unearthing his grave reinforces this poignant awareness of fortune in history. At this point, it is of little importance to mention that he was the largest landowner in a small mountain village of about twenty households. What is important is that during his brief life span Gompachi, though he possessed little formal education, composed over seven hundred poems in classical Chinese and left as many as seventeen volumes of poetry he selected and edited. These poems were not composed as literary diversions, or belles-lettres, like those often found among wealthy farmers in Edo times, but they served as the medium through which he expressed the rhetoric of revolutionary change on which he staked his youthful life.[1]

Of course I do not mean to imply that there was not an element of diversion in his poetry; there will always be aspects of diversion and entertainment in the pursuit of beauty and truth through poetic composition. Fukasawa wanted to be a man of refinement and lead a life of leisure so that he could escape from worldly affairs; he longed to bask in "a carefree life of elegance enjoying nature's beauties." But at the same time, precisely because of such longings, he felt a keen sense of opposition to the society in which these were denied him. He gave up his inner desire for a peaceful life of seclusion, broke through the comfortable shell of his life style, and felt the urge for a life that would smash through the trib-

[1] For a discussion of the role of Japanese poetry in classical Chinese (*kanshi*) in Japanese culture see Burton Watson, trans., *Japanese Literature in Chinese*, 2 vols. (New York: Columbia University Press, 1975 and 1976).

ulations of the new age with the spirit of a *shishi*.[2] All this found an outlet in his poetry; emotions of tranquillity and pent-up opposition surge through the lines of his poems.

Fukasawa Gompachi began composing poetry daily from about 1880, and he continued to do this until about 1885-1886, precisely the era in which the People's Rights movement peaked and ebbed. When Gompachi was in his early–mid-twenties, all parts of Japan experienced the greatest revival of *kanshi* composition of the entire Meiji period. (Kitamura Tōkoku and Hosono Kiyoshirō also composed in this era.)

Yamaji Aizan lists four periods during the Meiji era in which Chinese poetry was popular: 1881-1882, 1887-1888, 1899-1900, and 1907-1908. Of these the first was the greatest. It would not be wrong to say that these years also marked periods of reaction against Westernization; yet Meiji culture was not so much a series of pendulum swings between "Westernization" and "nativism" as it was the product of native counterflows within the larger and dominant currents of Westernization. Westernization was not a single flood tide rising unopposed: it would press forward only to meet with a reaction, be temporarily halted, then lurch ahead, only to be pushed back again. Through it all, Meiji culture made tumultuous headway, and herein lies its distinguishing style.

No one has yet found a conclusive reason as to why Chinese poetry enjoyed its heyday in 1881-1882, but there are two generally accepted hypotheses: one relates it to the Confucian revival that Motoda Eifu and other imperial advisors led in reaction to the *jiyū minken* movement, and another relates its decline to the craze for Westernization that peaked in 1885-1886.

In his article, "Chinzan and Shuntō," Maeda Ai[3] acknowledges that there were two schools, represented by Ōnuma Chinzan and Mori Shuntō, during the first (1881-1882) "boom" in Chinese poetry. In my opinion, though, these two schools

---

[2] *Shishi*—man of high purpose—is the term Restoration activists enshrined in the Japanese tradition.

[3] Maeda Ai, "Chinzan and Shuntō," *Nihon kinsei bungaku*, no. 8 (1968).

were only the crests of the waves that led to that first boom. One wave originated among those in positions of power, but the other was more broadly based farther down in Japanese society. The former stemmed from an instinctive desire for self-improvement by upstart bureaucrats who had finally succeeded in gaining access to power, and it happened to fit in with their needs for embellishment of the emperor system ideology. The larger movement, however, derived from an impulse on the part of wealthy farmers all over the country to discover in *kanshi* a medium of expression for their newly risen class. Without this latter movement, the wave from below, neither Mori Shuntō nor Ōnuma Chinzan would have received the attention they did.

Shuntō succeeded as a poet who could portray the ambitions of men in power. In October 1874, when he left Gifu for a rented house in the Shitaya district of Tokyo, he was already fifty-six years old, and he humbled himself to the point of lamenting that "I grieve at my wretchedness." Little did he know that he would become a popular favorite in Tokyo poetry circles and be surrounded by high government officials.

At that time there was a three-way rivalry between poetry schools; Ōnuma Chinzan's Shitaya poetry club led; less successful were Okamoto Kōseki's Kōjibō poetry club and Suzuki Shōtō's Nanamagari poetry club. Of the three, Chinzan's reputation was especially high, and people came constantly to request him to check their poems and correct them. He prospered so much that it was said "the middle of his inkstone wore thin." Mori Shuntō and Ōnuma Chinzan had originally been pupils at the Yūrinsha under Washizu Ekisai. Chinzan (1818-1891), who was one year older than Shuntō, went to Edo in 1835, and soon became famous by publishing his first anthology of poems.

Chinzan, like Nagai Kafū,[4] deeply appreciated and enjoyed the things of the Edo period. He did not take part in politics,

---

[4] Kafū (1879-1959) is chronicled in Edward Seidensticker, *Kafū the Scribbler* (Stanford: Stanford University Press, 1965).

even during the late Tokugawa political struggles, but instead indulged in poetry and wine. One could criticize him for being too conservative, but he reacted bitterly to the new Meiji government, and he was not afraid to declare that "the government of the emperor is not admirable." As a result, he was arraigned by the imperial police department at one time, and his life was even endangered. In this respect, his attitude is comparable to Narushima Ryūhoku's melancholy and depression.

On the other hand, Mori Shuntō (1819-1888) became famous under Yanagawa Seigan in Kyoto during the Ansei era (1854-1860), was associated with the antiforeign loyalist *shishi* in Restoration times, and volunteered to fight with the Owari contingents for the imperial cause. But his reputation as a poet was no match for that of Chinzan. Shuntō wandered from Kyoto and Osaka to Gifu and then to Tokyo. He complained about "being in distress for three years and wandering from place to place four times."

After he moved to Marishiten in Shitaya and founded the Mari poetry club, however, Shuntō's fame grew rapidly. His worldly shrewdness quickly realized the vanity of the new high government officials. He obtained support from Washizu Kidō, the judge of the Supreme Court, and son of his former teacher, and thereby quickly gained the patronage of high officials. In July of 1874 he published the first issue of *Shin bunshi* (New Verse), the journal of a new literary style in which he entered numerous pieces composed by high officials, thereby puffing up the vainglorious upstart *shizoku* from Satsuma and Chōshū.

According to Maeda Ai, thirty or more high officials such as Itō Hirobumi, Yamagata Aritomo, Hijikata Hisamoto, Tanano Seiri, Watanabe Kōki, Ōe Taku, Yoshikawa Akimasa, Tani Kanjō, and Gotō Shōjirō contributed to *Shin bunshi* between the first and thirty-second issues. Shuntō never hesitated to publish works of an inferior or vulgar quality in order to flatter government officials. He enhanced his literary reputation by publishing anthologies of their poems one after another, celebrating the alleged harmony between the government and its people. Wherever high officials gather, their lowly subordinates are not far behind. The Mari poetry club became crowded with pupils and prospered.

In contrast to this, Ōnuma Chinzan drank more and more. Remaining aloof from high government officials, he sought obscurity in solitude, yet he was idolized for his eccentric behavior. It is said that "nearly a thousand men passed through the gates of his house." But Chinzan, who shunned people, suffered from lung disease, and his failing health gradually became apparent. In November of 1875, a banquet for poets sponsored by Narushima Ryūhoku was held at Mukōjima. Shuntō came, but Chinzan did not.

In 1877 the Satsuma Rebellion broke out. High government officials, the patrons of the Mari poetry club, marched their troops to Kyūshū, took Saigō Takamori's head, and returned to Tokyo in triumph. At this time, Shuntō published numbers 24 and 25 of his journal, filling them with poems celebrating the government's victory and condemning Saigō.

While the common people of Japan spread rumors that "Saigō's star has come to the east" and showed their sympathy for the anti-government leader, Shuntō vilified Saigō by writing "even a dog does not eat the flesh of the dead and vanquished. How could such a man regain his soul and become a star in the sky?" At this time, Narushima Ryūhoku did not permit a single congratulatory poem to appear in his journal, *Kagetsu shinshi*; he treated the war with silent contempt. Chinzan, in turn, maintained his reclusive stance more firmly than ever and adopted an attitude of stubborn hostility toward the war. In the following year, 1878, he published a volume titled *Edo meishōshi*, punning on *shō*, for beauty and victory, and so ridiculed a new *Tokyo Journal (Tokyo shinshi)* that Shuntō had helped put together.

In April 1881 there appeared—in the form of a *sumō banzuke*, or championship ranking—a list called the *Tōkyō genkon bunga tairan* (Contemporary Tokyo literati and artists) presented for examination to the Empress and the imperial family, and edited by Yamamoto Daisuke. Among the more than one hundred literary writers and high government officials on the list, Ōnuma Chinzan was still ranked at the top, in the highest position as a poet. Mori Shuntō was placed above Uemura Roshū in fourth place, following Ono Kozan and Chō Baigai. Konagai Shōshū, Suzuki Shōtō, and others also rated high, but they were classified as "calligrapher-poets." Manaka Unpan, Mizoguchi Keigan, Takeuchi Shinzan, and others were placed in the middle group. Because Narushima Ryūhoku, Kurimoto Hōan, Fukuchi Ōchi, and others were high-ranking former Tokugawa officials, they were treated separately and placed at the bottom of a group of high officials. Others treated this way were Nakamura Masanao, Oka-matsu Okoku, Washizu Kidō, Shigeno Seisai, and Yamaoka Tesshu.

At the head of a group of high government officials was Prince Arisugawa Taruhito. Below him in the top category were Higashifushimi Bansui, Sanjō Ridō, Kitashirakawa Yoshifusa, and Iwakura Tomomi. In the second row were Itō Hirobumi, Ōki Takatō, Yamagata Aritomo, Yamada Kūsai, Kuroda Kiyotaka, Kawamura Sumiyoshi, and Katsu Kaishū. In the third row were Sasaki Takayuki and fifty-eight others. A glance at this list gives a rough idea of the basis for such literary evaluations.[5]

In 1881 Chinzan was still at the height of his popularity, but the poetic style of a new school led by Shuntō had grad-ually gained acceptance and popularity against the backdrop of the enlightenment movement, and the decline of Chinzan and his school had begun. In fact, it was probably the lower strata of local men of letters and People's Rights advocates who sustained his popularity.

In May 1879 Shuntō was invited to a banquet held for poets by the head of the Council of State, Sanjō Sanetomi. Shuntō pleaded with Sanjō to appoint his son Kainan to a government position. In 1881 Kainan got the position, and he soon be-came a close associate of Itō Hirobumi.

Chinzan, however, fared worse. In the fall of 1882, he was

[5] That is, the compiler fawned on the political elite by crediting them with literary achievements appropriate to their power.

stricken with paralysis and confined to his bed. One and a half years later, in the early spring of 1884, Hosono Kiyo-shirō, a *jiyū minken* advocate from Ogawa village in Minami Tama District, who was also known as a very active member of the Jiyūtō, took time off from his strenuous campaigns to visit his old teacher, Chinzan, at Okachimachi in Shitaya, to inquire after his illness. Many other local People's Rights leaders did the same.

Now a question comes up: why did Shuntō's "New Verse" (*shintaishi*) fail to satisfy contemporary revolutionaries while a conservative recluse like Chinzan had his poems well received by Hosono, Ishizaka, Fukasawa, and many local People's Rights advocates? The reader will have guessed the reason for this paradox. It is similar to the fact that poems by Kumoi Tatsuo, the Meiji rebel who seemed to have fought against the Restoration revolution, were appreciated and often recited by the *shishi* of the People's Rights movement.

Common people have learned through their long years of experience that "people intent on being up to date tend to become enemies." When Shuntō derided "the star of Saigō," the spirit of his poems had become utterly divorced from the people's hearts.

That Shuntō had deserted the cause was clear and beyond any doubt to Hosono Kiyoshirō, Fukasawa Gompachi, and others who lived at the lower stratum of society. As a matter of fact, it was the People's Rights activists who clearly saw through the priorities to which poets in the metropolitan literary circles subscribed, and they were not deceived by it. But Yasui Sokken, Kumoi Tatsuo, and Ōnuma Chinzan, to whom Chiba Takusaburō, Fukasawa Gompachi, and Kita-mura Tōkoku looked for guidance, clearly had the spirit of real poetry. Think again about the story of Yasui Sokken: after hearing about "loud cries of weeping" among commoners in Sendai in late Tokugawa days, Sokken composed a poem and then asserted that "after twenty years of scholarship this poem is what my learning amounts to. I will have to wait another twenty years before passing judgment on its implementation in government." How can one call this scholar of Ancient Learning an unregenerate, antiquarian Confucian or say that

Kumoi Tatsuo, Sokken's disciple, was a "reactionary former samurai"?

In his later years, Chinzan said that even if he starved to death he "would not beg for mercy from those sycophants." Young People's Rights advocates undoubtedly discerned that they would have to equip themselves with this same moral fiber. The biography of Ōnuma Chinzan goes as follows:

> Our teacher was already seventy years old. His heir was a wastrel, and the fortunes of the family were declining rapidly. A man suggested to Chinzan, "You are an old man of seventy. Why don't you hold a testimonial party to celebrate your long life and rescue your family from its dire circumstances?" Our teacher replied, "Since the time of the Restoration I have kept myself aloof from the world. Those other fellows have pursued wealth and fame. I despise them. I would gladly starve to death now, rather than beg mercy from them."[6]

When he learned about Chinzan's predicament, Ishizaka Masataka, the leader of the Santama district Jiyūtō, immediately sent rice, salt, wood, and charcoal to Chinzan and his poetry club. (It should be noted that it was Manaka Unpan, Mashimo Banshū, and Hiratsuka Baika, not Chinzan himself, under whom Ishizaka had studied.) This relationship struck mutually responsive chords—the People's Rights movement and Chinese poetry supported each other at the lower stratum of society during the first decade of the Meiji period.[7] Now let us return to young Fukasawa and his life.

HISTORICAL CONSCIOUSNESS AND POETIC SPIRIT

Fukasawa Gompachi, the first son of Fukasawa Naomaru, was born on April 28, 1861. By Japanese reckoning he was eight years old in 1868, the year of the Meiji Restoration, and he

---

[6] *Ōnuma Chinzan den.* Testimonial parties were a traditional device for raising money through contributions from those invited.

[7] See Yanagida Izumi, *Meiji bungaku kenkyū* (Tokyo: Shunjūsha, 1960), *Meiji shoki no bungaku shisō*, 2 vols. (idem, 1965), and *Seiji shosetsu kenkyū* (idem, 1966-1968).

turned twenty when the People's Rights movement reached its height.

This poem, which he wrote on the back of now-faded photographs of Napoleon Bonaparte and George Washington, shows his yearnings at that time.

> Once again I respectfully admire your meritorious deeds
>   in hundreds of battles.
> Your great achievements for the Republic shine over
>   Heaven and Earth.
> Should people seek to learn about your heart,
> it will seem a moon whose light reflects across ten
>   thousand miles of waves.

Gompachi's longings are also revealed in his admiration for the poems composed by Ōnuma Chinzan and Kumoi Tatsuo. His approval of and devotion to Kumoi are especially noticeable. Several volumes of Kumoi's poems, which were brush-copied by Fukasawa, can be found in an anthology he compiled of his own poems. The following poem, composed at the time of his death, is particularly noteworthy. In it is crystallized the defiant and proud spirit of Kumoi Tatsuo, the Yonezawa retainer, whose plot to overthrow the government was exposed and who was executed at the age of twenty-seven. This is the poem that Murakami Ichirō praised as "one of the finest death poems composed in any age in any country."[8]

> At death, I fear no dying;
> In life embrace not living;
> The brilliance of the sun
> Is rivaled by integrity.
> Execution has no terror,
> Though it be a boiling cauldron;
> But how insignificant my poor person,
> Against the Great Wall!

[8] Murakami Ichirō, *Kumoi Tatsuo no shikon to hankotsu* (Tokyo, 1968), *Dokumento Nihonjin*, vol. 3: *Hangyakusha*, p. 14.

In the past Kumoi Tatsuo has been regarded as having led "a rebellion of ex-samurai" or as "a feudal reactionary" in early Meiji. Despite these assessments, it is difficult to imagine how deeply People's Rights advocates ten years later grieved over his death, how encouraged they were by his resolution, and what inspiration they drew from it in their efforts to change the history of their times. In January 1881, when Nomura Motonosuke, a member of the Tokyo Ōmeisha, was campaigning in Sano, Tochigi Prefecture, a local associate came to see him at his inn. Their talk soon turned to Kumoi Tatsuo, and the man confided to Nomura that because "I could not suppress my indignation," he himself had been one of those who joined in the plot with Kumoi.[9]

Fukasawa Gompachi's experience with Kumoi was not as direct as that of this man in Tochigi Prefecture. His was an inner experience, which stemmed from understanding and assimilating Kumoi's ideas through "the power of imagination." The experience was all the more intense, however, because Gompachi obtained it through his own activities as a People's Rights activist who resisted despotic rule and risked his life in an attempt to gain freedom. Therefore, in Gompachi's eyes, Kumoi Tatsuo and Akai Kageaki[10] stood on common ground. Not only Akai and Kumoi; it seems to me that all those executed in the Meiji Restoration and who appear one after another in Fukasawa Gompachi's cursive notes or memos stood on common ground.

A note that Gompachi wrote in a copy of the biography of Sakura Sōgorō that he hand-copied and signed in October 1881, goes as follows:

Is "People's Rights" really something new, an import from the West for which Japan has never, since ancient times, provided any precedents or seeds? I will not discuss the reigns of the ancient emperors just now. But we can gen-

[9] *Tokyo-Yokohama Mainichi shimbun,* February 23 and March 18, 1881.
[10] Akai (1859-1885), a Meiji People's Rights activist who was executed after escaping from a prison where he was serving a nine-year sentence for revolutionary and insurrectionary activity.

uinely cite the peasant rebellions as a beginning of popular rights. It was simply assumed that peasants were ruled by oppressive governors and that they should obey official orders blindly. Nevertheless, they rose in revolt.
. . .

And on the front page he copied part of Ōshio Heihachirō's revolutionary manifesto of 1837.

In his attempt to rescue farmers in several hundred villages in the Shimōsa region, Sōgorō Sakura had made a direct petition to the Bakufu and for this was executed together with his family. He was vindicated posthumously, however, by being ranked among the Tōyō minkenka (East Asian People's Rights Leaders). Ōshio Heihachirō, of course, was the bakufu official who led a rebellion in Osaka that helped pave the way for overthrowing the bakufu. Such martyrs have been recorded permanently in the history of the liberation of the Japanese people. Young men like Fukasawa were inspired by them and tried to revive their tradition. Does this not have to be called a vivid historical consciousness?

Yoshida Shōin, a revolutionary of the Meiji Restoration, was, as everyone knows, executed by the bakufu during the Ansei Purge. Yet not even I had expected that Fukasawa Gompachi would have copied and preserved the complete text of Yoshida's prison farewell, *Ryūkonroku* (A Record of Leaving My Soul in this World).

Though my body may perish on the plains of Musashi,
Let my Japanese spirit remain alive.

How deeply did this cry of Shōin's penetrate the hearts of Gompachi and others? We can speculate about this, for the brush strokes of his memos are inked in deep black. He must have felt that Shōin and Kumoi Tatsuo were kindred spirits.

In addition it seems that Naomaru, Gompachi's father, co-operated with some friends to donate the stage curtain on the occasion of a stage play about Takano Chōei that was per-formed at the Shintomi Theater in 1886. In Gompachi's writ-

134

ing the name of Takano Chōei is listed with those of Kozeki San'ei, Watanabe Kazan, Sakuma Shōzan, and others.[11] We may not be able to provide conclusive documentary evidence as to why people in a Musashi mountain village were especially interested in Takano Chōei. But when we think about the following figures—Sakura Sōgōrō, Ōshio Heihachirō, Takano Chōei, Yoshida Shōin, Kumoi Tatsuo, and Akai Keishō— we come to understand that Gompachi intended to carry on the will of these men who were imprisoned and executed. It seems to me that Gompachi's resolution was crystallized in his notes; he copied a poem lamenting the death of Tamono Hideaki, who died in prison in connection with the Fukushima incident, and the wills of Kobori Shigeo and Kotoda Iwamatsu, who died on the scaffold because of their involvement with the Kabasan incident, and the farewell poem by Yasuda Komakichi.

It seems that Gompachi had a deep respect and affection for Akai Keishō, member of the Kubiki Liberal party and victim of the Takata incident, who was charged with conspiracy to overthrow the government. Gompachi wrote in detail about Akai's personality and convictions and copied out Akai's mother's farewell greetings at the time of her son's imprisonment. Moreover, he prefaced the following poem with the statement: "I respectfully offer the following poem to the spirit of Master Akai Keishō on the very day of his execution, July 27, 1885."

An evil mist shrouds these mountains and rivers,
I weep and read your poems, composed in the face of
execution, with reverence.

Your blood, which has poured from your heart,
will color the Heaven of freedom in future days.

[11] Takano Chōei (1804-1850), late Tokugawa scholar of Western learning who lived as a fugitive twelve years after escaping from prison after being jailed for writings critical of Tokugawa policies. Kozeki San'ei and Watanabe Kazan were involved in the same "purge" of 1839.

You willingly risked your life for freedom.
The heart of one of honor and courage shall surely fill
our Sacred Land.

Though our master has perished,
future generations promise they will never give up the
task of clearing the mist that surrounds these mountains.

In the Japan of those days Chinese was the only literary
medium capable of conveying the pledge to do away with the
conformist sychophancy that prevailed around the government. It was a form of expression appropriate for describing
familiar scenes and feelings. There is a short piece that Gompachi hurriedly composed on his return to the Shinkōin Temple in his own village:

A warm wind blows through a deserted forest,
about to embrace the evening's red sun.
Up the slope's path I halt for rest and gaze upon
the valley to the south.
The tolling of the bells.
Late autumn. A Zen retreat amid the mountains.

Buyō shishū, an anthology of Gompachi's poems, notes that
Chiba Takusaburō and his friends held a poetry party at the
Zen garden of this nearby house in December 1879. Whereas
Takusaburō wrote poems that are lively and masculine in style,
Gompachi (or Buyō, his pen name) wrote poems marked by
a delicate sensitivity. As far as one can see in Gompachi's
Shidaishū, his aesthetic concerns were like those of Hosono
Kiyoshirō, whose poetry I have discussed elsewhere.[12]
The seasonal and other themes to which these men de-
voted themselves reveal not only their personal aesthetic in-
terests but also the literary outlook and distinctively Japanese
attitude toward nature that lay submerged in their innermost
hearts:

[12] Irokawa, "Meiji no gōnō no seishin kōzō: Hosono Kiyoshirō ron," *Jimbun kagaku ronshū,* nos. 8 and 9 (Tokyo: Tokyo Keizai Daigaku, 1965).

In spring, I yearn to view cherry blossoms at a ruined temple, to listen to the sound of a flute at night. In summer, I want to hold a little banquet in the shade of trees, to take a stroll in the moonlight, in the evening. In mid-autumn, I am fond of singing poems under the full moon, of viewing rain pouring down mountains in the distance in twilight, of visiting a temple in the forest under the moon, and of listening to wild geese on a moonlit night. In winter, I consider it the highest bliss to fish alone in the cold, to drink wine in the evening by the river as the snow falls, and to spend a winter's day at a small cottage.

This is a serene and elegant world that, even today, remains deeply rooted somewhere in the hearts of the Japanese people—an aspiration to recapture a oneness with nature wherein the individual can find solitary and lasting tranquillity. It is a traditional attitude—Japanese, Oriental, Shintō, Buddhist—by which one lives in intimacy with eternal life and with death. This attitude is precisely the aspect of the Japanese mental character that is, as Watsuji Tetsurō and others have said, rooted in "climate." It seems to me that the fierce *shishi* spirit and revolutionary activities of the People's Rights advocates were two-sided; the solitary and tranquil world longed for here resembles the serenity and stillness of death. The tension in their poetic spirit is contained in this ambivalence; most of these poems belong to the world of serenity. On closer examination, however, it becomes apparent that it is usually a serenity kept under tight control; passion and tumult seethe below the surface. It is no longer the world of passivity, based on frustration and resignation, that prevailed a generation earlier. A storm of radical change was raging and roaring beyond the village. In the early Meiji period the temptations of success and social advancement for talented youths knocked seductively at the door, throbbing irresistibly within young men's breasts. As a matter of fact, many of Gompachi's young colleagues had left their home villages, and as he watched youths from his village leave for Tokyo even he, who praised "the joys of life in the mountains," must have felt alarmed. The following series of compositions from *Buyō shishū* show something of his uneasiness.

> A man of Japan in the Eastern Sea am I,
> Stouthearted, unafraid.
> In indignation and resolve
> I burst through raging surf.
> Once established in resolve and name,
> Successful in my goal,
> I will talk with friends about my Japanese sword.

and again:

> Alas! How can I achieve great things?
> I love green hills: my body will lie
> In a box three *ken* in length, overlooking mossy ground.
> Two tigers contend, but in a single game of chess.
> Men of seclusion, free from worldliness,
> Ride in palanquins and arrive at the house.
> Bush warblers sing and flit among the flowers.
> I submit to Heaven's will
> How can I cast doubt on it?
> As I turn my head about, I see
> Lightly colored scenes of spring, as in a dream.

How closely Gompachi's poetic mood resembles the elegant wish, expressed in this poem by Hosono Kiichirō, his friend in the Minami Tama area!

> I want no fame. Nor am I proud.
> I shall devote my life to letters.
> Today much goes on, and I fear for my country.
> In one way I want to go to the capital
> To debate the way of government.
> In another I prefer to withdraw to a rocky valley,
> to shun the wicked and the evil.
> I hope only to have a silver cup of *sake* one day,
> Enjoying the civilization of a Japan that has come to
>   flower.

One sees here the self-assured attitude of East Asian men of letters who shun vulgar fame and arrogance and prefer to find self-fulfillment in eternal and superior values within themselves. This attitude was the aesthetic consciousness that sustained the vigor of Meiji Japan—a consciousness that made it possible for these men to share with the nation's common people "silver cups of sake" at a great "spring banquet" as the flowers of Japanese civilization came into bloom.

THE LIFE OF LOCAL MEN OF LETTERS

Gompachi and his friends began their study of poetry by copying poems composed by prominent poets. About twenty volumes of those copybooks remain. Among these is an almost verbatim copy of the anthology *Meiji shisen*. There is also an Edo anthology, *Kinsei shishō*, selected by Gompachi himself. In addition, there are seventeen volumes of anthologies that consist of his own poems and selections. These anthologies are not solely his work but are combined with a collection of poems composed by thirty-two of his friends.

In analyzing these works, I came to understand the interesting way in which the *jiyū minken* movement of those days overlapped with that of Chinese poetry. The statistics are as follows: of the total number of 1,500 poems, 788—or half—are Gompachi's; the second largest number, 303, belonged to Nakashima Genchō. Nakashima had the pen name of Tankai and was a Zen monk and Gompachi's neighbor. The third largest group, 81 poems, was by Naganuma Orinojō, whose pen name was Kashiwadō (or Hakudō), and who was the principal of the Kannō School in Itsukaichi. The fourth largest contributor, with 34 poems, was Uchiyama Yasubei, whose pen name was Gofū, and who was a member of the Jiyūtō in Itsukaichi. Okano Motoyasu, a Zen monk with the pen name of Kōhitsu, in Nishi Tama, ranked fifth with 32 poems. The sixth, with 31 poems, was Izumi Mutsumune, who was also a Zen monk, with the pen name of Yūrin. Tsuchiya Tsunekichi, with 22 poems, is listed as the seventh. He had the pen name of Setsuhō (or Seppō) and was a member of the Jiyūtō in Itsukaichi. With 21 poems, Aburai Morio, whose pen name

139

was Suihoku, was eighth, and he was a member of the party temporarily living in Itsukaichi. The ninth, with 20 poems, is Satō Teikan, who had the pen name of Gagyū, and who was the secretary of the Jiyūtō in Sagami, Kanagawa Prefecture. Haneda Sōsen, with 15 poems, is ranked the tenth—a Zen monk, with the pen name of Kazan.

Then follow:

Takemura Kōjirō—pen name, Bidetsu—a People's Rights advocate

Itō Dōyū—pen name, Seikyō—a school teacher and People's Rights advocate

Tsuchiya Kambō—pen name, Shisui—a Jiyūtō member

Akabane Toshiyoshi—pen name, Shōtei—a Jiyūtō member

Date Toki—pen name, Ryōshū (or Rinshū)—a Jiyūtō member in Sagami

Yoshino Taizō—pen name, Ungai—a Jiyūtō member in Kita Tama

Last were Toshimitsu Tsurumatsu, Kubota Kume, Nakajima Nobuyuki, Kōchi Gyōhei, and Chiba Takusaburō—all school teachers, People's Rights advocates, and Jiyūtō members.

The anthology *Nyoran yokun* contains poems composed by twenty-five poets. Gompachi has the most. The poets whose works are included in the anthology are virtually the same men, with a few others such as Satō Shimpei (pen name, Ichijō, a member of the Jiyūtō in Itsukaichi) and Masuda Mokuryō.

From this list, we can surmise that the Tankōsha poetry club in Itsukaichi consisted of individuals from three groups: Gompachi and his Jiyūtō friends, a group of Zen monks led by Nakashima Genchō, and a group of school teachers led by Naganuma Orinojō. The members of this organization, the Tankōsha, all had the same hobby of poetry composition and were able to mobilize members to launch movements for local autonomy, for self-study, for establishing a national assembly, and for helping comrades in distress.

The headquarters of a group that called itself the Ibunkai was set up in Gompachi's residence, which he named the Tensokudō (The Hall of the Heavenly Principles). It was there that he met with members of the club and corresponded with Tokyo. It was probably from there that he often wrote letters to Ōnuma Chinzan, Kikuchi Sankei, Umasugi Ungai, Kurimoto Joun, Kokubu Seigai, Takabayashi Gohō, Ota Ka'in, and other nationally known figures. One sees everywhere in the anthologies that have been preserved red brush corrections inserted by those masters; the comments by Chinzan, Sankei, Ungai, and Gohō remain as they were.

Corrections by Ōnuma Chinzan are the most numerous. To begin with, Chinzan kept up acquaintances he had made with wealthy farmers and intellectuals in the Musashi area in late Tokugawa times. He kept close personal contacts with Kojima Shōsai, the *gōnō* scholar in Onoji Village (presently Machida City, Tama District) during the years of the Keiō period, and he often visited him. One finds in the Kojima household many books written by Chinzan.[13]

In 1877 membership dues in the Shitaya Poets Association (Shitaya Ginsha) cost one *yen*, but most instruction assumed the form of correspondence courses for which fees were roughly two *yen* per fifty poems corrected. Ōnuma Chinzan and the People's Rights advocates of the Tama area were on intimate terms, and he had many disciples among them. Since he became ill in the fall of 1882, however, most of them probably never met him personally. When we examine an extant pile of draft poems, however, we are struck with admiration to see how carefully and thoroughly Chinzan and the others corrected and commented on them. In these corrections and comments there is none of the arrogance that often characterizes eminent scholarly authorities. No wonder disciples in local areas were deeply moved by his manners.

Furthermore, beginning in 1882, Gompachi and the Tankōsha members sent their works to the Meibunsha and to the

[13] The Kojima Shiryōkan, in the care of Kōjima Sōichirō, in present-day Machida City, contains materials by Ōnuma Chinzan and others.

Kumpūsha in Tokyo and received instruction from these clubs. Correction fees per poem were arranged as follows:

> one and a half *sen* for Chinese quatrains of five characters;
>
> two *sen* for Chinese quatrains of seven characters;
>
> two and a half *sen* for eight lines of five characters;
>
> three *sen* for eight lines of seven characters;
>
> ten *sen* for free verse in ancient-style Chinese verse; and
>
> one and a half *sen* for Japanese poems (*tanka*).

In 1883 the group subscribed to poetry journals like *Shintoku yoshi* issued by the Kawasaki Study Society. Tankōsha members also contributed their own poems to the journal. The group valued the following works particularly highly: the *Dōjinshū*, compiled by Mashimo Banshū and Mizoguchi Keigen, with reviews by Ōnuma Chinzan; the *Kinkoshi*, supervised by Ōno Kozan; and the *Seinen shinshū*, compiled by Maeda Baishū, a commoner of Chiba Prefecture in 1883. Beginning in 1884, the Tankōsha group corresponded and gradually went on to establish an intimate relationship with the Koume Ginsō, a group of Chinese verse enthusiasts from the entire Kanagawa area, including the Tama districts, who were People's Right's advocates. The Koume Ginsō was named for Koume village, Mokōjima, Tokyo, where its editor, Wakabayashi Yoshinosuke, lived. It published a printed coterie pamphlet of twenty pages or so, titled the *Koume Ginsō Kadai*. Liberal movement leaders' names stand out among its contributors: Wakabayashi Yoshinosuke, Ishisaka Tenjū, Enomoto Nanrai, Usui Kōson, and others. They were also members of an "1884 Reading Circle" composed of Kanagawa Prefecture men residing in Tokyo. This was a club with which Kitamura Tōkoku was affiliated.

Thus one again finds that People's Rights advocates were also members of groups devoted to study and to Chinese poetry. Ishisaka Tenjū, a close friend of Tōkoku, probably led the politically oriented Reading Club, and Wakabayashi Yoshinosuke, a childhood friend of Tenjū's, took care of Koume Ginsō. Both men were energetic People's Rights advocates.

In particular, Wakabayashi was often advertised as a new and incisive speaker in the liberal *Jiyū Shimbun*. After his sudden death in the fall of 1885, it seems that the Chinese poetry group broke up, and Gompachi's correspondence with the club terminated suddenly. Accordingly we see the two sides of Gompachi's character: politics and poetry. He was master of the Jiyūrō (Liberty Tower) and manager of the Club of Learning and Lectures as well as "manager of the Society of Letters and master of the Hall of Heavenly Principles."

Fukasawa was not alone in this. It was quite common among many People's Rights advocates. For instance, an anthology titled *Royaku Ōmeishū* includes works by Gompachi and ten other poetry enthusiasts, all either members or sympathizers of the Jiyūtō. In addition, it is interesting that among these ten, eight were "wandering pilgrims" who had drifted into the Itsukaichi area from other parts of the country.[14]

POLITICS AND LITERATURE

On November 12, 1883, Fukasawa Gompachi wept bitterly on learning of Chiba Takusaburō's death. He had seen him and inquired after his health only a few days earlier. Takusaburō, who had no wife, no children, no blood relatives, and in fact no home, had breathed his last as a lonely stranger in another's house. Father and son, the Fukasawas had been warm and hospitable toward this ill-fated young man of high purpose. Now they arranged for his funeral, his will, and other matters as if he had been a member of their own family. It is thanks to their friendship that documents related to Takusaburō survived in the Fukasawa family storehouse.

[14] The names are Nakashima Genchō and Takemura Bidetsu of Omi, Aburai Morio and Itō Dōyū of Sendai, Kōchi Gyōhei and Toshimitsu Tsurumatsu of Ōita, Akaboshi Akira of Fukuoka, Kubota Kume of Mikawa, Satō Teikan of Sagami, and Yoshino Taizō of Kita Tama. If one adds to these Chiba Takusaburō, Akiyama Fumitarō of Minami Tama, Nagasaka Kishaku of Kai, and Ōya Masao of Sagami, we get some idea of how mobile men were in the Meiji period. I believe that Kitamura Tōkoku of Odawara also came to Itsukaichi around 1884, relying on his comrade Ōya Masao for help.

At about this time Gompachi's health began to fail, and he often went to Tokyo for medical treatment of a stomach disorder. In June 1884, he was temporarily hospitalized in Tokyo. This date can be ascertained because he frequently received post cards of inquiry during those days from *buraku* liberation leaders.[15] Men like Tamagami Takuki, Yamaguchi Jūbei, and Kashiwagi Toyojirō, *buraku* leaders in the village of Shimo Ichibukata of Minami Tama (now Moto-Hachiōji), had converted to Catholicism earlier. They learned about human equality, and in their attempts to realize this principle in politics, they participated in the democratic movement. They grew close to men like Uchiyama Yasubei and Fukasawa Gompachi, who had come to respect them as colleagues on an equal footing. It is a splendid commentary on liberal activists like Fukasawa that they were able to reject conventional discrimination based on status distinctions like *buraku*, samurai, or outsider, and commit themselves to the principle of equality among men of like mind. They seem to have held steadfastly to such ideas as human rights.

Gompachi's illness did not improve, but since the people in Itsukaichi relied increasingly on him after Takusaburō's death he could not allow himself rest for recuperation. Moreover, during 1884 and 1885 the People's Rights movement in the three Tama districts seems to have been gaining momentum despite its decline in other areas. From May through September 1884, activists like Hosono Kiyoshirō, Hirano Tomosuke, and Kiuchi Inosuke were pushing forward with rallies day by day in Hachiōji, Oume, and Fuchū in an attempt to combat suppression by government authorities.

In Itsukaichi, a movement to revive the disbanded Society of Patriots and to join armed uprisings like those in Gumma or at Kabasan began to emerge among teachers of the Kannō School. Kubota Kume, a close friend of Fukasawa, tried to join the Kabasan uprising but was unable to do so. Ōya Ma-

---

[15] Buraku dwellers, objects of longstanding discrimination as "Eta," had been "liberated" by law in early Meiji ordinances but continued to suffer discrimination until at least post - World War II days.

sao, together with Tomimatsu Masayasu, also promised to join, but much to their distress they were too late to do so.[16]

Then, beginning in August of 1884, rebellions by the Konmintō (Poor People's party) broke out repeatedly in the Tama area. Jiyūtō members were kept on the move constantly. In the middle of peace mediations it was reported that a party headed by Itagaki Taisuke, the head of the Jiyūtō, was about to come to Nishi Tama on a fishing trip. Uchiyama Yasubei was flustered by this report and sent letter after letter urging Gompachi to leave his sickbed. As might be suspected, Gompachi found it impossible to remain inactive. He had thus far done all he could to shield meetings of the "Learning and Discussion Society" from government suppression; now he organized a dummy society for Buddhist sermons, the Kenten Kyōkai, thus securing a lawful stage for his activities. Its membership list shows an almost complete overlap with those of the earlier literary and Liberal party members. People's Rights activists in the Nishi Tama region thus continued their activities by one means or another, even after the Jiyūtō had resolved to disband.[17] In January of 1885 they presented a memorial to the government calling on it to establish a national assembly earlier than the scheduled date of 1889, an act of unusual courage and daring, since it demanded revision of a clause in the imperial proclamation of 1881 and was thus subject to prosecution as *lèse-majesté*. This was in fact what happened to a similar effort on the part of an association in Kita Tama.

Accordingly, Yoshino Taizō wrote the draft carefully, and Gompachi took the lead in sponsoring it. This showed solemn determination on his part to assume personal responsibility if it should meet with government suppression. This continuous state of tension probably contributed to the advance of his illness. In April of 1885 Gompachi went to the Atami spa in

[16] *Ōya Masao jijoden*, unpublished manuscript (dating from 1927) in the possession of Ōya Hiroko.

[17] On October 28, 1884, the Jiyūtō met in Osaka and voted to dissolve, but it simultaneously petitioned that the announced (1889) date of a national assembly be advanced.

hopes of improvement. His colleagues, however, particularly young teachers from the Itsukaichi school, were unable to restrain their indignation over government suppression and the decline of the movement and shifted from speeches to armed revolt. In June of 1885, they joined the conspiracy led by the radical leader Ōi Kentarō.

This plot was undertaken in strict secrecy, and Gompachi was surely not informed of it. Tama activists led by Ōya Masao were to take money by force for military use. Radical teachers attacked the residences of wealthy farmers and village offices, one after another. It was at this time that Kitamura Tōkoku, asked to participate in this ring of conspirators, was driven to despair. When the "Osaka incident" came to light, Ōi and Ōya were arrested.[18] Fukasawa probably learned of this by reading the newspapers. His close friend Kubota Kume, who had fled, was arrested in Yamanashi. Gompachi grieved for him with these lines:

> Under a sorrowful and desolate full moon
> My spirit turns toward Yamanashi.
> I think of you this day,
> Feeling lonely and distressed.
> Throughout the East
> It is a time of confusion and darkness,
> I shed tears over hollyhock flowers,
> At their time of petaled bloom.

The Osaka incident was a serious blow for the radical teachers in Itsukaichi, and for a time tl.eir political movement foundered. As a result Gompachi and others changed their strategy several times and then decided to found an Assembly for Public Health (Kyōritsu Eisei Gikai).

Even now Gompachi became one of the three executive secretaries together with Baba Kanzaemon, the town head, and Kōchi Gyōhei, a physician. They prevailed upon Uchi-

[18] Discussion of the Osaka incident can be found in Marius B. Jansen, "Ōi Kentarō: Radicalism and Chauvinism," *Far Eastern Quarterly* 11 (May 1952): 305-16.

yama Yasubei, a member of a leading family, to be president. Thirty-five committee members were selected from among People's Rights advocates and concerned persons throughout the whole of Nishi Tama. In this way Fukasawa and the others promoted a movement for public hygiene and health and united the whole district behind it.

This hygiene assembly was a volunteer organization for preserving the health and sanitation of the people. The first article of its regulations stipulates that "our purpose lies in discussing and explaining methods of maintaining and promoting the health and safety of the general public, and to disseminate knowledge about hygiene." In this way the assembly was a foresighted movement to strengthen ties with ordinary people and to educate them.

The organization was not exclusively political: it was promoted in response to urgent needs to protect residents from cholera, typhoid fever, smallpox, dysentery, and other epidemic diseases that were rampant. In 1879, 15,784 people died of cholera alone; in 1883 and 1885 dysentery was epidemic, and in 1886, 18,405 persons died of cholera, and more than 32,000 died of typhoid fever and smallpox. Neither national nor prefectural governments did much to combat these diseases: appropriations for public health were less than half of what was spent to purchase one warship. It is natural, therefore, that freedom and popular rights advocates in the Nishi Tama area rose to action.

According to Article Twenty of the Regulations for the Assembly, "there shall be divisions as follows: 'The Department of Public Health,' 'The Department of School Health,' 'The Department of Infant Care,' 'The Department of Epidemics,' and 'The Department of Relief.' " Other units were also set up, and a committee member who was a specialist was assigned to each department. This showed extraordinary foresight for those days. My own view is that this assembly was a forerunner, not only of a voluntary movement for public health but also in the field of hygiene and medical science in Japan.

Among the thirty-five organizing committee members, there

were ten key officers who were related to ordinary people's livelihood. The movement was not just one of political philosophy embraced by "flighty young students." Rather, it tried to establish a regional commune, and it was a "movement by the people" brimming with potentiality. Other examples of this are in areas such as Okayama and Nagano, where they have been described by Naitō Masanaka and Gotō Hisashi.[19]

Later in 1888 Gompachi was elected to the Kanagawa Prefectural Assembly and took his seat in its chamber. But, probably because of his health, he was not particularly active. Instead it was his father, Naomaru, who participated in the Three-Point movement.[20] What did these men think of the Meiji Constitution when it was promulgated in February of 1889? Gompachi, together with Chiba Takusaburō, had been busily engaged in drafting a people's constitution. After Chiba's death his interest led him to continue subscribing to the *Meihō zasshi* and the *Kempō zasshi*, journals on law and constitution. It is not difficult for us to imagine how painful it must have been for him to read the articles of the constitution, granted by the emperor, which forcefully stressed imperial prerogatives. Nakae Chōmin said of the constitution that "having read it through just once, I merely smiled wryly."[21] This bitter feeling was surely not limited to Chōmin.

What had Chiba Takusaburō died for? How many of his colleagues devoted their lives to the cause of establishing a national assembly? The national assembly on which they had pinned such high hopes was first selected by an electorate so restricted that only one man in a thousand could vote. Immediately after the new Diet convened, on the morning of

[19] Naitō Masanaka, *Jiyū minken undō no kenkyū* (1964) and Gotō Yasushi, *Jiyū minken undō no tenkai* (1966).

[20] The "Three-Point Memorial" movement of 1887 brought the Jiyūtō into being again in alliance with its rival Kaishintō in response to government policies: the goals of the new federation were freedom of expression, a promised relaxation of land taxes, and a more forceful stand on reform of the unequal treaties that had been signed with the West.

[21] Nakae (1847-1901) was a leading theorist of the People's Rights movement.

December 24, 1890, Gompachi died before attaining the age of thirty. His father was plunged into deep despair by the loss of his only son. Naomaru brought his tumultuous fifty-one-year career to an end one and a half years later and followed his son to the grave. The moss-covered graves of father and son look down nostalgically on Fukasawa village, which had been their home.

From examining the attitudes toward literature and politics of wealthy Tama farmers who were leaders of the local movement one sees that they chose neither literature nor politics to the exclusion of the other. There was something calm and composed about their activism, some all-embracing attitude of life, education, and personality—something utterly different from the intense *shishi* types of the Restoration, and equally different from the young students, swashbucklers, China activists, or left-wing radicals of more recent times. In these People's Rights leaders we do not find a rigid division between simple-minded intensity of politics, commonly considered as characteristically Japanese, and a fastidious renunciation of the political in order to escape to an inner world inhabited by belles-lettrists and hermits. We find that these leaders combined both elements in a balanced and coherent fashion, and this enabled them—as members of a wealthy farmer class, rooted in the lives of ordinary people—to take Chinese poetry seriously.

Hosono Kiyoshirō composed this poem:

> I have finished my farm work
> and put away my plough.
> Now I pursue a life of three leisures:
> during the day I study the Chinese Classics,
> and also verse and odes,
> while at night I study laws and governance.

Hosono seemed to maintain a harmonious unity and balance between "farming," "literature," and "politics." Clearly landowning farmers and People's Rights leaders found this unity possible during that transitional era of early Meiji. Ultimately this unity proved to be illusory. Their happiness was short-lived, and suddenly they faced a severe ordeal. They then became keenly aware of what true modernity in "politics" and "literature" was. Fukasawa and his friends who lived in the 1800s were gone before that storm arrived.

As we have seen, the spirit of Chinese verse in early Meiji was renovated by the revolutionaries of the Meiji Restoration and spread astonishingly among lower level intellectuals during the movement for People's Rights. A new generation that made use of this Chinese poetry attempted to convey its own life, class aspirations, and political passions through that verse and infused it with a new spirit. Poetry in classical Chinese was revived in these turbulent years; in turn it played a role in stimulating historical change. Had this not been so, Natsume Sōseki, Mori Ōgai, and Hagiwara Sakutarō would probably not have considered Chinese verse to be the source of Japanese poetry, nor would they have gone on to preserve that tradition. It is astonishing that Japanese literary historians have so far been blind to this situation.

(Translated by Eiji Yutani)

· V ·

THE HEIGHTS AND DEPTHS OF POPULAR
CONSCIOUSNESS

THE VOICES OF THE INARTICULATE

So far I have been dealing with problems regarding cultural
creativity at the lower levels of society, primarily among intellectuals in agricultural villages. I have focused on "learned
men" among the common people, "articulate men" who could
manipulate words. I did this because I believe that these men
were situated at a focal point of conflict and tension that made
them particularly sensitive to the rumblings among the people. During the Meiji period this middle stratum found itself
between the government and the populace; it provided the
leaders of village communities and at the same time the lowest link in the chain of official power. Therefore, these men
were always exposed to pressures from both sides, and they
were in danger of being split up, especially during this period
of radical change. Their historical consciousness became all
the more acute, for they sensed the potential to foresee and
to play a crucial role in shaping the future. For these reasons,
I have viewed them as the "people's spokesmen" and have
paid close attention to their ideas and activities.

Is it really possible, however, to understand grass-roots
culture by restricting ourselves to the study of people in the
"middle stratum"? Is it really possible to have them represent
that larger majority of men who ended their lives without
ever articulating what they thought, felt, and did? I do not
think so. I am haunted by the fear that I will never be able
to arrive at a proper assessment of popular culture as long as
I confine my research to this "articulate" middle stratum.

In Shimazaki Tōson's masterpiece, *Yoake mae* (Before the
Dawn), a wealthy farmer, Aoyama Hanzō, who is the village
headman, a wholesaler, an officially appointed innkeeper, and
a student of national learning as well, works wholeheartedly

on his villagers' behalf. One day, however, he is astonished by a remark made by a farmer whom he trusts deeply. This farmer says to him, "Hanzō-san, does *anybody* really tell you the truth?" The inference is that no farmer would talk heart-to-heart with a village elder like Aoyama. This incisive and bitter remark should pierce us deeply as it does Aoyama Hanzō. We who have done our best to ascertain popular conscious-ness should certainly be made cautious and humble by this comment.

But then how can we expect to be able to get at the con-sciousness of the "inarticulate masses"? If we want to grasp that consciousness as a whole and not in fragments, we have to examine it in the abnormal forms in which it is revealed and in popular actions during a time of upheaval. On some occasions we may be able to come across traces of that con-sciousness, through cries, appeals, and protests; at other times, through detailed official records and reports and through the testimony of bystanders and eyewitnesses.

Documents dealing with agrarian disturbances of the sort that broke out intermittently during the agricultural depres-sion of the 1880s, and especially those dealing with the Chi-chibu incident, should provide excellent material for under-standing the mind of the masses. It has not been easy to discover such sources, though, and not many attempts have been made to examine popular consciousness through the records that do survive. I have made some effort to do so in my study of the Konmintō (Poor People's party) in Musashi and Sagami by analyzing the ideas held by leaders such as Sunaga Renzō, Shiono Kuranosuke, and Wakabayashi Taka-nosuke. But I have only dealt with that level in part, without attempting to grasp the consciousness of the masses who fought alongside those leaders and bravely continued to engage in underground activities.[1]

In this chapter I propose to plunge into this unexplored

[1] Irokawa, "Konmintō to Jiyūtō," *Rekishigaku kenkyū*, no. 247 (November 1960), pp. 1-30, and "Konmintō no shisō," in *Meiji no seishin* (Tokyo, 1964), pp. 197-217.

area by making use of official documents relating to several hundred suspects who were charged with insurrection in the Chichibu incident as well as other materials turned up by earlier researchers. Fortunately, a pioneering work by Inoue Kōji, *Chichibu jiken* (The Chichibu Incident), appeared in 1968, and I will draw on that. But my study cannot limit itself to the peaks of popular consciousness—the "high plain of Heaven"—represented by those who participated actively in the rebellion; it will also have to take into account those who stood aside and heaped criticism and abuse on the rebels. Moreover, I have to work out some way of incorporating the concepts of "conventional morality" (*tsūzoku dōtoku*) and "world renewal" (*yonaoshi*) that Yasumaru Yoshio worked out in his study of the followers of new religions like Maruyamakyō.[2] In short, this analysis of the Chichibu uprising has to be seen against the backdrop of the development of popular thought of many kinds.

What was the Chichibu uprising? First, I will provide a brief outline for readers not familiar with it. For convenience I will draw on a short essay I wrote for the *Asahi Shimbun* of October 22, 1968.

In June of 1918, a man appeared who revealed his identity as "a ring leader of the Chichibu incident." He had gone underground for thirty-five years because he knew he was under a sentence of death. His name was Inoue Denzō, and he had been living under the name Itō Fusajirō in Nozuke-ushi village (now Kitami City), near the Sea of Okhotsk in Hokkaido. Inoue is recorded in the Liberal party history (*Jiyūtō shi*) as a person who played a pivotal role in linking the Konmintō with the Jiyūtō. He was Chief Accountant and Staff Officer of "The Revolutionary Army" at the time of the uprising. On November 4, 1884, he sought shelter in caves of the Mt. Bukō together with his comrades after the main body of their troops had been routed by government forces. Thereafter he disappeared from sight.

[2] Yasumaru Yoshio and Hirota Masaki, " 'Yonaoshi' no ronri to keifu," *Nihonshi kenkyū*, nos. 85 and 86 (1966), pp. 1-25 and 46-65.

One day in October 1968, I visited this Inoue Denzō's daughter at her home together with Mr. Inoue Kōji. Fumi, as the daughter is called, told us about Denzō's life. She was about twenty when he died. "My father did not have a trace of tragedy on his face," she said; "he was always of good cheer. Our family too was a happy one. I continued to be proud of my father after he confessed to his real identity." In this way I learned that Denzō never felt remorse for his activities: to the end he lived and died convinced that what he had done was right. His last words to his son were simply "I am only sorry that the incident was not treated as a crime against the state. I would like you to return to Chichibu and perform a memorial service for my fallen comrades on my behalf."

More than 5,000 people (8,000, or as many as 10,000, by some estimates) participated in the Chichibu uprising. Of these almost 4,000 were found guilty, 300 were convicted as felons, and 7 men were sentenced to death. Five, including Tashiro Eisuke, the leader, were executed on the spot. The number of those who were killed in action is not known. Both the government and public opinion abused the rebels, calling them "rioters," and the incident was hushed up as a "disorderly riot." These slurs must have tormented Denzō the rest of his life. What then was the Chichibu incident about?

In 1884 an army of several thousand peasants, organized into two battalions, emerged suddenly out of mountain villages in the Chichibu district of present Saitama Prefecture, near Tokyo. Armed with hunting muskets, wooden cannons, swords, bamboo spears, and other weapons, they raised a banner announcing the "New Rule of Benevolence" and stormed Ōmiya, occupied the District Office there, and erected a sign reading "Headquarters of the Revolutionary Army." They dated their decrees "Year One of Freedom and Self-Government" and set out to "Renew the World" (yonaoshi). To this end they sent squads of guerrillas to each village to attack evil usurers. Then they marched toward Tokyo and battled with the military police and troops who had been sent to put them down. In ten days the rebellion was finally crushed at the foot of Mt. Yatsugatake. It was indeed a great event, of a sort rarely seen in the history of Japan.

This was no ordinary peasant uprising or "world renewal" disturbance. Nor was it a mere riot by a Debtor's party (Shakkintō) or by the Poor People's party (Konmintō). It was an uprising that, from the very start, set out to challenge the Meiji government. The rebels were able to do this because they accepted the revolutionary ideology of the Liberal party (Jiyūtō); they had a revolutionary faith that they could "reform the government, make freedom come to life, and join battle for the people"; they felt themselves at the point of creating a new morality, and they were sure that they were in the right and that the government was unjust.

Of course, I do not contend that each of the thousands who participated in the uprising arrived at this stage of revolutionary transformation. Nevertheless, we know that a song was being sung at Isama and other villages that urged people, "Do not worry about being out of money; the Jiyūtō will soon take care of that." Also, countless numbers of farmers believed that they could "join in arms with Mr. Itagaki, and turn out the tyrants of today in favor of a benevolent government"; we can surmise that such a hope spread widely among villagers. It is my guess that this vision was deeply held by at least one hundred or more organizers who formed the nucleus of the Chichibu Konmintō. If this is so, then the Chichibu rural uprising begins to assume the characteristics of a bourgeois and democratic revolution.

Because of harsh economic circumstances of those years, about sixty riots stemming from agricultural indebtedness took place in all parts of Japan in 1884. More than half of them took place in mountainous, silk-raising areas in the Kantō region. The total indebtedness of farmers and petty tradesmen amounted to two hundred million *yen*, a sum equivalent to two trillion yen today. One hundred thousand households were pronounced bankrupt in 1884 alone. This situation stemmed from the deflationary policy, made worse by heavy taxation, that Finance Minister Matsukata forced through in order to achieve the capital formation for Japan's early capitalism.[3] The

[3] Matsukata Masayoshi (1835-1924), Meiji statesman who directed the Finance Ministry through the decade of the 1880s. He reversed the inflationary

Komintō were fundamentally a form of uprisings resistant to such financial policies.

Up to now the Chichibu uprising has been interpreted in one of two ways. Scholars like Hirano Gitarō assumed that the Shakkintō (Debtor's party) was identical with the Kosakutō (Tenants' party) and asserted that class conflict and confrontation between wealthy farmers and landlords on the one hand, and poor farmers and tenants on the other, caused these riots. On the other hand historians like Horie Eiichi have simplified the development of leadership in the People's Rights movement to see it change hands and directions from an initial, ex-samurai stage to a second period of leadership by rural elite and wealthy farmers, ending with a preponderance of ordinary, cultivating farmers. They see the Chichibu incident as the ultimate stage of this development. But I do not believe that either thesis accords with the facts. If it was the task of the Meiji Restoration to achieve a bourgeois revolution, then the *jiyū minken* movement was one that the Japanese people tried to bring about by themselves. It is true that the People's Rights movement was begun by former samurai, but it was the rural elite (*gōnō* or wealthy farmers) who developed the movement all over the country. Local Jiyūtō everywhere came into being as parties of *gōnō*. We should emphasize, however, that the Jiyūtō organization that led the Chichibu incident was essentially different from other local Jiyūtō. Up to now a good deal of misunderstanding has resulted from the failure to appreciate this fact. We cannot grasp the true essence of the Chichibu incident by relying exclusively on official documents and court records pertaining to a few ringleaders. Mr. Inoue Kōji's study has helped to break the bottleneck of misunderstanding about the incident. His long search for materials has led him to an exhaustive examination of the records of some three hundred farmers' interrogations, records that have been held by the Gumma Pre-

---

policies of the 1870s with strict monetary policies that produced hardship in the countryside, but he also established the basis for a sound currency with orthodox economic policies of capital accumulation that were followed by the adoption of the gold standard in 1897.

fectural Government. He is the first to have provided profiles of the ideas and activities of about one hundred Konmintō village organizers who built such an astonishing organization. Through his work it has become evident that members of the Jiyūtō in Chichibu, namely, the core of the Konmintō, did not belong to the radical wing of the Jiyūtō that was led by Ōi Kentarō. Rather, they were men who believed in the Jiyūtō as a "visionary party of revolution." Mr. Wakasa Kuranosuke has recently collected materials about a village organizer in Fuppu named Ōno Fukujirō that show that he collected about fifty new pledges of membershp in the Jiyūtō during four short days immediately before the uprising. This shows that party leaders were organizing and preparing for an insurrection by pursuading people to join the "party of revolution," and it is particularly moving because at this very same time, the "other" Jiyūtō was dissolving itself in Osaka. It was people like Ōno rather than Ōi's Jiyūtō who were the real driving force behind the Chichibu uprising.

Like Inoue Denzō, Kikuchi Kampei was sentenced to death and suffered many hardships in Abashiri Prison for twenty years. Even after the main force was put to rout, Kikuchi commanded men like Ōno and went on fighting for revolution from Gumma to Shinano Prefectures. What sustained this determined group of men who resisted to the bitter end? It was their belief that "Kampei and the other officers would avoid pitched battles with government troops." They were optimistic that wherever they might go, they would find bases of commoner support on which to rebuild the Konmintō army. This was a sort of Jiyūtō romanticism that by maintaining dogged resistance they would induce uprisings in the neighboring Yamanashi and Shinano regions.[4] In present-day parlance, it was the ideology of Che Guevara.

A monument to unknown soldiers, the majestic "Tomb of

[4] Inoue Kōji, *Chichibu jiken*, Chūko Shinsho Series no. 161 (Tokyo: Chūō kōronsha, 1968). Roger W. Bowen, *Rebellion and Democracy in Meiji Japan: A Study of Commoners in the Popular Rights Movement* (Berkeley: University of California Press, 1980), relies on the author, on Inoue, and on other sources to provide an account of these events.

Monument erected in 1933 to those killed
in the Chichibu war

the Fallen Rioters in Chichibu" was erected in the name of
Kikuchi Kampei on Managashi Hill facing Mt. Yatsugatake on
November 9, 1933, just when the prewar left-wing movement had completely collapsed. The fortitude on the part of
Tokuda Kyūichi and others, described in his book, *Gokuchū
jūhachinen* (Eighteen Years in Prison), became widely known
after 1945. Yet the names of Meiji heroes who "went underground for thirty-five years" or were "imprisoned for twenty
years" have never been restored. In fact, the story of several
hundred unknown soldiers who bravely faced death for their

ideals, and the story of the ideology that sustained them, has never been told, though years have passed.

The Thoughts of Unknown Soldiers

At this point I would like to deal with that ideology here. According to Inoue's account, of the 5,000-8,000 people who joined the Chichibu uprising, from 100 to 130 can be considered core organizers. By themselves, they would not have been able to mobilize more than some 3,000 people for an armed insurrection. But those 3,000 were not just "tag-along followers"; they had been mobilized in advance by organizing cadres so that they would respond promptly to an emergency call. The Konmintō core organizers included several dozen local "directors" who were on the scene at the time of the insurrection. A "core organizer" was defined as a village organizer (the general representative of the village) and field organizers within it. These men Inoue calls "militants" or "activists." As of May 1884, there were about 30 formally registered Jiyūtō members in Chichibu; half of them were included among these 130 or so "core organizers." Therefore, half of the Chichibu Jiyūtō members were leaders of the Konmintō, and the other half had nothing to do with the uprising. Accordingly, it would probably be more correct to say that the incident was led by the Jiyū Konmintō than by the Chichibu Jiyūtō.

The following are all Jiyūtō members of this type: Tashiro Eisuke, the commander, 58; Katō Oribei, second in command, 37; Inoue Denzō, treasurer, 31; Sakamoto Sōsaku, commander, 30; Ochiai Toraichi, commander, 34; Takagishi Zenkichi, commander, 38; Ogashiwa Tsunejirō, commander, 42, an organizer from Gumma; and Kikuchi Kampei, staff officer from Nagano, 37. In addition to these leading figures there were 100 or more village or area organizers. These people took the initiative in joining the Jiyūtō just prior to the uprising, and by persuading farmers to become members in this revolutionary Jiyūtō they participated in planning the uprising through massive recruiting efforts, as demonstrated by Ōno Fukujirō.

These unlettered persons, and their thoughts and consciousness, are my concern. The only "articulate" men among them were Inoue Denzō and Kikuchi Kampei; the rest, though they may have been literate, do not seem to have been able (or to have tried) to persuade the others to accept their ideas the way the *gōnō* popular rights advocates did. Tashiro Eisuke, whose distinguished family had held the post of village head for generations, was fifty-eight at the time of the uprising. Probably because he traveled a lot, working as a kind of lawyer and performing faithful public service, he had a rather distinctive air and charm about him. After the Restoration his family had fallen on difficult days. Eisuke had only about an acre of upland fields, and sericulture, to support himself, and even those fields were about to fall into a usurer's hands. This man was quickly promoted to the position of general commander because of his popularity and capabilities—he had continuously given assistance to others as a "man of the world" (*sekenshi*). He also had political acumen and perception; he was tenacious in conducting preparations for simultaneous uprisings in the Tokyo-Saitama and Gumma regions. Tashiro was by no means an insurrectionist, but a prudent political realist who did everything possible to achieve his ends by lawful means before resorting to violence.

Katō Oribei, the Deputy Commander, had something in common with Inoue Denzō. He was regarded as a money-lender/gambler with many henchmen, but this was not so. Even the prosecuting attorney who interrogated him reminisced that "Kato had the strongest character" of the leaders of the uprising. When asked to take a leading part in the uprising, he first tore up I.O.U.s in his possessions amounting to one hundred and fifty *yen* before joining in the rebellion. From the fact that his eldest son later became an elementary school teacher in the village, we can surmise that Oribei came from a good household.

Ogashiwa Tsunejirō, like Eisuke and Oribei, could also appropriately be called a "man of the world." He was forty-two and a roofer by trade. He had no fixed abode and moved about. But he was an excellent orator and apparently a popular person, engaging from time to time in storytelling as an entertainer. He was hard-working. After coming to Chichibu, he had part-time work in sericulture while organizing the farmers. People were attracted to him because, as a man who had seen something of the world, he had a wealth of topics of conversation. An affable man, he won the people's trust, and the villagers whom he had organized fought tenaciously to the bitter end of the uprising.

The Konmintō trio—Ochiai, Takagishi, and Sakamoto, all from the village of Yoshida in Chichibu district—were given humorous nicknames. They were all poor farmers who had a natural aptitude for organizing the uprising, and it was they who undertook the tortuous and protracted work of organizing the farmers. Early in 1884 the three joined the Jiyūtō. Legally, they carried on formal recruitment and petition campaigns among the masses that attracted many people; at the same time they illegally persuaded Tashiro Eisuke and Katō Oribei to set up a general headquarters for the insurrection, established liaisons with party headquarters in Gumma and Tokyo, and carefully built the basis for their organization.

Ochiai Torakichi, a big man weighing sixty-five kilograms, cultivated about two acres and also made charcoal. Sakamoto Sōsaku, an enthusiastic sericulturist, sent his products to a cocoon exhibit in Kodama district and received a certificate of merit. Both of them were hard-working men. Takagishi Zenkichi was a farmer and "big brother" to the other two. He was a very simple and honest person of great integrity. There is an interesting episode about him. When the date for the uprising had been set, "bucktoothed Sōsaku," as Sakamoto was called, selected a posthumous Buddhist name, Gozan Dōshii Koji, wrote it on a white sweat band, and set off for battle with no intention of returning home alive. Even after the main body of troops was routed and the leaders dispersed in all directions, he directed a company of soldiers with drawn sword and proceeded to Shinano, another theater of action, where he resisted to the bitter end and was finally executed.

As we thus observe the way men like Sōsaku lived, we can understand how they formed their ideas and developed a critical spirit toward the social system in which they lived. They were hard-working, persevering men of independence who practiced the precepts of conventional morality. Sōsaku made extraordinary efforts to improve agricultural techniques in an attempt to protect his livelihood, but no matter how hard he worked or how much he persevered he was unable to avoid destitution and was faced with bankruptcy. At such a point these people were forced to realize that the cause of their destitution did not lie in themselves, in their lack of effort or inadequate productive capacities; it lay outside of themselves, in the relations of production imposed by society. No doubt they first realized this in their dealings with usurers and government officials who treated them unjustly; and for this very reason they repeatedly tried to reason and plead their case in a courteous, respectful manner. But what results did they obtain through such channels? Their petitions were ignored by local officials, and they were hauled before the police where they were beaten and dismissed time and again. Then the Jiyūtō view of the social order allowed them to become critical of the very top of the existing power structure.

As Inoue aptly puts it, "crisis brings the difference in men's personalities into sharp relief." As we read the police records on several hundred participants in the uprisings in Gumma and Saitama Prefectures, we are surprised to come across unforeseen expressions, firm conviction, and defiance on the part of hitherto unknown commoners. Perhaps crisis brings the fine qualities of the commoners, qualities usually obscured, into sudden, sharp relief.

Kimura Matakichi (real name), from the village of Kami-Hinosawa, answered police questions as follows: "I am Kōno Naoshichi, fifty-four years old. My status is commoner, and my occupation, construction laborer. I am illiterate, and I have no previous criminal record." He went on to tell that he had marched as far as Managashi in Shinano; there while he was eating breakfast in camp, he was suddenly fired upon and fled. This semiproletarian agreed to the assertions by his associates that "all usurers charge unjustifiably high interest rates, so it is quite all right not to repay loans." He calmly told the police that he first was an organizer and presented petitions to the police, then repeatedly pleaded with creditors for extensions of his payments, only to be refused; finally he had risen in revolt. In a battle at Kanazaki village through which the Arakawa River flows, he had fought with a rifle under the direction of a battalion commander, Arai Shūzaburō. He said to the police of Oshikano that "I fired my gun of my own free will." Pressed by the police officer, "Did you fire to kill officers? Is it true, then, that you fired from the second floor with the intention to kill?" Matakichi replied calmly, "Yes, sir. There is no doubt about that."

In that village of Kami-Hinosawa, about fifty men with semi-proletarian backgrounds like his, together with intellectuals like a Shintō priest, Miyakawa Tsumori, participated in the insurrection; many of them were prosecuted. Muratake Shigekagu became a platoon commander. He too had started out as a peaceful petitioner against usurers. Becoming indignant at their atrocious deeds, he soon joined representatives from twenty-eight villages and went to petition the Ōmiya police chief. But the officers defended the creditors and ignored the people's claims. He confessed that, not knowing what else to do, he willingly participated in illegal mass meetings, and when he finally learned about the plans for the rebellion, he thought it a good way to rescue his fellow countrymen and agreed fully. His written refutation is very straightforward and dignified. Thanks perhaps to his age of forty-six, he was serene and by no means pretentious. Notice the following question and answer: Question: "What did the fifty-odd rioters you led do?" Answer: "There was a company of forty men with bamboo spears. There were four guns. About ten men formed a company of swords. All these soldiers formed three lines. I was in command for their battlefield movements. We burned and destroyed houses."

This peasant platoon leader was criticized during the battle as being a clumsy commander and was replaced, but Muratake was a sincere man. He did not leave the battle and continued to fight as a soldier in the ranks. Even after the main body of troops from Chichibu was routed, he continued fighting to the foot of Mt. Yatsugatake and was captured at Uminokuchi. Men like him, endowed with superior human and moral qualities, would never betray the people and could provide genuine leadership. Morikawa Sakuzō and Kōno Naoshichi, from the same village as Muratake, pressed on to Shinano with him but were arrested at Managashi. They were sentenced to fifteen years' imprisonment.

MOUNTAIN VILLAGE COMMUNES

It is reported that villagers in the Isama village of Chichibu district sang the following lines:

> Do not worry about being out of money: the Jiyūtō will soon take care of that.

Katō Oribei lived in this village; under the leadership of five organizers, 180 people were mobilized. The village contained only 175 households, so these 180 people represented an extremely high proportion. Arai Shigetarō was a typical field organizer in the village. When he was interrogated, he said that he and another organizer had mobilized 30 out of 35 households in Urushigi. Tanaka Senya said this about Arai in his work, *Chichibu bōdō zatsuroku* (Notes on the Chichibu Riot): "Shigetarō abandoned his family occupation in Urashigi, and trained his wife and daughter in the use of the halberd." He went on to the judgment that "There were a number of people like him who accepted the false doctrines of liberty and neglected their work." Arai Fukutarō differentiated between the aims of the Jiyūtō and Shakkintō (Debtors party) by saying that "The purpose of the Jiyūtō lay in mob violence, to smash district offices and police stations and thereby abolish schools and reduce taxes, whereas the Shakkintō aimed at burning public tax and title records and certificates of loans kept in local government offices."

In 1884, mountain villages in Japan literally turned into communes. Songs of liberation were sung, a triumphant spirit prevailed, and the calendar was revised to read "Year One of Freedom and Self-Government." This was by no means a dream. Twenty people from Isama village alone were prosecuted by the authorities. But that particular commune did not have a long life. Arai Shigetarō learned on the afternoon of November 4 that the leaders had fled in all directions, and he became suspicious that Eisuke and Oribei might have run away with the village money. He became enraged and declared that he would "find them and beat them up." Unable to find them, however, he crossed the pass to Shinano only to decide that he would "never be able to accomplish my goal in this way," and he ended by turning back. Tragically enough, he was arrested by Gumma villagers on his way home. It seems that Ogashiwa Tsunejirō, commander of a Gumma freedom brigade, met a similar fate. Thus, the communes in Japan were still primitive and short-lived. At the very moment of their birth, internal conflict and strife led to their collapse.

Villagers in Fuppu were as stalwart as those in Isama, and the first shots of the Chichibu uprising were fired there. Fuppu, too, took on the structure of a commune. Of the 52 pledges to join the Jiyūtō collected before the uprising by Ōno Fukujirō, 28, a little more than half, came from Fuppu. They included commitments by a lad of nineteen as well as by an older man of sixty-six. In this impoverished mountain village of eighty households, there were field organizers such as Ōno Chōshirō and Ōno Fukujirō under the command of Ōno Naekichi who strove to convert the entire village populace to membership in the Konmintō and Jiyūtō. They were called "The Fuppu Company," and their unity was solid. They fought in the vanguard and did not give up even after the situation became desperate. The platoon commander was a certain Ishida, and Ōno Chōshirō testified that Ishida led some hundred and forty villagers.

Nearly all of them were impoverished sericulturists. They were oppressed, to the point of ruin, by usurers and money-lenders in neighboring villages who enjoyed the protection of the police and the courts. For example, Ōno Shinkichi and twelve other villagers in Fuppu borrowed money from a finance company in the village of Kanezaki. The principle and interest amounted to 108 *yen* and 20 *sen*. Ōno Chōshirō, too, was pressured to return an 85-yen loan to a finance company in Ido village, and Fukujirō was called upon by Noguchi Sōgorō, a moneylender of Ido, to repay the debt of 21 *yen* he owed him. At the time of his arrest Fukujirō had in his possession papers that, among other things, listed the debts of each poor farmer.

Yet the uprising was not just an expression of debtor discontent. This organizing cadre—Ōno Fukujirō, together with Tajima Ryūsuke—led fourteen or fifteen soldiers in a rapid march toward an assembly area in Kami Yoshida village on the night of October 31. With sword in hand, a white sweat band around his head, and his sleeves tucked up, he encountered a police squad, was arrested, and was confined to the house of Minano village headman, Koike. He hid the papers that Tajima carried under a tatami and declared that he was just "going along with the crowd" and managed to get off with a light fine. Later he was released. But when he sneaked back into Koike's house to regain the papers he was arrested again and sentenced to seven and a half years in jail. The papers in question contained documents with five articles of procedural instructions for the uprising. For instance, one article said, if the leaders were captured, others were to "blow the police to bits with explosives" and "resist all local and school taxes, but not the national tax." Thus the uprising was not a mere riot by debtors; indeed the article above made clear that national taxes were different. Also included among these papers was a *tanka*

> In eight more years we celebrate
> A less polluted world

showing the expectations they held of the national assembly that had been promised for the end of the decade.

After having done all that he could legally do, Fukujirō declared that he had "resolved to resort to force, to destroy the Nakasendō rail line, to cut down telegraph poles . . . and to rescue poor people." His declaration indicates that he intended to confront state power and authority frontally. We have to take notice of these utterances from a group of field organizers.[5]

Ōno Naekichi, the Fuppu organizer, was Fukujirō's and Chōshirō's superior. At the time of the uprising, he pressed the villagers to participate, sword in hand, asserting "You have to support us, for we go to oppose the Imperial government," and he vowed that he would cut them down if they refused. Inoue Kōji's account of this has made Ōno justly famous. Ōno's fierceness is sufficient to convince us of his hostility to the government and his antagonism against powerholders.[6] As a farmer Naekichi was so impoverished as to be on the verge of bankruptcy, but within the village, as an alleged Jiyūtō member, he was given duty as Deputy Commander under Arai Shūzaburō, the Commander of "A" Battalion.

His plucky fight began on the afternoon of November 4 after the leaders had fled. Shūzaburō, seriously wounded, gave Sakamoto Sōsaku the battalion commander's flag. Leading a force of five hundred soldiers, Naekichi attacked the police station and town office of Motonogami. Later he led them over the mountain and down to the new Chichibu road toward the Kodama County plain. It was reportedly after 11:30 at night when he approached the village of Temae Kaneya in Yahatayama township. There he attacked the main force of the Third Battalion of the Tokyo garrison that had been hurriedly dispatched.

Soldiers from the garrison were at first unable to cope with the rioters' strength and withdrew to a bamboo

[5] Materials relating to the Chichibu incident have been published by Saitama shimbun as *Chichibu jiken shiryō*, 6 vols. (Tokyo: Heibonsha, 1970-1979). Materials relating to events in Saitama Prefecture, including the written statement of Ōno Fukujirō, are in the care of Mr. Wakasa Muranosuke and were kindly made available by him.

[6] Ōno's statement to the villagers began with *osorenagara* (in all deference), a phrase normally used by Tokugawa commoners when addressing higher authority. In this context, however, it was a formal and not an obsequious usage.

thicket from which they opened fire on the rioters' right flank. The rioters had thus far vied with each other, stepping over their dead, but now they proved unable to withstand the bombardment, and withdrew to a house across the street. They piled up tatami as a barricade and kept on fighting until about 1:25 a.m.[7]

According to Saitama Prefecture Police Inspector Kamata Chūta's *Chichibu bōdō jikki* (True Account of the Chichibu Riot), the farmer's troops raised a war cry and opened fire as soon as they saw the soldiers of the Tokyo garrison. The peasant troops closed in on their enemy to a range of about two hundred and seventy meters and then erected the tatami barricade against the garrison soldiers. Captain Hirata of the Third Battalion tried several assaults without success. Finally he led his entire force in an all-out charge that dislodged the farmer soldiers.

Ōno Naekichi died in this battle and became one of the unknown war dead. His body was not identified, and he was buried somewhere in a mountain forest. His sortie aimed at breaking through the Nakasendō route is significant because it shows that the fierce fighting spirit of the Konmintō was a spirit that lasted even after the dissolution of the main camp. What were the ideas that sustained such a spirit?

It is to be found in the ability to say, "The Imperial government lacks justice; justice lies on the side of our 'rebellion.' " These rebels' words and deeds show their conviction that "justice is on our side and not on the government's." It was no easy thing for commoners to say those words, but I believe Naekichi's death shows that these people experienced such a revolutionary transformation in values.

Unit Commander Arai Shūzaburō, who was slashed and seriously wounded by a policeman whom he had taken prisoner, was a commoner of Nishinoiri in Obusuma district, near Chichibu. At one time he had taught in an elementary school and on hearing about an opening for a teacher in Isama village, he had come to see Katō Oribei. It seems that he joined

[7] From a special issue of the *Doyō shimbun* of November 1885.

the planning for the rebellion during his stay at Isama village. He said he "found it unbearable to sit by and look at the poverty and hardship of the villagers" and "roused myself to action." He gave his captors the following scornful answers.

> The policeman asked again: "What did you intend to achieve by committing such a rash act?"
> The defendant laughed and said: "I intended to become a great general."
> QUESTION: What do you mean by "a great general"?
> ANSWER: "A great general of Japan's Army."

Arai's defiant refusal to treat this police officer with the respect due a government official clearly shows the people's changing outlook—they were shedding their submissiveness to political authority, a submissiveness that has been the weakness of Japanese commoners throughout our history. Arai was only twenty-three then, but others thought him over forty; his personal bearing, responsibility, and strength must have won their respect. Farmers in Chichibu accepted the leadership of men like Arai and risked their lives for the cause of "leveling the world." Here we see their growing consciousness of "rebelling against authority and government" and realize that they had taken a long step toward the spirit of resistance. This must have been particularly so in the case of the thought and consciousness of the more than one hundred organizers of the rebellion.

Shimazaki Kishirō, from Chigaya in Kami-Yoshida of Chichibu, was a field organizer and captain of a guerrilla band who fought stubbornly in Saitama, Gumma, and Shinano. When the war situation became most desperate—after learning of the defeat that Ōno Naekichi and others had suffered and receiving a report that a force of government soldiers and police were approaching—he got to his feet and said,

> I am going to Shinano, to recruit a large number of men there, and then return here. All who hold their lives dear may go home. . . . (But when I return), come back immediately.

Ōkawara Tsurukichi, a thirty-four-year-old horse dealer from Hirahara village in Minami Amaraku district, was one of those who did return home in response to this directive, but he stated that "the general from Chigaya ordered us to rush back as soon as he returned from Shinano with additional troops, and of course I was following instructions." At that time almost thirty men followed Shimazaki to fight in Shinano. These are refreshing words and deeds, and they give us insight into Meiji popular consciousness.

Ōno Naekichi, who declared that "You must support us because we go to oppose the Imperial government"; Arai Shūsaburō, who asserted that "I intended to become a great general of the Army"; Chiba Takusaburō, who wrote that "The king may die, but not the people"; and the Fukushima farmer Yanaginuma Kamekichi, who was imprisoned for a speech in which he said, "Men are all equal and have the same rights, but high ranks are granted to wicked persons like emperors or kings, who are arbitrarily given power"—in men like these, three of whom were lower school teachers, we find clear expression of the conviction that human rights are prior to king or authority. Of course I do not contend from these few cases that the Japanese people in those days were moving toward republicanism or that they harbored hostility toward the emperor at that time. The issue is not that simple; I recognize that complex ideas, mired in the mud of tradition, lay beneath such statements.

Nonetheless, the statements by leaders expressing Jiyūtō doctrine could emerge and attain currency only because of the village organizers' highly politicized consciousness of radical change. Men like Kikuchi Kampei and Ide Tamekichi, the Jiyūtō members of Shinano, and Inoue Denzō, a leading Chichibu member, were able to tell participating villagers about their expectations of nationwide and simultaneous uprisings; they were able to justify the cause of their "revolutionary army" in terms of the "early establishment of a National Assembly," a "reduction of taxes," and an "overthrow of despotism"; and they were able to proclaim a "new government of benevolence and virtue" thanks to the mediation provided by village organizers who worked among people and found it possible to use their resistance against repayment of debts as a bridge to a new consciousness.

But once the war situation deteriorated after November 4 and the Jiyūtō leaders' illusions of spontaneous uprisings in Gumma, Tokyo-Saitama, Yamanashi, and Nagano proved false and the rout began, the determination to carry on lay solely with the convictions held by a core of several hundred disciplined village organizers. As I said earlier, their conviction was based on a revolutionary optimism that it would be possible to avoid pitched battles with government troops, and that as long as the core of the group of organizers held together they would be able to find communal bases for recruiting an army of the poor and go on fighting for an indefinite period of time. Kikuchi Kampei, Sakamoto Sōsaku, and Shimazaki Kishirō, who marched to Shinano, embraced a Jiyūtō type of romanticism: the expectation of a spontaneous, nationwide uprising, as well as a Che Guevara type of guerrilla ideology. But the potential of these ideas was not to be realized in modern Japanese history down to the nation's defeat in 1945. Therefore, it would seem that the spirit of popular thought that underpinned the Chichibu incident was based in the main on the developing political consciousness of this core of middle men: the hundred or more village organizers.[8]

Abandoning Conventional Morality

Inoue Kōji's analysis of the 261 men of known background who were convicted out of the 3,400 arrested for participating in the Chichibu rebellion comes to the following conclusions. Two-thirds of the participants were literate, a much higher ratio than expected. This disproves contemporary descriptions of them as "ignorant and illiterate." When we examine age groups, the following picture emerges. There were 83 persons—the most numerous group—in their thirties, 63 in their twenties, 53 in their forties, and 34 in their fifties. Thus,

---

[8] Unpublished materials described in note 5 above.

those in their thirties and forties make up over half of those convicted. The youngest was seventeen years old, the oldest, seventy-two; he allegedly joined the uprising with a cane instead of a bamboo spear in his hand.

In terms of property the participants were almost all middle and lower ranking farmers, worthy of the name *konmin* (poor and distressed), although there were also some wealthy farmers, landlords, and merchants. Of the 261, 70 percent were farmers, of the others 15 were charcoal burners and forestry laborers, 11 were day-laborers and construction workers, 11 were small business proprietors, and 5 were carpenters and plasterers. We know from these figures that the rebellion was an all-village movement supported by the working members of society.

Yet the Chichibu incident was reported to have been a riot instigated by gamblers. In fact there were only 7 former convicts among the 261 sentenced, and of those 7, 1 was an army deserter, and 5 were gamblers. These data show how government propaganda and demagoguery distorted the truth about the incident. If the uprising had indeed been instigated by a group of outlaws, as alleged, it would have no significance whatever in the history of popular thought. For me it is clear that the organizers in Chichibu were upright, honest men who practiced conventional morality and thus were diametrically opposed to the hoodlums and outlaws with whom they have been identified.

In this respect I want to consider in some depth the connection between conventional morality of the common people and ideas of social change. Was the Chichibu incident just a riot instigated by "hoodlums," as alleged by the government, press, and popular demagogues? To begin with, could "hoodlums" lead and direct people? My answer is, obviously not. Gangsters and gamblers infringed on the *tsūzoku dōtoku* (conventional morality), from which the Japanese masses derived their energy for self-discipline from Tokugawa times, and through which they established their autonomy and independence. Hoodlums transgressed this ethic of inner discipline; they were good-for-nothing scoundrels who found it impossible to live up to the masses' moral code of hard work, frugality, honesty, harmony, modesty, and filial piety, and instead sank into wickedness, idleness, dissipation, extravagance, truculence, arrogance, and unfilial behavior. When people condemned a man as a "hoodlum" or as a "good-for-nothing," he was stigmatized as something less than human, as an idler and an outcast. He would be denounced and ostracized by the community.

A popular movement like the Chichibu uprising could never have been led by such hoodlums. On the contrary, the Konmintō of Chichibu sprang from fidelity to conventional morality, which contained principles suited to sustaining the livelihood of small-scale producers during a time of social upheaval. That is why the people strove to uphold it during the depression and exploitative taxation that accompanied Matsukata's financial policies. To save themselves from ruin, the people of Chichibu labored with all their energy, practiced draconian economy, exercised resourcefulness, utilized the efforts of all family members, and struggled to bear all types of hardships. But, despite their extraordinary diligence, frugality, and honesty, they were unable to withstand the evil claws of usurers and the exploitation carried out for purposes of primitive accumulation of capital during the 1880s. People realized keenly that however faithfully they might observe the laws of the state, the rules of society, and a conventional morality that imposed brutal demands on them, they could no longer maintain household and happiness. Traditional, conventional morality had run into a dead end. Only then did they face a dilemma, for the conventional morality that they took to heart did not contain anything that allowed them to scrutinize critically the social system as a whole. "Although we work and work, we are never better off." Why is that? Are we to blame? Does our selfishness prevent us from fully conforming to conventional morality? Or, conversely, are the "laws of the country and rules of society" at fault?

At this juncture the people looked for clues to an answer in their recent historical experience during the Tokugawa period. They reminded themselves of how village loans had been made during the famines in the 1780s and 1830s. When taxes or debt had become more than they could bear, village officials and leading farmers had "mercifully" arranged for postponement of payments; loans might have been stretched over a period of as long as fifteen years, and lenders would wait for payments on principle and content themselves with interest for years at a time. Meiji usurers behaved very differently. Loans were contracted outside the village, interest rates were high, and loan collectors were heartless. Cancellation of debts was unthinkable, and there was no alternative to appeal for postponed repayment. At first the people did so in a courteous manner and humbled themselves like beggars. But then they began to complain about the usurers' inhumanity, and they did so in groups of three, four, and five. They had to submit their pleas time after time to usurers and finance companies.

According to conventional morality, a man was duty-bound to repay his debts. But excessive profits and cruel extortions were immoral and infringed on the ethics of "honesty, harmony and compromise; therefore, they are unpardonable," so the people believed. From this conviction, personal pleas by debtors led to attempts at persuasion by their representatives, then to group negotiation, and finally to direct petitions. This process of transformation, however, could be carried out effectively only under the direction of leaders, and these leaders had to be models of virtue in the eyes of the villagers. Only such men, men who maintained the strictest of discipline for themselves, and who upheld conventional morality to the utmost, could be astute and self-assured critics of the larger society. Only when such leader-organizers had taken conventional morality as far as it would go, and applied it resolutely to themselves and to their adversaries, only then would its limitations be clear, and only then would the moment for breaking out of it be at hand.

Let me demonstrate this breakthrough by following the steps of three Konmintō members—Sakamoto Sōsaku, Takagishi Zenkichi, and Ochiai Torakichi—to see how they began on the path of conventional morality and legal action and, step by step, together with the masses, moved to break through the limitations of that morality and legality. It was in December 1883, that the three men filed their first petition with the District Office in Chichibu. They requested the District Chief to admonish moneylenders privately, but they met with a flat refusal. Each of them must have addressed several petitions to the usurers individually before this. In March 1884, the three changed their tactics and presented petitions, following appropriate legal ordinances. But since the officials in charge refused to affix their seals to the petitions and foward them, they were blocked from gaining legal redress of grievances.

By August 1884, the organizing activities of the Konmintō were already making headway; liaison conferences were being held in valleys and forests. Sakamoto and others were elected to represent the villagers in negotiations with moneylenders to obtain a four-year deferment of loans and permission to repay these through annual installments over forty years. These requests were based on Edo period precedents.

But the creditors stubbornly rejected these requests, since they had the backing of the police and courts. On September 6, about one hundred and sixty organizers met in the forest again. Time after time they were taken to the police station, but they did not let up in their efforts to organize the people. In the early part of September, the trio invited Tashiro Eisuke and Katō Oribei to take over leadership at the center, meanwhile launching for the third time a legal petition against creditors and police. They volunteered to become general representatives of several dozen villagers and appealed to the police chief of Ōmiya to admonish the creditors, but they were turned down once again. But they did get a concession from the police: permission to negotiate openly with each creditor individually. Thus by this time the trio, village organizers, and the mass of impoverished people had adopted virtually the same position. On October 5, a crowd of some six hundred debtors collected in the town of Kojikano, thus throwing the police into consternation. This crowd milled about for ten days and caused a stir of incalculable proportions in villages near Chichibu.

This petition campaign made it possible for the ordinary individuals in the Konmintō to gain personal experience about disputes, and it taught them the limitations of the methods being used. Not only that; the experience fostered a powerful sense of solidarity among them all. In an attempt to capitalize on this, the leading organizers shifted their strategy to group negotiation. In these negotiations Arai Shūsaburō and others made eloquent speeches as representatives of the groups of debtors. By appealing to conventional morality and legality, they put the usurers on the defensive. But "creditors" who were protected by "laws" and government officials "were so strong that they refused to comply with demands." (At a similar incident in Hachiōji, one usurer declared, "I will not retreat one step as long as the Meiji government exists.")

At this juncture a cry for the use of force arose among the people, but the organizers tried to keep it down. They had appealed to the police three times to admonish creditors in order to show the masses the limitations that were inherent in conventional morality, even when pushed as far as it would go, and to make the masses aware of the larger enemy—state authority—that stood behind the individual usurers, who were only the immediate enemy. At the same time they appealed to the masses to convince them that the courts, police, and prefectural offices were all "in league with" usurers, and that as long as those usurers were protected under "laws" enacted by the government, no fundamental solution could be expected. A *yonaoshi* (world renewal) had to be carried out to break up this "league" of official instrumentalities. In truth, then, the people did begin to experience the *yonaoshi* process, and it began to constitute a part of their very being.

Leading members gathered at the residence of Inoue Denzō in Kami-Yoshida, Chichibu, on October 12, and decided to stage an armed uprising. Later, they met with one hundred and twenty or thirty village organizers in Iwadonosawa and agreed with them to continue petitioning as long as this route seemed feasible. As it turned out, of course, the petitions were all rejected. What is more, creditors appeared at the Ōmiya Court with summons to be distributed to their debtors. Farmers who received them became panic-stricken, and their panic spread. They pressured their leaders, who were conducting a campaign within the bounds of law, to call for an immediate uprising. Tashiro Eisuke, General Commander, stood in front of Inoue Denzō and the crowd and begged for another month of time. They would not listen to him. He then begged for "fifteen days' delay; even a one-week postponement." That, too, was refused.

Tashiro and Inoue tried to persuade the farmers by arguing that if they would wait for another thirty days, "people in Yamanashi, Kanagawa, Nagano, and Gumma as well as in Saitama Prefecture will surely rise simultaneously," and then "it will be easy for us to present to the national government a direct petition about the reduction of taxes."[9] One sees in Tashiro's arguments a combination of Konmintō demands and Jiyūtō revolutionary romanticism: expectations of overthrow of a despotic government, an early opening of the national assembly, the abolition of evil laws, and a new government of benevolence. One also sees the idea of criticizing the social system as a whole. But the people insisted on an immediate rising of their own, and they would not wait. Tashiro's belief in "waiting until the time is ripe" was shaken. On November 1, 1884, three thousand peasant troops began to march and launched an attack against government agencies.

What kind of laments did the people stifle before their spontaneous uprising? How heavy was the heart of each participant? We cannot know. Take the tragedy of a certain Iwata farmer who joined the Konmintō. His wife turned on him in a fury. It was probably mealtime. "It's all well and good for you to join in this Jiyūtō," she said, "but what will you do about these three children?" She suggested he stop eating. Iwata was so enraged by her words that he took out a sword and killed two of the children.[10]

Farmers in mountain villages were gentle, self-depriving, and patient, and they held government authorities in awe.

[9] *Tashiro Eisuke kyōjutsusho*, published in Tokyo newspapers in 1885.
[10] Inoue Kōji, *Chichibu jiken*.

How did they overcome this deeply rooted passive attitude and undergo a transformation so as to confront governmental power proudly? The answer is that they pursued conventional morality, the basis of their own inner morality and self-discipline, and then broke through its limitations. Only after they had presented petitions time after time with diligence and sincerity, and had gone through self-reflection on their own shortcomings, did they finally reach the point at which they could endure no longer. At that point they projected the criticism outward, against their arrogant adversaries, to make a searing denunciation of those adversaries' immorality and injustice. Only then did they discover their own moral superiority; only then did they turn self-abnegation into self-affirmation; and only then did they undergo a true transformation of values. It seems to me that there is something here reminiscent of the moral, spiritual, and nonviolent resistance movement of Gandhi's Satyagraha.

This transformation was of the same spiritual quality as that in the conversion experience of Nakayama Miki, the founder of the Tenri Sect; Deguchi Nao, the founder of the Ōmoto sect; and Itō Rokurōbei, the founder of the Maruyama sect. This transformation in values, however, did not take place through the religious medium that had guided those religious teachers but rather through the political thought and world view of "freedom and people's rights." Those doctrines and that world view helped them to make the transition from conventional morality to the consciousness of social transformation.[11]

Sakamoto Sōsaku and Itō Rokurōbei were different. The difference was the one between the Jiyū-Konmintō and the Maruyama sect. It was the difference between politics and religion. But Sakamoto and Itō did share some assumptions that made it possible for them to undergo transformation. Both were upright moralists and tough-minded men of self-disci-

[11] For the spiritual process of conversion that Miki, Nao, and Rokurōbei experienced, see Yasumaru and Hirota, *Nihonshi kenkyū.* Also *Ōmoto shichijūnen shi,* vol 1., and Murakami Shigeyoshi, *Kindai minshū shūkjōshi kenkyū,* rev. ed. (1963).

pline. Both tenaciously and consistently upheld conventional morality, and both discovered ethical principles that justified a break with it, through inner transformation.

Itō Rokurōbei, the son of a poor farmer in Noborito village in Musashi province, gave his private conviction the ultimate authority of divinity through a magical, religious medium. In his search for "Peace under Heaven," he developed principles for a sweeping critique of the social system. As a result, his passion for social change captured the minds of farmers who were in desperate straits during the 1880s. The number of followers of the Maruyama sect suddenly grew to become several hundred thousand. From time to time these adherents, together with the Konmintō people, criticized governmental misrule; they grew to become a formidable force threatening the lower reaches of state authority. Because plans for social change held by this sect were illusory and impractical, however, it failed to organize a rational reform movement. In contrast to this, there were few magical or cultist aspects about the people of Chichibu who rose in rebellion. Although they held a mistaken view about the revolutionary nature of the Jiyūtō they were rational in their thinking about overthrowing their adversaries. The sense of realism came into being in their cool calculation, in overcoming conventional morality, in attaining a broad perspective of society, and in weighing the balance of power between them and their foes. They would not have been able to attain this rational political awareness except for the ideological medium, the revolutionary world view that the movement for freedom and people's rights provided.

As Yasumaru Yoshio and others have shown, in the late Tokugawa period the Japanese people underwent a spiritual revolution and created a new autonomy of character by a self-discipline that concentrated massive supplies of energy. This spiritual revolution came about through their acquisition of the ethical modes of thought inherent in "conventional morality." Through practicing it, the people believed, the unlimited wealth and potential lying in the human heart could be brought forth; abundant harvests, restoration of ruined villages, peace and security in the home, and personal happiness and prosperity could be achieved. The Japanese people came to realize that values like honesty, thrift, and hard work actually did bring results. They rejected traditional fatalism that led to acceptance of one's lot in life and non-rational, magical methods of seeking to improve life, and turned instead to the more rational, active, and self-generated ways of conventional morality. Though this moral rationality liberated men to a certain degree in their personal, everyday lives, however, it proved illusory and sterile when they applied it to the social structure as a whole. The ideology of the Chichibu Konmintō, on the other hand, broke through this bottleneck.

Desires for change among the masses that were left unfulfilled by the *jiyū minken* movement or such vanguard-like groups as the Chichibu Konmintō were evoked and organized by popular religions founded by people like Nakayama Miki, Deguchi Nao, and Itō Rokurōbei. About the same time the *hōtoku* movement of moral and economic betterment of Ninomiya Sontoku developed in competition with these new religious movements. It satisfied similar popular aspirations. Taken together, these movements probably made up the entire picture of popular consciousness that developed in agricultural villages during the 1880s. What they shared is their birth from the womb of conventional morality. Each sought to perfect it, rationalize it, and finally overcome it. There seems to be no doubt that, if we set aside the traditions of townsmen in urban areas, the basic characteristics of popular thought in this period are to be found here.[12]

In previous chapters I traced the processes through which Chiba Takusaburō and Fukasawa Gompachi accepted traditional ideas and reinterpreted them into an ideology of change. Readers will have noticed that their attempts were rather different from the way in which popular ideas at the level of the

[12] Takao Kazuhiko, *Kinsei no shomin bunka* (1968). In this work the author compares the thought of conventional morality (as Yasumaru and others term it) with the ethics held by merchants in the Osaka-Kyoto region and sees it as an aspect of popular thought in less developed, rural areas.

Konmintō grew. In the case of wealthy farmers like Fukasawa advocating popular rights, conventional morality was not a direct premise of ideological transformation. Instead, the basic education received by these farmers was the Confucianism of Japan's ruling class. They developed universal aspects of Confucianism from a popular standpoint and thereby recreated it into an ideology of change. In other words, Confucian ideas such as "Heaven," "True Kingly Way," "benevolence," "deposing evil rulers," or "changing the mandate" were taken away from the ruling class and were applied in a broader, more universal fashion from the standpoint and interests of the people, the ruled rather than the rulers. There we saw immense energy directed toward fashioning an ideology of change.

I have also discussed how theories of liberty and popular rights based on Western ideas of human rights were catalysts inducing these radical changes. But there was a substantial difference between "articulate" rich farmers and the "illiterate" lower stratum in the way they developed their ideas, even though we generally classify them together as the "common people." How much greater the gap between so-called "urban intellectuals" and the lower stratum must have been!

THE CLASH OF IDEAS AT THE LOWER SOCIAL LEVEL

Before going into the problem of qualitative differences in the structure of thought between the class of intellectuals and the masses, I have to say a few words about the fierce ideological struggle that was raging unseen among the masses themselves. The truth about the Chichibu uprising could not be told to the press or to the general populace due to the government's strict censorship of the news and its deliberate, demagogical spread of false rumors. Newspapers were denied direct access to information about the uprising. Despite these restrictions, thanks to newspapers belonging to some factions of the People's Rights movement or travelers to the scene of the incident, it gradually became known that this incident was neither an ordinary peasant uprising nor a disturbance

181

incited by gamblers but rather a serious revolt linked with the Jiyūtō.

Against this backdrop, we find that an ideological offensive designed to roll back the tide of Jiyūtō ideas and the earnest wishes of people in rebellion began to take shape among the commoners themselves. This offensive was rooted in the fear that, although the uprising had been thwarted, socio-economic conditions of the 1880s were so desperate that the ideas held by Inoue Denzō, Kikuchi Kampei, Ōno Naekichi, and Shimazaki Yoshishirō might continue to spread in the countryside. It was quite possible that these farmers, like Sakura Sōgorō, might have been idolized and worshiped as martyrs and models of popular virtue, and then their ideas might become part of a tradition of protest and social change. Consequently it was natural that the entire police force under Yamagata Aritomo, Minister of Home Affairs, should become nervous about this situation and be wary about the possibility that other and similar incidents might break out. The police organized a series of campaigns and gave orders to "check and eliminate" ideas of guerrilla warfare.

Still such an ideological campaign of encirclement and containment could never be successful if waged solely by the government, even if aided by newspapers, since circulation at that time ran only into some tens of thousands. Who, then, played this ideological role for the government? Who halted the revolutionary ideas held by Ōno Naekichi and his associates and branded them "outlaws"? In pursuing this problem I will pay attention to anonymous *sekenshi* (men of the world), the "village propagandists" and "petty agitators" at the lower stratum of rural society among the common people.

We have two pamphlets, *Chichibu bōto taisan kudoki* (Persuading Chichibu Rioters to Disperse) and *Jisei Ahodarakyō* (A Mock Sutra for Trends of the Times), both drafted at about the same time in November 1884.[13] The former, a ten-page pamphlet selling for ten *sen*, was privately printed in Tokyo.

---

[13] Handwritten copies of these two works were provided by the Chichibu City Library through the good offices of Mr. Inoue Kōji.

Though erroneous in places, it told the people of the nation how massive this uprising was.

The first pamphlet reports that although some Jiyūtō members participated in the uprising, its main force consisted of five thousand rioters, led by Tashiro, who went on a rampage to punish moneylenders.

> The battalion commander of this mob of rioters was Tashiro Eisuke, who was assisted by Kikuchi Jūrō, Inoue Seizō, Ozawa Katsuzō, Yagihara Masao, Arai Enji, and Ochiai Torazō. Other rioters had entrenched themselves in such mountains as Mt. Tsukuba and Mt. Kaba and were not there at the beginning, but they all joined the disturbance once it started. With three thousand guns that had been handed out to many villages, the rioters raised their war cries and suddenly attacked the finance company of Sueno village, burning all records of loans. Then they forced their way into the village offices of Kanai and burned all the documents there. They then careened off to other areas, stealing countless amounts of money.

The style of this work is that of the *chobokure*, a street performance by beggar priests who chanted to the accompaniment of pounding a small wooden block.

It has none of the preaching tone found in the other pamphlet, *Jisei Ahodarakyō*. This document is owned by the Kashihara family in Nagatoro, Nogami-chō, Chichibu. It was brushed on seventeen sheets of Japanese paper, no doubt shortly after the incident, and it was published sometime the next year. The work seems to have been drafted in November or December of 1884. In style, cultural background, and content, the writer was probably a wealthy farmer or merchant familiar with conditions in the district; he may also have been a local intellectual with a flair for writing. Perhaps he was a preacher of moral songs, which were popular in the area in those days. He may also have been from Gumma Prefecture. At any rate, as my analysis will show, this text was ingeniously composed for ordinary people.

It is fascinating to see how cleverly the author of *Jisei Aho-*

darakyō tried to influence conformist, "tag-along" followers of the movement to abandon it and how he raised doubts in their minds about the rightness of the movement for popular rights and managed to obliterate the true significance of the Chichibu incident. We have to be astonished by his determined attitude in trying to halt and roll back the dangerous ideas disseminated by *Konmintō* organizers. He has a historical perspective. In criticizing the Chichibu incident, he puts it in a context of the Meiji Restoration, *yonaoshi* (world renewal) rebellions, the series of rebellions of former samurai, violent Jiyūtō incidents such as the Fukushima and Kabasan incidents, and the Konmintō disturbances in Kanagawa Prefecture. Let us examine the tricks and arguments he employs to win people over to his side.

> The Restoration of Imperial Rule came into being. The reform of abolishing the domains and establishing prefectures was promptly carried out. Commoners kept their counsel and bided their time as gambler bosses bragged about inciting *yonaoshi* rebellions. These gang bosses recruited many poor and ignorant people, and spoke of *unlawful things* such as smashing rice dealers, destroying sake brewers, claiming articles from pawnshops, and retrieving notes from moneylenders, and *demanded* that they follow them. Violence helped these people in the short run, but in the long run it does them no good. . . .
>
> As you know, impoverished people in village communities near Hachiōji, Kanagawa Prefecture, descended on their creditors in large numbers and demanded that they give them four years' grace. On top of that they said 'We want to repay our debts by yearly installments. Cancel as much of our debt as possible. Why don't you answer? Are you deaf and dumb?"
>
> They became violent, and pressured creditors by pulling their ears and poking them in the mouth. These rascals *know no compassion or mercy*. . . .

In the first place, the author of the book regards *yonaoshi* participants and the Konmintō as "criminals" who break promises, demand obedience by force, and use violence—all of which violate conventional morality. He conveniently ignores the causes of the popular uprising—why villagers fell into such extreme circumstances—and merely abuses them with the epithet "outlaws." His trick is to denounce the people as morally inferior and make them recoil from such a frightful view of themselves.

Why did this method achieve its intended results? For the masses it was crucial to understand the process of self-reprisal and sincere effort on their part that proved futile prior to their participation in uprisings. But the author of *Ahodarakyō* purposely omits this crucial background process and instead depicts them as having rioted without reason. In so doing, he probes their most vulnerable spot, for people's conventional morality had told them to blame themselves before blaming others; they had a long spiritual and moral tradition of this kind of self-guilt and looked askance at anyone who was not rigorously critical of his own behavior. Official apologists and moralists were fully cognizant of this vulnerability. They ignored the usurers' lawlessness and exaggerated the violence of the rioters out of all proportion, distorting the facts to brand them "criminals" who "know nothing of compassion or mercy."

In the second place, he emphasized the fact that officials were superior and sure to triumph. It would be "fools" indeed who would challenge such superiors. Even Saigō Takamori, who wielded power and influence, had been able to do no more than "cast sand against the wind." How much more foolish it would be for ordinary commoners to attempt rebellion! So went this logic of counterattack.

The authority and power of the government cannot be rivaled. Fools do not understand the reign that pacified storms throughout the four seas. In the autumn of 1882 the Fukushima incident broke out. Now this year disturbances took place at Tsukuba in Ibaragi. . . .

Saigō's revolt, the Fukushima incident, and the Kabasan incident were discredited as follies that dared to challenge the absolute, superior entity that was the Meiji government.

Ordinary people knew from their experience in day-to-day living that, regardless of why or wherefore, it was foolish to rebel; defeat was certain. The author of *Ahodarakyō* raised this piece of folk wisdom to the national level and tried to persuade people to refrain from inquiring into the details of things that were beyond their comprehension. Due to centuries of feudal submissiveness to authority, after all, the masses had the idea that government, as "superior," was necessarily made up of wise and capable officials. It is difficult to imagine, then, how intensely the common people must have been struck and moved by Ōno Naekichi's declaration that "You must support us, for, in all deference, I am going to oppose His Imperial Majesty."

In the third place, ordinary people were most afraid of being labeled "self-serving," for to be so condemned meant ostracism from the village. Conventional morality dictated that yielding and harmony as well as integrity and hard work were virtues that had to be observed strictly within village communities, and in *Ahodarakyō* these very virtues were used to indict the people. The author accuses them of seeking to change established state laws purely to suit their own convenience, or in a "self-serving" fashion, thus violating their own moral code. What is more, he makes this indictment in an authoritative, categorical manner, without dwelling on fine points of motives or causes behind the uprisings.

> Moreover, in Chichibu, Saitama Prefecture, the villagers appointed the boss of Kumachi village (Tashiro Eisuke) commander. They made *self-serving* demands such as reducing taxes, abolishing schools, changing conscription laws, or repaying debts in annual installments over time. . . .
>
> After the battle cry was raised, people in the Districts of Hiki, Kodama, Hatara, and Hanzawa all followed along. With hunting guns on their shoulders they thought nothing of marching by night or of the dangers of crossing mountains and valleys. . . .

Fourth, the author argues that the Konmintō members, "just a mob of country bumkins," were uncomprehending fools. Throughout the feudal era, insulting epithets such as "boors," "the poor," "fools," "idlers," "morally inferior," and "ignorant and lowly" had been heaped upon commoners, so these traits had become inseparably linked in the people's minds. Hence to be poor, to be a peasant, and to be of the lower classes surely meant that one was stupid, foolish, lazy, and morally inferior. Such self-deprecatory assumptions on their part reflected their acquiescence in "the worship of the powerful," the presumed superiority of "metropolitan culture" over "countryside boorishness," and the slave mentality of feudal consciousness that by rights should have been overcome by this time. But since it had not, the tract's author took unfair advantage of this weakness in the people's psychological armor.

Yet even this author could not help describing the fierce and courageous battles the Chichibu people fought against the police and army units. In the battle at Kanaya, Kodama district, Ōno Naekichi and others died. Twenty-eight were killed, and many others were seriously injured. This gives some idea of how high the fighting spirit of the peasant army was—a peasant army that was, in the author's view, impervious to reason. The writer made no mention of these things.

Several hundred police inspectors and policemen tried to persuade these *boorish rioters* to desist, but the latter did not understand a thing. Instead, these violent rioters closed ranks and fired in formation. Policemen therefore wavered, calling to one another, "Don't die for nothing!" Hearing this, the rebels grew all the more brazen. Declaring victory, they began to hold a drinking bout. . . . Rebels and soldiers who chanced to meet, between Hachiman-Kodama and Kanaya, began firing on each other. Few soldiers and policemen were hurt, but twenty-eight insurgents were killed, and many were wounded. The rebels who managed to run away did so badly flus-

tered, hurrying off in confusion. The chase was on. . . .
The rioters could not stand. In Nagano Prefecture, they
were unable to sally forth toward Saku District, a southern and remote area, and beat a hasty retreat. They again
recruited a number of people here, and plundered lots
of money and clothes in Takano, Managashi, and Umi-
jiri. They committed outrages and violence, fiercely resisting and opening fire on the police. Policemen in Nagano were wounded or died. For the time being they
grew weary and withdrew a bit. Then the rebels found
themselves faced with honorable soldiers of His Majesty's troops from Takasaki who were stationed between
Iwa-Murata and Usuda. A squad of military police advanced nobly in the direction of the pass to Yamanashi.
. . .

Notice the distinction made between despised "rebels" and
"honorable government forces," which emerges clearly in the
use of honorific language for the latter. The "rebel army," no
matter how heroic its resistance, is treated no different from
those who commit "acts of fierce violence" or "robbery and
plunder."

Fifth, the author then switches tactics to play upon the
lacrimose sentimentality to which the common people were
vulnerable in discussion of family matters, insinuating that
rebellion against the government only brings suffering to elderly parents, wives, and little ones left behind. His pseudo-
humanism is displayed in "tears shed" for those weak and
innocent victims. This is a trick played by government authorities in all periods of history. The government looks down
on errant children with loving concern—it is the "rioters"
themselves who, through acts of lawlessness, cause the suffering:

When captured, the cornered rats turned out to be
worthless ragamuffins of the petty Shakkintō. Be that as
it may, aged parents, wives, and children left behind no
doubt constantly worry about them and visit the Niō in

188

Ogano. The homophone of "Niō" (guardian gods of a temple gate) is "meet again." Out of parental love, wifely devotion, and filial affection, elderly mothers and fathers, wives, and children endure foot-sore pilgrimages to Niō, praying to see their loved ones again. Ah, it is enough to bring the tears, just to hear about them!

Such popular preachers knew all about the vulnerability of the common people in the Meiji period; they did not live as "individuals" but as "familial" beings who shouldered the memory of their ancestors and found meaning in life only when surrounded by parents, wives, children, and relatives. Accordingly, the government frequently frustrated the emerging consciousness of independence and autonomy on the part of individuals by keeping in front of them the crisis of the "familial" community, to which they were destined to belong.

Finally, in the following ingenious conclusion to the effect that "you have been troubled by a nightmare," see another skillful trick:

Well, the commanding officer and other chiefs were taken prisoners . . . but the top chief had stolen money, amassed a fortune, and run away somewhere. The others are now as though bewitched by foxes and badgers and feel that they have awakened from a dream. Now they must surrender themselves to the police, and for what? If only they had not been caught in that net of shrewd persuasion and wrongdoing! If only they had been careful and prudent and had not allowed themselves to be taken for a ride by flatterers!

May they devote themselves wholeheartedly to their family business and observe what is right so that the devil will disappear in this new year of the monkey [1884]. May there then be perfect peace throughout the four seas forever under the Emperor. May the people enjoy riches and long life. They will sing odes for a splendid reign. Ah, happy day!

189

It is a commonplace trick to bring disgrace on the revolutionary leaders' personal conduct and to alienate them from the masses. The writer expertly stirs up people's suspicions by lamenting "If only they had not allowed themselves to be taken for a ride by flatterers," and he simultaneously tries to persuade them that happiness and long life are imminent, thanks to the benevolent administration of the sovereign. Such a demagogic technique, perfected during Japan's long feudal period, remained effective in dividing the people from each other: many *yonaoshi* uprisings and popular struggles during the Meiji period were disrupted from within by this traditional argument. At any rate, one must admit that the emperor system was indeed fortunate to have these anonymous popular ideologues who took it upon themselves to counterattack dangerous ideas among the people through astute use of the arguments outlined above. These local "intellectuals"—numerous preachers and "men of the world" who assumed an "I told you so" attitude toward the people and posed as loyal servants of those in power—provided genuine social support for the modern emperor system.[14]

It was between these "preachers" and the village organizers that the real ideological struggle at the lowest level of society was waged, for the ideological struggle between emperor system ideology and popular consciousness was by no means initiated by official apologists like Katō Hiroyuki and Inoue Tetsujirō;[15] their very names were unknown to most ordinary people. Instead, the common people were induced to persevere in the face of life's hardships and to accept the emperor system ideology in terms of their own conventional morality by hundreds and thousands of anonymous teachers like the author of *Ahodarakyō*.

If *jiyū minken* intellectuals and theoreticians such as Ueki

[14] Ōe Kenzaburō, "Katsuji no mukō no antō," *Gunzō* 24 (July 1969): 180-91.

[15] Inoue Tetsujirō (1855-1944), like Katō Hiroyuki, an establishment intellectual, was also a Tokyo Imperial University professor, German-trained, and played a leading role in formulating official state morality appropriate for school instruction.

Emori, Ōi Kentarō, Baba Tatsui, and Nakae Chōmin had thought about these contortions in the historical development of common people's consciousness, if they had comprehended the ways in which the masses themselves thought and felt and plumbed the significance of the ideological struggle taking place at the lowest level of society, revolutionary thought in Japan would surely have evolved very differently from the way it actually did. But let us stop longing for what might have happened in history. A full century separates us from the Meiji Restoration; we can now observe its events in a more cool and detached manner.

From Peak to Valley

When did the self-discipline in conventional morality, which had been such an important element of people's thought, begin to weaken their independence and autonomy; when did it become a social, exterior norm, to which they had to conform? I believe that in Kantō villages this turnabout came at about the time that Nagatsuka Takashi wrote his novel *Tsuchi*.[16] In Chapter VII, I shall describe some particularly tragic cases. Certainly the third and fourth decades of Meiji (1887-1907) constitute a transitional epoch in the history of the Japanese people's social awareness and a point at which their "conventional morality" no longer liberated, but began to subject them to, the existing order and ideology. For example, in 1900, sixteen years after the Chichibu uprising was suppressed, a collection of "counting jingles" titled *Hontobushi* circulated in the town of Urawa, Saitama Prefecture. Each jingle, from "one" to "twenty" extolled a particular virtue in conventional morality.

> Go on, read these jingles! They're true, not false!
> Honest, really!

[16] Nagatsuka Takashi's *Tsuchi* (The Soil), published in 1910, a classic of realism, remains a standard picture of grinding poverty in rural Japan. A translation is in preparation by Ann Waswo.

We do not know who wrote or walked around singing these didactic jingles, but they became popular in Ōmiya and Chichibu and spread to Nishi Tama. In Minami Tama and Saga district, *Tōkyūjutsu* (a kind of conventional moral homily) and *Shinkyō tanrenkyō* (Teachings to Train Minds) became particularly popular among wealthy farmers, spread astonishingly around the early 1890s, and faded away by the end of the period. Such shifts indicate that the character of popular thought was undergoing drastic changes, reflecting fundamental shifts in productive relationships in agrarian villages during the Meiji period. Thus,

1. To be human means to follow the Way that all men must observe. That's true, it does!
2. It is foolish to waste a single day, for it will never come again.
3. If you care about yourself, get out and work: money doesn't appear out of thin air.
4. There will always be people living in this world. So they have to live in harmony with themselves and with others.
5. Can there be anybody in this whole wide world who doesn't wish he had something he doesn't?
6. The universe is the same as men's lives: Mind is more important than appearances. That's true, that's true!

Here the "conventional morality" extolling "diligence," "frugality," "harmony," and "filial piety," which formerly roused people to liberation and change, has become petty and vulgar, telling them to accept passively the world and their place in it. The implementation of conventional morality is now seen as an end in itself—the people are to concern themselves only with profit and loss, like *petite bourgeoisie*; they have lost sight of conditions in the larger world round them and no longer have a realistic understanding of their changing situation.

A similar transformation should be noted in the philosophy of "heart" in popular, conventional morality. In these jingles all problems are reduced to one's heart and attitude; all that is necessary to secure happiness in the world is to maintain the heart's tranquillity and remain content. But earlier in the development of the people's consciousness, conventional morality was humanistic; it allowed ordinary people to believe in unlimited progress, to overcome resignation and submissiveness, and to transform themselves into independent entities. By mid-Meiji, however, this philosophy of "heart" had degenerated to a passive level of acquiescence; people were instructed "do not spread rumors about others," "do not grumble," or "the heart is more important than the whole universe."

Nakayama Miki (1798-1887), the founder of Tenrikyō, relied on the authority of her absolute God, Tenri Daijin (The Diety of Heavenly Principles), to criticize government authorities bitterly as men who "rule the world in arbitrary fashion"; she preached that "because common people are children of the gods, if they take care of their hearts, reform themselves, and lead moral lives, they can bring about an ideal world." When one compares self-discipline and the philosophy of mind as preached by her with that of the jingles about truth, one is deeply moved by the difference.

> As men gradually become of stout heart, this world will prosper. Fellow creatures throughout the world are all brethren. They can never be said to be strangers.[17]

Compare these statements with *hontobushi*. "Can there be anybody in this whole wide world who doesn't wish he had something he doesn't?" One immediately sees that the thrust of ideas is in opposite directions; by the 1900s conventional morality had become commonly accepted ideas of social deceit. It was no longer an ideology to challenge authority but was incorporated into the ruling ideology. A vicious cycle ensued: the more earnestly ordinary people practiced it, the more they reinforced the existing state structure from below, and the less they could imagine their own extrication from it.

[17] Quotations are from Nakayama Miki's *Ofudesaki*, vol. 1, part 9, and vol. 13, part 43.

What is more, once this conventional morality gained common acceptance by society, would-be reformers were inevitably ostracized and denounced as heretics for seeking to transgress it, not only by government authorities, but by the common people in ordinary communities as well. Only sixteen years after Chichibu, its leaders—men like Ōno Naekichi, Inoue Denzō, and Sakamoto Sōsaku—would no longer have been able to live in their home villages. Thus, quite unnoticed by city intellectuals and literary men, the emperor system fastened itself on to and helped create these momentous changes in the lowest stratum of society, becoming a pervasive and powerful ideology that would determine the course of Japan's modernization. Which of the Meiji thinkers or writers realized this was taking place?

The ideological struggle waged every day among ordinary Japanese, then, was not the sort of refreshingly clear-cut encounter in which state ideology was flagrantly brought to bear against the people, in the way that our intellectuals would have had us believe. Instead, it was a battle of consciousness and vision waged between groups of commoners themselves, each armed with a different version of false consciousness that assumed the form of "conventional morality."

In Chichibu, where clean, cold water still runs today, and in villages lying in the valley of the mountain regions of Gumma and Nagano, old people and women who managed to avoid arrest continue to tell their children vivid anecdotes about the way "rioters of Chichibu" waged a heroic struggle, recalling and embracing that group consciousness and vision. As long as that story is told, the common people will never submit to authority, regardless of whatever oppression may be brought upon them by government or whatever slanders and abuses may be thrown at them. As Ōe Kenzaburō has said,[18] the power of group consciousness and vision carries far more weight than the power of individual consciousness and vision. According to Wakasa Kuranosuke, until quite recently popular versions of the *Ahodarakyō* about the Chichibu riot

[18] Ōe Kenzaburō, note 14 above.

were told by an old woman in Bamba, Chichibu, and an old man at Jōhōji village, Minami-Kanda district. They say that the old woman, timid and in fear of punishment, never sang in front of other people, but that she once let some trusted friends listen to her song. As for Jōhōji village in Gumma, that was where Arai Shūsaburō—the dauntless soldier who led a battalion of the Chichibu Revolutionary Army, and who was later executed—once taught elementary school.

(Translated by Eiji Yutani)

· VI ·

CARRIERS OF MEIJI
CULTURE

THE ESTABLISHMENT OF THE JAPANESE
INTELLECTUAL CLASS

Although studies of the popular rights (*jiyū minken*) movement have made considerable progress since World War II,
less than a third of the picture has been elucidated. At present, many areas remain to be explored. Even so, several
hundred political and educational organizations connected with
popular rights have been identified. In Kōchi and Kanagawa
Prefectures alone, there were over a hundred, so in all of
Japan the number of organizations must have been well over
a thousand.

These organizations, which were created by people in the
early years of Meiji, were more than cultural centers that
served as places for character formation; they were also bases
of all other movements. They provided places where people
were really able to breathe the air of the new age, to experience true self-government, and to dream of their future in
an ideal Japan. Associations like the ones in Nishi Tama villages that I have described earlier are only examples of this;
similar organizations were probably flourishing throughout
Japan during this period. Although I cannot quantify this on
the basis of primary materials at present, when I read the
dozens of reports, records, and travel accounts of city journalists of *Tokyo-Yokohama Mainichi Shimbun, Chōya Shimbun, Yūbin Hōchi*, and *Jiyū Shimbun* who were invited to
address these local associations, such activities at the lowest
stratum of society in the 1880s stand out very vividly for me.

Take just one association, the Itsukaichi Arts and Sciences
Discussion Group (Gakugei kōdankai): it was able to produce
a number, even dozens, of new personality types among its
members. If there were one thousand such associations in the
Meiji era, think of the latent intellectual and cultural poten-

tial that must have been present! I have emphasized that the People's Rights movement was more than a political movement in the narrow sense; it was also a movement of learning and arts on a national scale, one that brought forth a large number of local intellectuals. The unprecedented activities in agricultural and mountain villages during the 1880s were supported by the intellectual as well as political aspirations of the common people, and those activities were the fountainhead of "Meiji vitality." Many young people who were to become very well known experienced their first intellectual stirring in provincial towns. Kitamura Tōkoku wandered through the Tama areas obtaining personal experiences that would later form the basis of his thinking; Makino Tomitarō, who appeared at a Jiyūtō outdoor meeting brandishing a great banner, was from an influential merchant family in Sakawa, Tosa, and later established a science association; Kinoshita Naoe grew up inspired by the call to freedom in villages of the Japan Alps in central Nagano Prefecture, and Masaoka Shiki participated excitedly as a youth in local political discussion meetings in Matsuyama. There were unprecedented activities in the 1880s. In such a setting these and other young men developed the bases for their thought and their spirit of freedom, as well as the writing styles that distinguished them throughout the remainder of their lives.

The Chinese verse (*kanshi*) and travel accounts written by Kitamura Tōkoku, who probably went to the Itsukaichi area around 1884 and 1885, show almost identical forms of expression, and follow the same lines, as those of Fukasawa Gompachi and Chiba Takusaburō. This shows that Tōkoku began forming his ideas from this same rural point of origin. In fact, he deeply admired Akiyama Kunisaburō, a wealthy farmer and respected man of letters in Kawaguchi village of Minami Tama district, and he maintained that admiration and affection for him all his life.

If the People's Rights movement had continued without setback for another ten or more years, the formation and constitution of the Japanese intellectual class would most certainly have been different. At the very least, it is much less likely that a man like Fukasawa Gompachi would have given up cultural activity, cut himself off from rural and city intellectuals, and thus been deprived of a leading role in the formation of modern Japanese culture. Probably the tragic isolation suffered by Tōkoku, Tōson, Sōseki, and Naoe would have been considerably alleviated. Of course this is only conjecture. In reality the failure of the People's Rights movement largely doomed the effort for creation of a new culture from Japan's grass roots.

The local notables who had played the leading role in the democratic movement retreated after the political blows they suffered in the crushing of that movement. They found themselves under attack from the disadvantaged, such as the Poor People's party (Konmintō), on the one hand and from governmental authorities on the other. As a result they abandoned what had been a forward-looking position. For example, Hosono Kiyoshirō, who had been a prominent activist in the Tama area, tried to make himself a mediator between Konmintō debtors and creditors. Then, after he was appointed to the post of village head by the government he became an antagonist of the Poor People's party. About the same time his stature as a serious poet of Chinese verse declined, and his earlier freedom and self-reliance began to weaken. A spiritual change was reflected in his work, and the freshness of his poetic spirit disappeared. He retreated to a high-flown and rootless literati consciousness unconcerned with social affairs. Since I have discussed this change in detail elsewhere, however, I will not dwell on it further here.[1]

There were several revivals of Chinese verse later in the Meiji years, but the broad and vigorous poetic spirit of the earlier 1880s that combined with reformist thought was not to be seen a second time. This ebb of cultural creativity was not limited to *kanshi*; it was true of other literary arts, thought, technology, and related forms of village cultural creativity.

This change in the local People's Rights movement resulted in a lost rural charm; ambitious and promising youths found nothing to keep them in their villages, and instead a

[1] Irokawa Daikichi, "Meiji gōnō no seishin kōzō: Hosono Kiyoshirō ron," *Jimbun kagaku ronshū*, nos. 8 and 9 (Tokyo Keizai Daigaku, 1965).

"flight" of local intellectuals to the cities took place. Most of the numerous study circles and associations that were organized during the 1880s melted away as they lost their more active members to the cities or else became more narrowly oriented to practical concerns, transforming themselves into study groups for agriculture or sericulture. People gradually lost pride in their villages; they adopted, so to speak, a "speculative" attitude, convinced that "success could only be had in the cities." The old notion, common since medieval times, that the "culture of the capital" was superior to the "boorishness of the countryside" returned once more, and as urban-centered outlooks strengthened in villagers' minds, the feeling of a gap between cultural levels of "country" and "city" became accentuated.

Moreover, Japanese capitalism and the Meiji government that fostered it depended for its capital accumulation on the sacrifices of the farmers, and these were mercilessly demanded of them. The entire country experienced a serious depression that began in the latter half of the 1880s: more than 600,000 small farmers went bankrupt, and over 2,000,000 people saw their households break up. The radical sector of the People's Rights movement resisted this by resort to force and clashed with army and police units a number of times, but the coordinated Jiyūtō uprisings they had hoped for never took place, and as a result the Kabasan, Chichibu, and Iida incidents were suppressed one by one.

In this maelstrom the local notables disintegrated as a class. Some of them fell into ruin and lost their property; others fled to the cities, and still others became parasitic landlords by accumulating land and solidifying their preeminence in their locality, cultivating contacts with local bureaucrats appointed by the central government. Thus, concurrent with the establishment of capitalism, the landlord system became common everywhere in the countryside. The intellectual, cultural, and economic vigor of the villages disappeared, and they reverted to conservative backward areas. By the latter part of Meiji no one could have thought in terms of "advanced villages, backward cities" anymore.

Meiji culture ultimately came to flower in those "advanced

TABLE 1
Founders of Meiji Culture and Their Date
and Place of Birth

Founder	Date	Place
Religion		
Ebina Danjō	1856	Fukuoka, Yanagawa
Uemura Masahisa	1857	Edo
Uchimura Kanzō	1861	Edo
Kawaguchi Ekai	1866	Osaka, Sakai
Suzuki Daisetsu	1870	Kanazawa
Deguchi Onisaburō	1871	Kyoto, Sogabemura
Literature		
Tsubouchi Shōyō	1859	Mino, Ōtamura
Mori Ōgai	1862	Shimane, Tsuwano
Futabatei Shimei	1864	Edo
Masaoka Shiki	1867	Ehime, Matsuyama
Kōda Rohan	1867	Edo
Natsume Sōseki	1867	Edo
Tokutomi Roka	1868	Kumamoto, Minamata
Kitamura Tōkoku	1868	Odawara
Baba Kochō	1869	Kōchi
Takayama Chogyū	1871	Yamagata, Tsuruoka
Shimamura Hōgetsu	1871	Shimane, Kusamura
Kunikida Doppo	1871	Chiba, Chōshi
Tayama Katai	1871	Gumma, Tatebayashi
Tokuda Shūsei	1871	Kanazawa
Shimazaki Tōson	1872	Nagano, Magome
Higuchi Ichiyō	1872	Tokyo
Takahama Kiyoshi	1874	Ehime, Matsuyama
Yosano Akiko	1878	Sakai
Masamune Hakuchō	1879	Ibaraki, Okadamura
Nagai Kafū	1879	Tokyo
Arts		
Asai Chū	1856	Edo
Koyama Shōtarō	1857	Niigata, Nagaoka
Okakura Tenshin	1862	Yokohama
Kuroda Kiyoteru	1866	Kagoshima
Yokoyama Taikan	1868	Mito
Shimomura Kanzan	1873	Wakayama
Hishida Shunsō	1874	Nagano, Iida
Hagiwara Shuei	1877	Nagano, Higashi-Hodaka

TABLE 1 (*cont.*)

Founder	Date	Place
Thought		
Kuga Katsunan	1857	Aomori, Tsugaru
Miyake Setsurei	1860	Kanazawa
Shiga Shigetaka	1863	Aichi, Okazaki
Tokutomi Sohō	1863	Kumamoto, Minamata
Ōnishi Hajime	1864	Okayama
Nishida Kitarō	1870	Ishikawa, Unokimura
Learning and others		
Katayama Sen	1859	Okayama, Yugemura
Yokoi Tokiyoshi	1860	Kumamoto
Ume Kenjirō	1860	Shimane, Matsue
Hozumi Yatsuka	1860	Ehime, Uwajima
Kuroiwa Shūroku	1862	Kōchi, Kawakitamura
Nitobe Inazō	1862	Iwate, Morioka
Makino Tomitarō	1862	Kōchi, Sakawa
Iwamoto Zenji	1863	Hyōgo, Ideishi
Yamaji Aizan	1864	Edo
Tsuda Umeko	1864	Edo
Nagaoka Hantarō	1865	Nagasaki, Ōmura
Naitō Konan	1866	Akita, Kemauchimura
Toyota Sakichi	1867	Shizuoka, Yoshizumura
Minakata Kumakusu	1867	Wakayama
Tanaka Ōdō	1867	Saitama, Tomiokamura
Kinoshita Naoe	1869	Nagano, Matsumoto
Honda Kōtarō	1870	Aichi, Yazukuri
Kōtoku Shūsui	1871	Kōchi, Nakamura
Minobe Tatsukichi	1873	Gifu, Shimoyoneda
Yanagita Kunio	1875	Hyōgo, Tahara-mura
Noguchi Hideyo	1876	Fukushima, Inashiro

cities," but we must never forget where its seeds germinated and its roots took form. To make this point clear, let us review the points of origin of the people who became "carriers of Meiji culture." Table 1 lists the names of those who surely were outstanding pioneers in a number of fields.

I have not included in the table a group born around 1850,

which I would call the "first generation of Meiji youth," because they are more political than cultural in their character
and contribution:

Baba Tatsui	Kōno Hironaka	Suematsu Kenchō
Hara Takashi (Kei)	Ōishi Masami	Taguchi Ukichi
Hoshi Tōru	Okumiya Keishi	Tanaka Shōzō
Itō Miyoji	Ono Azusa	Ueki Emori
Kaneko Kentarō	Suehiro Shigeyasu (Tetchō)	Yano Fumio

Compared with this group, those in the table, our "founders
of Meiji culture," might more appropriately be called "the
second generation of Meiji youth"; they were born between
the latter half of the 1850s and the 1870s. Many of them were
bruised in spirit and pessimistic in outlook; they set out with
doubts about the optimistic views of politics that had been
held by the first generation. If we look at their birthplaces on
the map (see Figure 2), we find there were few from the
northeast region, and many from west of the Tokyo plain, but
the distribution extends rather evenly from the old castle towns
to farming, mountain, and fishing villages throughout the
country. The reason why so many seem to be from Edo is
probably because so many of the shogun's retainers congre-
gated there and because so many people from other parts of
the country moved there in search of employment after the
Restoration.

Again, in terms of background, the majority were from the
class of local notables, wealthy farmers and farmer-mer-
chants, a group that included part of the "rustic samurai"
(gōshi); this indicates that roughly half of them were from
"the villages." The rest were from the former samurai (shizoku) class, with former Tokugawa retainers particularly numerous. It is worth noting that as many as twenty-five of these
"carriers of Meiji culture" came from areas where the People's Rights movement was very active—Nagano, Toyama,
Ishikawa, Okayama, Shimane, Kōchi, Ehime, and Kumamoto.

These people were pioneers in their fields during the 1880s

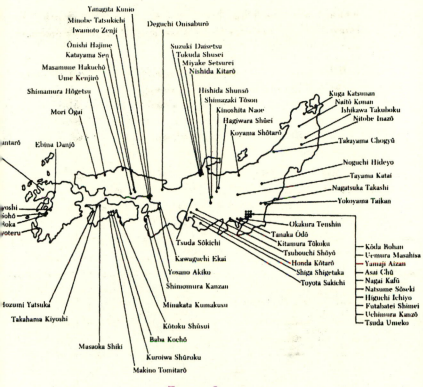

FIGURE 2
Founders of Meiji Culture and Their Birthplaces

and 1890s, but around that time leadership began to shift to several thousand new people who were trained in the new schools and who engaged in cultural pursuits on a full-time basis. As a result, a clearly distinguishable stratum of "culturally advantaged" individuals emerged to form a genuine "intellectual" class. The bulk of that group, as I have suggested, was no longer made up of new, local intellectuals who had been fostered by the Meiji Restoration and the People's Rights movement. Instead, this class was formed out of urban refugees from farming villages, immigrants who sought advancement in life, together with intellectuals from local castle towns, all of whom converged on cities like Tokyo.

During the Meiji period the people's spirit of resistance to clique (*hanbatsu*) government pulsed with the blood of national energy and rural vitality, which was later poured into urban intellectual circles. As a result, Meiji culture was vigorous and creative: the rugged determination and quick wit of Japanese farmers and merchants at the base of society gushed to the surface. Perhaps this is why Meiji culture contained little of the balmy, Indian summer calm of the middle-class culture that emerged in Taishō days. Meiji culture was intensely experimental; originality and imitation were intermingled, and Westernization and nativism mingled in bewildering fashion. Furthermore, post-Restoration nationalism and the hardships experienced by commoners resonated constantly in the hearts of those who were creating that culture at the front line in the city. The difference in gravity and earnestness between Sōseki and Ōgai, on the one hand, and Mushanokōji and Akutagawa on the other, can be found here.[2]

In this way Japan's intellectual class was formed by the confluence of rural and city intellectuals, and it was given a special historical flavor by the upsurge and defeat of the People's Rights movement as a great cultural tide. As our table shows, most local intellectuals came from the class of rural notables (*gōnō*), and many people with cultural talent emerged from regions where the People's Rights movement was strong. Even so, this type of rural intellectual did not dominate the

---

[2] Studies in English of the four writers discussed are, for Natsume Sōseki, Edwin McClellan, *Two Japanese Novelists: Sōseki and Tōson* (Chicago: University of Chicago Press, 1969); for Ōgai, Richard John Bowring, *Mori Ōgai and the Modernization of Japanese Culture* (Cambridge: Cambridge University Press, 1979); for Akutagawa, Howard S. Hibbett, "Akutagawa Ryūnosuke and the Negative Ideal," in Albert M. Craig and Donald H. Shively, eds., *Personality in Japanese History* (Berkeley: University of California Press, 1970), and most recently, Donald Keene, *Dawn to the West: Japanese Literature in the Modern Era*, vol. 1: *Fiction* (New York: Holt, Rinehart and Winston, 1984). Mushanokōji is discussed by Tatsuo Arima in *The Failure of Freedom: A Portrait of Modern Japanese Intellectuals* (Cambridge: Harvard University Press, 1969), pp. 98ff.

new intellectual class of Japan. Instead, former samurai, a portion of the old merchant class, and urbanized intellectuals became the mainstream.

Nevertheless, Meiji intellectuals retained deep emotional ties to the villages and the farms that had sent them into the world. It is easy to forget that Tokutomi Sohō—who hoped for Japan's modernization through democracy (*heimin shugi*), held up the ideal of the "country gentleman" (*inaka shinshi*), and popularized the virtues of "practical learning"—had learned these from the wealthy gentry of his Kyushu youth.[3] Tanaka Shōzō, "a Shimotsuke farmer," as he called himself, typified the diligence and sincerity that were among the fine qualities characteristic of commoner morality in Japan, and his life of struggle was an expression of the agrarian political radicalism.[4] Again, the never-ending intellectual curiosity, spirit of inquiry, optimism, and nature-loving character of Japanese farmers cultivated by cosmopolitan scholars like Makino Tomitarō, Minakata Kumakusu, and Noguchi Hideyo helped give their work world stature. Nor would the achievements of Katayama Sen and Toyota Sakichi have been conceivable without the strong curiosity, practicality, and persistence typical of farmers.[5]

We can regard Yanagita Kunio as a man who expressed a mysticism and a life philosophy that were embodied in the

[3] For Tokutomi (1863-1957), see Sugii Mutsurō, *Tokutomi Sohō no kenkyū* (Tokyo: Hōsei Daigaku, 1977), and, in English, John D. Pierson, *Tokutomi Sohō 1863-1957: A Journalist for Modern Japan* (Princeton: Princeton University Press, 1980).

[4] For Tanaka Shōzō (1841-1913), Kenneth Strong, *Ox Against the Storm: A Biography of Tanaka Shōzō* (Vancouver: University of British Columbia Press, 1977).

[5] Makino Tomitarō (1862-1957), born in Kōchi, was a botanist known for his studies of Japanese flora. Noguchi (1876-1928), born in Fukushima, was a bacteriologist who made major contributions to the study of yellow fever and other tropical diseases. Katayama Sen (1876-1928), born in Okayama, was a pioneer labor leader and communist who is the subject of Hyman Kublin, *Asian Revolutionary* (Princeton: Princeton University Press, 1964). Toyota Saikichi (1867-1930), born in Shizuoka, was an inventor and industrialist who began with the automatic loom and textiles and later launched the Toyota Motor Company. For Minakata, see the Introduction, note 5.

outlook of Japanese farmers; Masamune Hakuchō and Naka-
zato Kaizan as men who personified the bottomless and
swamplike, nihilistic social distrust held by farmers; and Deguchi Nao as the systematizer of the farmers' faith and morality and responsiveness to nature. In so doing we realize
that although Japanese intellectuals have been criticized for
isolating themselves from the people, many Meiji intellectuals owed the seeds of their culture to dominant genes among
the populace. In turn, they themselves helped bring these
seeds to maturity.

Of course the common people considered Yanagita, Minakata, Tanaka Shōzō, and Deguchi Nao to be "giants" and quite
different from themselves. It is true that although these people concentrated the common people's qualities on a larger
scale, they also had a more cosmopolitan, universal quality.
Undoubtedly the common people of Japan gave birth to such
figures, but the factors that made them "giants" were of their
own creation, and the power of that creativity and universal-
ity made it possible for them to nurture ordinary people. If
this basic interaction and symbiosis of city and country had
only remained vital and lasted longer, Meiji culture might
well have gone on to become a truly "national culture" of all
the Japanese. These "giants" could then have established a
broad popular base within which they could have realized
their own personal aspirations while flourishing together with
that base. At the very least, one such "giant" would not have
found it necessary to detail his suffering in the words that
follow:

> If I think that Japan alone is "my country," then I will
> be disappointed. However, I am a world citizen, not just
> a citizen of Japan. If I think that the prairies of North
> America, the woodlands of South America, the wilder-
> ness of Siberia . . . and forest lands in Canada are all
> "my country," there is no need to explain that Japan is
> small. Nor is it necessary to be indignant at the high-
> handedness of aristocrats and powerful merchants. . . .
> If I think that only Japanese are "my brothers," then

I will be disappointed. However, if I consider all men who recognize truth as truth and falsehood as false-hood—regardless of their language or the color of their skin—to be "my brothers," I need not be disappointed. The Boers who were struggling for their freedom and independence in South Africa are my brothers. The Fil-ipino Tagalogs, who have been fighting to establish the first free country in the Orient for the last three years, are also my brothers. The Finns, who insist on the im-portance of ethnicity at a time when all other yellow races seem about to come under the sway of the Russian Czar, and who suffer the calamity of expulsion as a result, they too are my brothers. Let Japanese politicians obey what-ever their government decrees; let Japanese philoso-phers insist that nothing is more important than loyalty and patriotism. We will never need to feel disappoint-ment in the whole of humankind. As long as all within the Four Seas are brothers, whatever is good in other countries will come to ours sooner or later. We can hope to receive from the politicians and philosophers of other countries what we cannot receive from the politicians and philosophers of our own country.[6]

OPENING THE EYE TO THE INNER LIFE

As I stated in the introduction, Japan is a very special coun-try. Whether we credit its singularity to theories of climate, to insularity, or to the long history of national seclusion, it is clear that the Japanese people have many deficiencies in cul-tural sensitivity that might have been smoothed out through contact with other peoples. Above all, concepts of the house that stressed the importance of elders, of family, of status, and of village communal consciousness (*kyōdōtai*) since me-dieval times bolstered the idea of a single national lineage

[6] Uchimura Kanzō (1861-1930), a major Christian intellectual and pacifist. The quotation is from "Kibō no kuiki," published in *Yorozu chōhō*, March 1901.

and helped make it a permanent fixture that limited the growth of a modern culture in Japan.

During the People's Rights movement this idea of a single lineage was shaken; for a time it seemed as though this obstruction to modern culture might be broken through from within. The growth of a mass consciousness in that period gave hope that the Japanese people might manage to transcend the traditional values placed on elders, status, and communal consciousness, and that they might develop a broader and more free and liberal social consciousness through the avenues of popular rights organizations and communes. Of course, no Japanese "communal social consciousness" could have been identical with the social-contract type of commune described by Locke or Rousseau, for that was based on the principle of individualism. Our communes had as their point of origin a cooperative consciousness based on territory and tried to create a new democratic content within traditional forms. But in the end even these attempts failed with the collapse of the People's Rights movement.

So, after the 1880s and the development of the parasitic landowner system, when Japanese "folk society," which had been essentially different from European "civil society," began to show characteristics of a more bourgeois culture, that new society proved to be even more different from its European counterparts. Many Japanese intellectuals responded with cries of despair. Each time they came into contact with the masterpieces of modern Western literature and art, and with Christianity, all of which conveyed the spirit of Western civil society, they were struck by its beauties and felt ashamed of the deviations and shortcomings of their own society.

It is not surprising that when the young spirits of Japan in the 1880s and 1890s discovered the romance of individual dignity or human liberation in Protestantism—or when in the words of Byron and Goethe, they suddenly awoke to become conscious of the "self"—they were brought to a change in values as though in response to a sudden wind. From that moment, these young men seem to have begun to feel that they were a race apart, virtual aliens among native Japanese.

Takamura Kōtarō, as I mentioned in the introductory chapter, experienced this in Paris:

> Living in a corner of this bottomless world capital
> where France exists transcending France,
> I forgot, at times, my nationality.
> My native land was remote, small, petty,
> it was like some bothersome village.
> I was first enlightened to sculpture in Paris,
> had my eyes opened to the truth of poetry,
> and recognized the reasons for culture
> in each citizen there.
> Saddened and helpless,
> I saw an unmatchable gap.
> I felt nostalgic for, yet denied,
> everything Japanese, the way the country was.[7]

For young people like Kitamura Tōkoku and Natsume Sō-seki, who reached their twenties after the collapse of the People's Rights movement, it was natural to rebel against the psychological atmosphere of Meiji society. It seemed hopelessly dark, archaic, and dehumanized. Why should they not have been captivated by the (illusory) brightness of European-style modernity and civil society and regarded it with tremulous desire? The introspection and the modern sense of self they experienced became the source of their later creativity. They contributed treasures of the human spirit more international and universal in nature than anything the Japanese masses had ever been able to produce. It would be provincial and shortsighted to dismiss such sensitive reactions to European culture just because they were far removed from the psychic processes of the ordinary people of Japan. However attached an intellectual may be to his own country, he has to be able to observe it in a critical, detached manner and reach an initial stage of despair regarding its condition. Only then will he be able to understand his country and people in

[7] See chap. I, note 6.

a global context; only then can he ask meaningful questions about Japan's "real modernity."

What needs to be emphasized is that we have to mend our foolish tendency of looking down on the masses, and we have to stop trying to cloak their thinking to make it resemble that of our intellectuals. Until and unless intellectuals attain a universal understanding through a sincere and genuine individuality, they will not be able to renew contact with the spiritual world of the masses in the way that Kitamura Tōkoku, Tanaka Shōzō, and Uchimura Kanzō did. At present—in our current stage of historical study—it is more important to give serious weight to the consciousness of the masses. Ideally that consciousness should merge with the thinking of the intellectuals, and undoubtedly one day it will. But it will never do so through "enlightenment" activities by intellectuals who take it upon themselves to "lead" or "elevate" the masses; it will have to be worked out by the people themselves in a process of independent thought and individual transformation.

In 1891 Kitamura Tōkoku, who was then twenty-three, wrote a poetic drama called *Hōraikyoku* (Ballad of Eternal Youth), in which he had Yanagida Motoo, a wanderer living in obscurity, deliver the following monologue:

My eyes, strangely enough, look within and not without
They pierce every mystery within me, without exception
But more surprising still, the eyes that stared within
      when I was in the light
now search without instead, once it is dark. . . .
I seem to feel two conflicting spirits
One divine, the other human, within me
That will struggle without end un il I die, forever
      tormented and ill.

This kind of agony was unknown to Japanese of ea. lier times. Tōkoku pondered this agony deeply, and he laid the foundation for consideration of the "self" or "ego" in Japan in his "Discourse on the Inner Life" (*Naibu seimei-ron*, 1893), "My Prison" (*Waga rōgoku*, 1893), and "Secret Palace within the

Mind of Each" (*Kakujin shinkyū-nai no hikyū*, 1892). He sought the dignity of the individual, which is the basis of the modern view of man, in this "inner life," and he tried to discover this "inner life" in the history of the Japanese people ("a great underground river") in the form of an aspiration for basic freedom. It cannot be said that he succeeded. But the reason he was able to direct his search in this area was that, as someone personally interested in people's rights, he had worked together with the people and, though frustrated, continued struggling to revive the idea of popular rights. Yet even in his case, it was probably Meiji Christianity that facilitated the transformation from a primarily political People's Rights idea to the "inner world" and allowed it to take root.

Meiji Christianity, particularly Protestantism, was profoundly influential among Japanese intellectuals, probably as much so as Marxism in these Shōwa years. Many Japanese in the Meiji period who were not able to see the West at first-hand received some understanding of modern civil society by entering the world of Christianity and coming into contact with the atmosphere of "God," "missionaries," and "the church." Of course, there must have been a great deal of exoticism and romanticism mixed in. But for Japanese who had been surrounded by myriads of gods and deities, accustomed to a mixture of Buddhism and Shintō, who had lived for centuries in a mental environment that effortlessly embraced all kinds of ideas and principles, Christianity, with its insistence on the "encounter of the individual with the only True God," must have been truly shocking and revolutionary.

On many counts, Japan's baptism in Western modernization took place through Christianity. Not all Japanese converts, however, were able to reach the equivalent of Tōkoku's "inner life." For many, the more intense their encounter with Christianity, the more intense their subsequent renunciation of it and the deeper their confusion. According to a history of the Christian church in Japan (*Nihon Kiristo kyōkai shi*), of the 7,700 people baptized between 1891 and 1899, 3,795 later left the church. Moreover, many intellectuals like Shimazaki Tōson and Masamune Hakuchō, although they did not

211

formally remove their names from church rolls, left Christianity during these years.

Such intellectuals were in search of a modernization structured along a rationale quite different from that being worked out by the imperial government. There were also some, like Kitamura Tōkoku and Taoka Reiun, who had doubts about modernization altogether. But on the whole until the middle of the Meiji period resistance to the emperor system had first priority for such people, and they were concerned with the values appropriate to a "bourgeois modernity" (*shinminteki na kindai*). Symbolic of that effort was the controversy about Christianity and the Imperial Rescript on Education that raged in 1892 and 1893.[8] In this controversy the Christian community gave important intellectual support to progressive intellectuals, and the regime did not by any means have things its own way. But the churches were unable to criticize the royal family because of the taboos surrounding it—nor were there any Christians who were prepared to come forward to defy those taboos and risk imprisonment or death as martyrs—and the controversy gradually died down in an inconclusive and unsatisfactory manner. Shortly afterward, the Sino-Japanese War of 1894-1895 broke out. Virtually all Japanese were caught up in the current of patriotism, and the influence of the Christian church declined rapidly.

VIEWS OF CIVILIZATION

When Japan launched foreign wars like the Sino-Japanese War of 1894-1895, the expedition to Peking in 1900, and the Russo-Japanese War of 1904-1905, many changes occurred in the thought of intellectuals as well as in the consciousness of the common people. What sort of influence did Japan's joining the circles of Western imperialist powers have on the national

[8] The controversy in question was touched off by Uchimura's hesitant refusal to bow to the Imperial Rescript on Education at its first reading in the First Higher School where he was teaching English. This provoked Inoue Tetsujirō and others to a series of writings in which they argued the incompatibility of Christianity with Japanese patriotism.

consciousness? Despite the importance of this problem, it has not been studied adequately. There are two or three examples like Ariizumi Sadao's analysis of changes in the consciousness of one wealthy farmer,[9] but it is extremely difficult to carry out sound, basic studies of the changes in national consciousness as a whole. At this writing it is not at all clear when such research will come.

The Japanese victory in the Sino-Japanese War brought Fukuzawa Yukichi to the nation's attention once again. When this great enlightenment thinker published his *Outline of a Theory of Civilization (Bunmeiron no gairyaku)* in 1875, he gave the Japanese nation the prospect of a "civilization" that was not a monopoly of the West but something shared by all mankind. He called on Japan to adopt this universal "civilization" as quickly as possible while resisting the Western powers. As the revolutionary People's Rights movement rose in strength and as Japanese-Chinese relations became strained over the Korea question, however, Fukuzawa advocated that Japan extricate itself from Asia. In his essay titled *Datsuaron* (1885), he argued that Japan should distance itself from "bad friends" in Asia. In other words, he changed his view to argue that it was right and proper for Japan, together with the Western countries, to intervene in the affairs of "barbarous" Asian lands because Japan represented "civilization" and had the mission of awakening less advanced neighbors by the use of force. Ten years later Japan, which had adopted this "civilization" and built up military strength, defeated the Ch'ing empire, the symbol of Asian "barbarism." A joyous Fukuzawa, on seeing Japan's victory in this war, told the nation, "the great work of the Restoration is now achieved. This victory was nothing other than the victory of Japanese 'civilization.' "[10]

[9] Ariizumi Sadao, "Meiji kokka to shukusaijitsu," *Rekishigaku kenkyū* (November 1958).

[10] Fukuzawa's *Bunmeiron no gairyaku* has been translated by David A. Dilworth and G. Cameron Hurst (Tokyo: Sophia University, 1973) as *An Outline of a Theory of Civilization*. On Fukuzawa, Asia, and the Sino-Japanese War, see Kenneth B. Pyle, *The New Generation in Meiji Japan: Prob-*

After this a deep split developed with respect to intellectuals' views of "civilization." Uchimura Kanzō issued a statement of self-criticism and apology for his earlier mistaken public statement that the Sino-Japanese War was "a war of justice and civilization," and he went on to question the meaning of civilization in imperialistic countries. Kinoshita Naoe and Kōtoku Shūsui pursued the question more radically from the standpoint of the laboring class. All three, Uchimura, Kinoshita, and Kōtoku, transcended their identification as Christian or socialist to set out arguments in *Yorozu Chōhō*, the largest daily newspaper at that time. They exposed the falseness of the Meiji government's "modernization" and "civilization" and criticized them bitterly. Since their view of "civilization" revolved around a universal idea of humanity, whether Christian or socialist, they did not need to show any mercy toward offenders against justice at home or abroad, Occidental or Oriental. Kōtoku's *Imperialism (Teikoku shugi)* of 1901 can be interpreted as an essay in which he tried to show the ideal of a truly civilized society from the standpoint of the working people through a criticism of the existing order.[11]

In those days, however, what method besides Westernization was available to a backward country like Japan to become civilized and modernized? It was natural that Japanese in the Meiji period were unable to imagine any concrete models of societies achieving civilization and modernity except by Westernization, which in fact meant imperialism. The only possible alternatives were concepts like Okakura Tenshin's "principles of Asia" as set forth in *Ideals of the East (Tōyō no risō*, 1903) and the banners of anti-civilization hoisted by Taoka Reiun.[12]

---

lems of Cultural Identity, 1885-1895 (Stanford: Stanford University Press, 1969), and Hilary Conroy, *The Japanese Seizure of Korea 1868-1910* (Philadelphia: University of Pennsylvania Press, 1960).

[11] For a general and brief treatment of Uchimura, see John F. Howes, "Uchimura Kanzō: Japanese Prophet," in Dankwart A. Rostow, ed., *Philosophers and Kings: Studies in Leadership* (New York: George Braziller, 1970). Kōtoku is studied in F. G. Notehelfer, *Kōtoku Shūsui: Portrait of a Japanese Radical* (Cambridge: Cambridge University Press, 1971).

[12] Taoka (1870-1912), from Kōchi, was a People's Rights advocate who be-

For these people, the principle of "civilization" could no longer be monistic; "Western civilization" became something that had to be overcome by the principles of Asia, the "Ideals of the East." In Tenshin's early notes, "The Awakening of the East" (*Tōyō no mezame*, 1902), he viewed even the Sino-Japanese War as one that the West had instigated to foment dissension among the Asian nations. Basic to this view was the idea of opposing Western imperialist control by emancipating Western colonies in Asia. In the case of Tenshin, however, his early radicalism weakened as Japan's own imperialism developed.

The Russo-Japanese War was an important turning point. Japan's surprising victory against the great Russian empire aroused the fear of aggressive yellow power among the Western nations, which were swept by theories of a "yellow peril." Against this Tenshin made an attempt to explain the causes of the Russo-Japanese War. In *The Awakening of Japan* (1904) and in *The Book of Tea* (1906), both of which were published in English, he introduced Japan's traditional aspirations for peace and aesthetic values, and while grasping to find a non-Western type of modernity he denied the idea of a "yellow peril." Even so, the fierce enthusiasm that he displayed in 1902—when, together with fighters for the independence movement in India, and indignant at the cultural destruction wrought by Western imperialism, he insisted that "Asia is one"—was no longer to be seen in his later writings. Tenshin's groping stopped in midstream.[13] The fact that Japan traveled down the path of imperialism—the "way of force" in traditional East Asian thought—produced this abrupt change in the depth of some intellectuals' thought, but the majority were little aware of this subtle transition.

Japan's victory in the Sino-Japanese War (1895) raised in

---

came increasingly iconoclastic. His criticisms of capitalism and the family system were banned with some regularity. He was relentless in his criticism of modern nationalism and mechanization and advocated a retreat from modern society to primitive, utopian communism.

[13] Irokawa Daikichi, "Tōyō no kokuchisha Tenshin: shono shōgai no dorama," Introduction to *Okakura Tenshin*, vol. 39: *Nihon no meicho* (Tokyo: Chūō kōronsha, 1970), pp. 7-63.

earnest the curtain on imperialism in Asia, and its victory in the Russo-Japanese War (1905) masked the coming of the struggle for liberation of peoples in Asia and Africa. The news that Japan had defeated one of the great Western imperialist powers roused the spirits of Asian, Arab, and African peoples. This "Japan shock" of 1905 engulfed not only thinkers like Tagore, Sun Yat-sen, Gandhi, and Lu Hsün but also ordinary people; Arab laborers working at Suez, black people in Africa, and people in Turkey, India, and the Philippines; it gave them a strong and deep premonition that the future held hope for them. There is much testimony regarding the repercussions at that time, and it pains our hearts as Japanese today. For in reality, just as these people gained strength from their illusion about Japan and rose to struggle for their own national liberation, Japan betrayed these expectations and hopes.

This rupture in world history seems to have thrown people like Futabatei Shimei into a quandary. In his work *Watakushi wa kaigiha da* (I am a Skeptic; 1908), Futabatei describes a fundamental skepticism toward life as well as art, saying, "Is not twentieth-century civilization destined to be meaningless?" Yet in *"Yo ga hansei no zange"* (Confessions of the First Half of My Life), he lamented that "my life is torn between two opposite poles: my innate passion for imperialistic patriotism and my socialist ideals. I alternate constantly between these two and am unable, even now, to free myself from that anguish." It was not a problem of private inclination. Rather, it was a position for which there was no solution—this was the fundamental riddle he faced. Not only he: Natsume Sōseki and Mori Ōgai also felt themselves torn between these poles near the end of Meiji; they, too, struggled. They could not understand the trend of the times that Japanese intellectuals faced, the worldwide divisions and deep fissures in the minds of the people that were caused by the completion of the emperor system and the surfacing of internal crises. These trends permitted no peace for men of conscience.

Of course, people live in various ways. There were men like Nagai Kafū, who closed his eyes to this historical change, who was intoxicated by the aesthetic illusion of the modern

West, and who continued to write explicitly about his hatred
and dislike of Meiji civilization in his works (all in 1909): *Fu-
ransu monogatari* (Stories of France), *Shin kichōsha nikki*
(Diaries of a Person Recently Returned from Abroad), *Kan-
raku* (Pleasures), and *Reishō* (A Smile). Another, Takamura
Kōtarō, kept his criticism of Meiji civilization to himself and
instead struggled in search of an inner world of self and the
formation of his inner life.

Ishikawa Takuboku denounced Kafū's life style as that of "a
spoiled dandy from a country town who, after living in Tokyo
on his father's money for a few years and being played up to
by Shinbashi and Yanagibashi geisha, returns home to complain about the cloddishness of local girls to everyone he meets.
His affectation is disgusting. He is the oldest son of a noto-
riously wealthy family, and has nothing to do from morning
to night." Takuboku went on to complain that if Nagai "can't
really love his country, he should just leave. . . . If he can't
leave, he should think of improving it. Ultimately the improvement of the people's life in a country has to start with
self-improvement."[14]

Takuboku's great indignation probably stemmed from his
awareness of the masses of obscure Japanese commoners whom
he saw at the bottom of Meiji society and who created the
civilization that Kafū so despised. Takuboku came to have
harsh feelings toward urban bourgeois intellectuals who tried
to cast off these common people on the basis of their own
fascination with the West and its modernism; since he himself
had lived at the lower depths of society, it is only natural that
he denounced them. In addition, Takuboku was personally
convinced that Meiji writers were evading the troublesome
problem of government authority.

Would Takuboku's sound and sensible criticism, however,
be enough to dispose of Kafū's view of "civilization" in Japan?
Hardly. What better evidence is there than the fact that even
today, sixty years after Kafū published his *Shin kichōsha nikki*,

[14] Ishikawa Takuboku, *Hyakkai tsūshin* (1909). See also Seidensticker, *Kafū
the Scribbler*, p. 33.

the same sort of books continue to appear? Young Japanese intellectuals who came into contact with the essence of modern Western culture return home, not as fascinated, frivolous imitators, but as people who have been shaken to their very depths. When they return home they fall into despair at seeing the "citizens" and "civil society" of their motherland. I suspect that this pattern of thinking is likely to continue for a long time to come.

(Translated by Noboru Hiraga)

· VII ·

MEIJI CONDITIONS OF
NONCULTURE

Desperate Farming Villages in the Meiji Era

In 1905, northeastern Honshu (the Tōhoku area) suffered from extremely cold weather that resulted in the worst crop failure since the Temmei (1781-1789) and Tempō (1830-1844) periods. In Miyagi Prefecture, the crop registered only twenty percent of a normal year's production, and as a result, 280,000 of the approximately 900,000 people in the prefecture became destitute. Since the Restoration, good harvests had been rare, and there were lean years six times, in 1869, 1884, 1897, 1902, 1905, and 1910. Consequently, farmers in the Tōhoku region became acutely and chronically poverty-stricken toward the end of the Meiji era. As described in one account:

Before the wounds due to the poor crops of 1902 could heal, the Russo-Japanese War started. Just at the time the war required sacrifices of many kinds, people were affected again by unprecedentedly bad crop conditions. Even middle-class farmers, who owned part of their land but also rented some, experienced economic difficulties; many dropped down a peg, losing what they owned. . . . Many lower class farmers had neither rice to harvest in the autumn nor any means of work, and when starvation loomed, those living in the mountain villages gathered nuts and dug wild plants for food. But when winter snow arrived, even this became impossible and these people, like those on the plains, could do nothing but fold their arms and wait for assistance.[1]

Horror stories from these crisis years are numerous. One dates from January 25, 1906. Endō Hisaharu, 53, a farmer of Hitotsuguri-mura, Tamatsukuri district, Miyagi Prefecture, had lost his means of livelihood due to poor crops. He and his

[1] Fujiwara Ainosuke, ed., *Meiji 38 nen Miyagi-ken kyōkōshi* (1916).

219

family of four had been without food for days. On this particular evening, a neighbor passed in front of his house and
heard a pitiful moan, "I think I'm dying." The neighbor immediately brought some rice cakes and tried to feed them,
but it was too late. Hisaharu was too weak to eat and died
the next morning. His wife, Matsu, 56, had lost the use of
both arms through rheumatism; the following day she, too,
died. The only survivors were his sickly eldest son and his
small grandchild. The cause of the deaths was reported as
chronic bronchitis, but it is said that at the village office they
admitted that the cause of death had been a "prolonged lack
of food."

Ujiie Tomosuke, 51, also a farmer in Hitotsuguri-mura, and
his family of five, lived in a small rented house. The walls
had completely disintegrated, and they had hung up straw
mats instead. These did not, however, keep out the icy wind.
The roof, too, was so dilapidated that the sky showed through;
it afforded no protection from rain and snow. "Even during
the coldest season," the account goes, "the family wore thin
rags for clothes. Their sleeves did not even reach their elbows
and their pants legs came to their knees. The shirt of the
baby, Tōsuke, was so short that his stomach was not even
covered." Of course, there was no bedding. "They sat around
the fire for warmth, spread straw on the ground, and slept
with straw mats covering them."[2]

Saitō Hiroshi, who provided the above materials, also wrote
an excellent article titled "Desperate Farming Villages in the
Meiji Era." He prefaced this with the following poem by the
Emperor Meiji, written in 1905:

> Be alert, my prefectural governors
> To see whether smoke rises from the hearths
> of my humble people's houses.[3]

[2] Ibid.

[3] Reference is to the legendary Nintoku Emperor, who was credited with
Confucian virtues by the eighth-century *Nihon shoki* and quoted as saying
"We ascended a lofty tower and looked far and wide, but no smoke arose in
the land. From this we gather that the people are poor, and that in the
houses there are none cooking their rice." Forced labor was abolished, palace expenses cut, and the enclosure allowed to fall into ruins, but "For the

This is truly biting criticism. After reading it, I thought of the following questions: Why did people bear these conditions so patiently and stoically? Why did they just submit and starve? Why did they not protest? Explode? Seek assistance? It cannot be because hunger deprived them of the energy. Human beings are living creatures who can see what is happening to them in time to try to take steps to avoid such fates. Nor is it satisfactory to say that the government under the emperor system erected a control network that extended to every corner of the village and dominated the people with tacit help from landlords. No, the question goes deeper. Was there not some sort of internalized spiritual factor that made these people bind themselves voluntarily? If so, what was it? Was it only the "conventional morality" discussed in the previous chapter? Was it the rules and regulations of the communal village, or was it the manifestation of some basic distrust and despair that farming people had known for hundreds of years? We must investigate this problem thoroughly: What was it that pushed people to suicidal starvation? What was the source of the strength, the endurance that made them so patient in destitution and death? With this problem in mind we need to reread Nagatsuka Takashi's 1912 novel *Tsuchi* (The Soil) and Mayama Seika's 1909 *Minami Koizumi-mura* (The Village of Minami Koizumi).

These books make it clear that farmers in Tōhoku, however desperate their situation, found it unbearable to ask other villagers for help. They particularly dreaded being stigmatized by biting terms of contempt—*annya, gassutari, gasshitakari, hoitotakari*, which were reserved for the starving and indigent—and found it preferable to starve in silence.

> There were many people whose means of livelihood was gone, and who, even if they had not eaten for two or three days, felt it debasing to ask others for food; they managed to stay alive by eating unspeakably strange

space of the three autumns the people had plenty, the praises of his virtue filled the land, and the smoke of cooking was also thick." W. G. Aston, trans., *Nihongi: Chronicles of Japan from the Earliest Times to A.D. 697* (Tokyo: Tuttle reprint, 1972), p. 279.

things. Among the poor people in Kawasaki-mura Mo-
toshakin, Shibata-gun, some left the village telling their
neighbors that they were going on a pilgrimage to the
Grand Shrine of Ise, but actually went to other villages,
where no one knew them, to beg for food there. But in
their own villages they never complained of their hard
life.[4]

What kind of self-discipline, and what kind of values, were
at work here, when villagers were ashamed to ask their
neighbors for help even when they had had nothing to eat for
several days? Why was it possible to beg away from home,
unknown, but preferable to starve in silence in their own
village? If the village community had been a real communal
body (kyōdōtai) it should have been possible to find help within
it without having to go outside. Yet in fact the morality of
common people in the Meiji period led them to do the exact
opposite.

It requires stern self-discipline to starve in silence. Had
the masses generated this by themselves, it would be little
short of astonishing. But this self-discipline collapsed when
these people went to other villages. As a result we can only
surmise that such individual consciousness was combined with
and reinforced by the silent coercion of that "communal" village. Such behavior was recognized as "shameful" only within
the home village where the individual was controlled from
within. That sense of shame had indeed become a socially
accepted path of behavior, but it had not developed into
something approximating the consciousness of (Western) civil
society. Moreover, village society had changed; the community no longer constituted a body that guaranteed the security
of life and equality among its members. It had become instead a fictive communal village, an organization based in part
on compulsion and dominated by landlords. As a result poor
people had no means for help, either within or without their
village. The "family" would have been their last hope, but
that family was too often destroyed as a result of continuous

[4] Fujiwara, *Meiji 38 nen.*

years of crop failures, as family members had to go off to seek help on their own.

Farmers like Endō Hisaharu were unable to leave their villages and starved to death. But the daughters of such poverty-stricken people could become workers in silk-spinning factories or they could be sold as prostitutes. The boys went to other places to work, becoming fishermen, construction workers, or miners who crawled along the narrow shafts pulling baskets of coal by sashes tied around their foreheads. In this way the families were scattered about, but no matter where they went they could not easily free themselves from the fatalistic view that bound them.

Mayama Seika used these, almost clinical, phrases about the life of Tōhoku farmers: "miserable, unspeakable life," "ugly life," "defeated life," "degrading," "people unable to escape agony no matter how they struggle, unable to imagine another existence," "insects that crawl on the ground," "misery, whether they remain or leave."[5]

These farmers believed that their poverty and distress stemmed from their own or their parents' crime of not being able to endure the self-discipline enjoined by a stern conventional morality, and this helpless resignation made their plight even more serious. The miners who worked in the pits despised themselves as "lowly criminals," whereas the girls who lay in brothel beds crushed by the heavy bodies of sweating men considered this a "duty." The depth to which they had sunk was crystallized in this "abyss of consciousness." The real consciousness of the populace at the bottom of society was expressed in humiliating terms, like "lowly criminals," or "working in the world of suffering."

Women workers at the silk-spinning factories, who were held in dormitories, as if in detention, sang dreary songs like "Bring the rice bowl closer/ Look at the mixture of rice and barley/ What, no rice? Eyes fill with tears." In reality, songs like this, in which women workers express a grudge, were

---

[5] Mayama Seika, *Minami Koizumi-mura* (1907-1909). A representative novel of the naturalist school.

surprisingly few, but since they could remember that at home their parents were struggling to fight off hunger by eating the roots of wild vegetables, it was to be expected that there were few expressions of indignation or demands for improvement in conditions. One exception to this was a publication titled *Jokō Aishi* (Pathetic Episodes in the Lives of Female Mill-hands). Capitalists cleverly utilized the common people's perception of their own poverty and consciousness of being lowly "criminals" to control them. On the other hand, progressive intellectuals could not attain a similar true understanding; as a result their appeals for the people's liberation did not penetrate to the popular level and consequently found no acceptance.

No matter how much intellectuals might emphasize the common people's relative poverty, they could never generate revolutionary change without an understanding of the real conditions in which the masses lived. Advocates of socialism in early Meiji Japan called for the liberation of the people but failed to capture their hearts. Quite the contrary; a man like Kōtoku Shūsui could be cut off from the masses and labeled a "traitor," and he met a tragic, solitary execution. One of the causes for such a tragedy lay in this separation of the intellectuals from the masses.

Consciousness in the Lower Depths

Of course, the entire populace at the very bottom of society was not subsumed under this dark and negative image we have discussed. For instance, Kanji, the destitute farmer who is the principal figure in *Tsuchi*, is described by Nagatsuka, the author, as "brutal," but he displays an astonishing vitality that borders on lawlessness as he claws his way up from the bottom of a deep abyss. His struggle shows the populace as it really was. That reality can also be seen in the reckless defiance with which the coal miners started uprisings that shook the authorities.

What I want to use here, however, is the diary of a private

first class from Sakura, Chiba Prefecture, to give another view of human nature at the very bottom of society. It shows a character type that will surprise our intellectuals. Ōzawa Keinosuke was discharged from the Second Infantry Regiment in 1899 after fulfilling his two years' service. At the time of his discharge there was a popular parody of a song that was regularly sung on National Foundation Day, February 11. The song was "Takachiho Peak, Rising Above the Clouds."[6] The parody retained the melody while altering a few crucial lyrics. It went as follows:

> The lofty tower that rises above the clouds
> Shining electric lights as well
> An engagement of slightly more than two years.
> Today we parted and I am on my way
> Worshiping the sacred emperor's palace
> With figured silk from afar
> Holding back the tears that flow
> Seeing the flowery capital along the way
> Leaving for home, bidding farewell
> To my dear castle of Sakura in Shimōsa.

This is probably a typical ballad of a soldier regretfully parting from his favorite woman at the brothel. Its significance, however, is that it borrows the melody of National Foundation Day and sings of the palace and the emperor in the same context as the brothel. Soldiers enjoyed themselves by indulging in dangerous "disrespect" of this sort. In this era the emperor was not yet a "living god." The populace used the emperor to make their own image of passion stand out more conspicuously. The couplet, "Worshiping the palace from afar/ Holding back the tears that flow," indicates their true feeling and reads well. We tend to forget the fact that soldiers, who stood at attention in front of their superiors to hear the "Imperial Rescript to Soldiers and Sailors" read to them, were

---

[6] The mountain in question, in Hyūga, was the spot where, according to the traditional mythology of an "unbroken line" of emperors, the Emperor Jimmu's great-grandfather descended at the Sun Goddess's command to rule the Divine Land.

clever enough to create a humane and relaxed world for themselves while giving the appearance of being respectful and proper at all times.

One sees this even more clearly and directly in another song. The voice singing was changed from man to woman, and the soldiers translated their own feelings into womanly concerns of a prostitute. Soldiers and prostitutes are alike in that both are "captive," and so a relationship of unconscious sympathy and human compassion was established. The "sorrow of the [woman's] work" and the craving for the day when her "term of service" would end and she could know the pleasures of freedom once again were specified with an accuracy that only the populace at the bottom of society could have understood.

These lyrics were jotted down with brush on military stationery imprinted with the words "wartime use." They must have been written as a memo when Private First Class Ōsawa, who received orders to report for duty again in June 1904, was on a ship heading for the battle of Port Arthur. Military correspondence, in addition to four volumes of Ōsawa's journal, have been discovered together with these notes.[7]

> I parted from my beloved man
> For the sake of my parents
> I was sold to another province,
> Whether north, south, east, or west, I do not know.
> I have these painful duties to perform
> But it's for my parents and it can't be helped.
> Though I don't begrudge my duty
> I may be hurt having private parts
> Examined by cold-hearted doctors
> A treasure box that I wouldn't even show my parents
> I hate to have examined.
> If it is the emperor's rules

[7] Irokawa Daikichi, "Nichiro sensō to heishi no ishiki," *Tokyo Keizai Daigaku sōsetsu 70 nen kinen ronbunshū* (1970), pp. 451-66, and "Nichiro sensō ka no aru nōmin heishi no kiroku," *Jimbun shizen kagaku ronshū*, no. 24 (Tokyo Keizai Daigaku, 1970), pp. 195-290.

There's no way out, there's no way out.
If you're sorry for me, just buy up my contract
I receive customers for my family's sake,
I refuse them for my lover's sake.
I can't wait for my contract to run out,
So we can live together
Holding hands together,
Two pillows on one bed
We'll lie in bed and talk.
The warship that my parents gave me,
I'll let you ride on top
Hoist sail to the winds of this intransient world
Take the helm, and enjoy in zest
The joy of rowing
The pleasure of starting
Nothing compares with this delight
Since this was the bond in which
The Izumo shrine's deity presided over our union
How grateful, how grateful
When we each part at the end of the path of love
Drop anchor there
Visit the shrine to give thanks
The two of us together.
How happy an event, how happy!
(Wartime use)

At first glance this song appears to be a prostitute's love song, but in fact it contains the strong reality of the people's consciousness of that day. It is probably one of the finer products among army songs during the Russo-Japanese War. The allegorical and metaphorical qualities of this song must have been effective in wartime. With the text of lyrics changed to say "I parted from my beloved man (woman) for the sake of my parents (country)/ I was sold (sent) to another province/ Whether north, south, east, or west, I do not know./ I have these painful duties to perform/ But it's for my parents (country) and it can't be helped/ Although I don't begrudge my duty/ I may be hurt having private parts/ Examined by cold-hearted doctors (old soldiers)" and so on, the song becomes a chant of grief by new soldiers who were sent to an unknown continent and were frightened about spending their lives in an army camp.

Then why make such revision in the text? It is because the following lyrics were written on the same pages as the private first class's notes. It clearly served as a lyric to depict a wife lamenting the departure of her husband for the front in the Russo-Japanese War.

> At this time I part from you who go to the west
> *Far, far away for the sake of our country*
> Parting with you for awhile
> Waiting only till we meet again
> *North, south, east, or west* in that unknown ocean
> Completely losing all hope
> Parting, you go far to the west
> Another letter, but none in return
> Even if we share a bed overnight
> Our feelings form the path of our love. . . .

The lines in italics are the same as the other song. Moreover, boundless emotion is concealed in places where "parting, you go far to the west" is repeated, and "North, south, east, or west . . . completely losing all hope" is added. It would not be an exaggeration to say that these two songs were composed under almost identical concepts. Why is it that this song also becomes the sorrowful chanting of new recruits?

The sadism that prevailed among the "old soldiers" of the Imperial Japanese Army was, on a miniature scale, an exact model of Japan's darkly hierarchical class structure and a sign of its perversion. It is difficult to convey the inner workings of this perverted psychology, but metaphorically speaking, it was similar to the sinister expressions of the madam of a brothel who had herself begun as an ordinary prostitute and now looked down on the new girls. New conscripts, getting such looks from the old soldiers, cowered before them and trembled with fear like a small bird toyed with by a cat. These feelings were similar to the hatred that prostitutes felt toward their medical

examiners and madams. Therefore, it is not difficult to surmise the empathy with which new recruits hummed this song.
It was a source of consolation and support for a life of submission until the day that they themselves became old soldiers.

On the other hand, the old soldiers, too, probably experienced the masochistic sensation and sensuous zeal contained
in the song. The passage, "I can't wait for my contract to run
out/ So we can live together" must have had meaning in the
context of their anticipation of discharge from military service.

Popular psychology was different from that of Japanese intellectuals, and it, too, was expressed in this song. For example, there is not so much as a suggestion of the sentimentality shown by intellectuals toward "women who were sold."
Intellectuals looked down from the high standpoint of "humanity" at "fallen women" and no doubt felt compassion, but
such notions are completely missing here. Composers and
singers were casual and carefree, on the same plane, as these
women. That is the source of the reality we find here once
again.

For instance, we find no essential difference in popular attitudes between the terrible drudgery of the mine worker
crawling along the shaft dragging his bucket of coal or that of
the tenant farmer, work that moralists considered sacred, and
the work of the prostitute, work that was no less essential for
the sake of the "family," although it was conventionally thought
of as shameful. How much more realistic is the song's mention of "duty" for love of "parent" or "beloved." As we see,
the lyrics, "I have these painful duties to perform/ But it's for
my parents and it can't be helped," make no room for a view
of morality that takes the prostitute's work out of its context.
These women were driven to this, but they did not feel the
loss of self-respect and did not consider themselves to be slaves
deprived of human nature. As the lyric puts it, "I receive
customers for my family's sake/ I refuse them for my lover's
sake"—a tough-spirited retort. They, too, had a choice, however limited, and could refuse customers. Moreover, their

customers were more often than not familiar friends in similar circumstances. So even these women, at the very bottom of the social abyss, managed to retain some ability to construct and secure an environment of their imagination.

This section of the song thus takes a complete turn; it is cheerful. Intellectuals may think that life comes to an end if a person falls into this sort of "abyss" and that people in this situation have no hope or dreams. On the contrary, these women managed to hold a vivid image of pleasure and of happiness. Its expression may be sentimental, but the strong sensual desire that lies behind it is difficult to cover up. Their flight of imagination expands endlessly: "I can't wait for my contract to run out/ So we can live together/ Holding hands together . . . We'll lie in bed and talk . . . Take the helm, and enjoy in zest/ The joy of rowing/ The pleasure of starting/ Nothing compares with this delight. . . ." This enraptures both the soldier and the prostitute. There is even an impudence in their conviction that if only the heart is true, one can find happiness, whatever the circumstances to be faced. It tells of a positive mental attitude, that even the humiliation of to-day's "duty" can be endured because there is joy and hope in the world of fantasy. Of course, we have to remind ourselves that after that view of life was shattered, and only sapped spirits remained, all that would be left was a selfish desire for life.

Nevertheless, such a mental outlook probably appears amoral, one that would astonish our upper class people and intellectuals. But the common people's vitality and recalcitrance, though they were not conceptualized or articulated, are to be found here; one also discovers here a special sentimentality as well as a tenacity of will and raw desire. Remember the characters Oriki in Higuchi Ichiyō's *Nigorie* (Muddy Stream, 1895); Kanji in Nagatsuka Takashi's *Tsuchi* (The Soil, 1910); Oshima in Tokuda Shūsei's *Arakure* (Tough, 1915), and the heroine in Imamura Shōhei's *Nippon Konchūki* (Japanese Insects, 1963 film). The intellectuals' insisting on the pre-modern nature of the common people in total neglect of this mental structure is futile.

On the other hand, this kind of soldier's song also functioned to create support for the idea of the emperor system. For example, it ends on a note of relief for women in an "abysmal" situation or provides consolation for discontented soldiers. At the beginning the three elements—"painful duty," "emperor's rules," and "passion" of the people—contradict each other. So far as this goes, the song is a song of sorrow, but in later parts these contradictions are harmonized in the world of imagination to conclude "How happy an event!" At that point the precious bud of criticism is nipped. Even though we change the phrases "for my parent's sake" and "for the sake of country" to "for the sake of country" and "for the sake of emperor," and if we replace "the duty" in bed with the "military service," the "doctors" with "higher officials or veterans," and "my contract runs out" with "discharge from military service," this song performs the ideological function of making soldiers affirm the existing system and comforts them through the analogies of "family" and "country," "parent" and "emperor." On the popular level, the emperor system's "central ideology" was accepted in this vivid, concrete form, and through amplification, it was sentimentalized, solidified, and constantly recreated.

In the village of Funaoka, in Miyagi Prefecture, at the foot of Mt. Zaō, 222 people verged on starvation after the disastrous flood of 1910. In February of the following year, the village officials conducted an inspection of forty-five households that were considered "destitute and in need of emergency relief," and their report, "Survey of Poverty-Stricken People," was submitted to the office of Shibata district. Upon examining this report, we find that almost all of the forty-five families lost all their land and became protoproletarian day workers. According to the report, almost all of them had "nothing but the clothes they wore," some were "groaning on sickbeds," the breadwinners were "unable to keep the pot boiling because of decreasing wages," and some who were out of work were "destined for starvation if nothing was done." The account of these cases disclosed that almost all of them were families that had invalids, elderly members, and children, or were without a male breadwinner; that is, the bread-winners had gone off to work in other places and had not been heard from again. This shows the reality of life and not the theory: loss of land and employment by farmers, people sick with incurable diseases, the elderly and children in agony, and most of all the disintegration of the "family"—the institution that was supposed to be ministering to all these needs. These people needed social services, but there were none.

This plight was no longer one that could be overcome through conventional morality. It was the inevitable result of a situation in which insult was added to injury in the late Meiji years: higher taxes, burdens of war (in the Russo-Japanese War almost all the soldiers from Funaoka who were sent to the front were conscripted from the poor; of 87 draftees, 30 were listed as dead, wounded, or disabled), chronic crop failure and famine, exploitation by landowners and loan sharks, and the spread of trachoma, tuberculosis, rheumatism, asthma, and stomach disorders.

For this reason, not only "the destitute" but even farmers with small landholdings suffered. The report goes on: "After the flood damage, this family was deserted by its head and consequently was driven to desperation. Their belongings, even the little furniture they owned, were all taken by creditors. The family now has no bedding, no sliding doors, and no *shōji*. Its plight is simply unbearable to contemplate." Under such conditions, an exodus of farmers from Funaoka followed; in 1910, the year of the report, 41 girls left the village for silk factories while many others fell into the hands of brothel owners. Over 100 families fled to the wind and snow of Hokkaidō. In 1903, emigrants to Hokkaidō from Miyagi Prefecture numbered 1,000, but in 1907, the number increased to 16,000 people.

Saitō Hiroshi comes to these conclusions:

Escape and desertion from such a situation was not limited to unhappy youths. The household head or his heir might leave for work elsewhere or the entire family might

232

move. Families were for Tōhoku farming people divided and scattered, and the "warmth" of family life was destroyed. The family system, which should have been a support for modern Japan, ironically had to be destroyed instead in order to sustain life. Without the breakup of families the lower level of modern Japanese society could not have sustained itself. A supportive and orderly family system did exist among large wealthy landowners in the countryside and among the upper classes in cities, but it was built upon the rubble of the broken homes of these poor emigrants and migrant laborers who constituted the vast majority of middle and lower class Tōhoku farmers.[8]

This is the tragic historical background to the development of Japan's proletariat. Some moved to big cities while others went to factories and mines hoping for a solution to the "tragedy." Studies have been conducted on the workers' conditions, but almost no research has been devoted to their thought or consciousness, and this is a serious shortcoming.

In Funaoka village the landowner class came forward belatedly, in 1913, and organized a cooperative, the Funaoka hōtokusha (The Association for the Repayment of Kindness), "with the purpose of carrying out the aims of the 'Imperial Rescript on Education' and the 'Imperial Rescript of 1908,'[9] to conduct rural reform and promote public morality." This association attempted to revive villages on the verge of disintegration in cooperation with other organizations such as the Aikoku fujin-kai (The Women's Patriotic Association), Mura heiji gikai (The Village Society on Military Affairs), Seinendan (Young Men's Association), and the Jinushi-kai (The Landlord Club), which had been organized around the time of the Russo-

---

[8] Saitō Hiroshi, "Zetsubō no Meiji nōson," *Kyōyō shogaku kenkyū*, no. 3 (Dokkyō Daigaku, 1968).

[9] The 1908 Rescript (*Boshin shōsho*) was issued to combat the breakdown of discipline that was seen as accompanying the economic growth that followed the Russo-Japanese War and was, the government feared, producing a rise in socialist thought. It was part of an effort to restore and reify traditional rural values, and it charged the populace to pursue frugality and hard work.

Japanese War. Thus by then the government and political parties supported by landowners and bourgeoisie, greatly shocked by the unexpected seriousness of this agricultural crisis, finally took a series of measures in response to the crisis. Only then, it seems, did intellectuals become aware of the importance of all this.

The Age of the Lost Ideal

Inaka kyōshi (The Country Teacher) is a novel by Tayama Katai published in 1909.[10] It tells of an "elementary school teacher, an ordinary young man who could be found anywhere," who was born on the Tokyo plain and died of illness at the age of twenty-four with his ambitions and dreams unknown to other people. Tayama wrote of reading the autobiography of a man named Kobayashi Shūzō, the young man who became the prototype for his principal figure. What came into his mind was the thought that this young man died "on the day that Liaoyang fell—a day that marked the greatest glory of Japan's expansion, a day the nation was wild with joy—lonely and unable to work, unable even to go to the front as a soldier. . . ." He was drawn by the death of this unknown young man, and to recreate the setting of his life he walked around the villages along the Tone River from Hanyū to Gyōda in Saitama Prefecture many times. For that reason his book provides an excellent source for the stagnant atmosphere of the farming villages of that area around the end of the Meiji period.

One night the fire alarm in front of the school rang loudly. He went to the other side of the bamboo grove and saw the sky was a hazy red. (Author's note: One farmhouse was burned down. What would be the fate of this family?) In the countryside where money is so precious, it takes a lifetime of hard work just to build a house. (But what of my friends who did not concern themselves

[10] The novel was issued by the University of Hawaii Press, translated by Kenneth Henshall, in 1984.

at all with poor farmers and could only think about "making it" in Tokyo?) He thought about these friends in Kumagaya and Gyōda who were engrossed in study and intent upon achieving future distinction, and compared them with those who spent a hard life in the countryside. As he walked along he thought about his friend—powerful, a wonderful life style! That would be splendid. But many people lived ordinary lives. There was no need to strive for your own distinction to the point of sacrificing the happiness of your family and ailing mother. You should be satisfied with living an ordinary life. (Being so convinced, he looked around once again, and the meaning of the village, which he could not see before, was now clear to him.)

He had once gone to see the ditch where an old man had buried himself in the dirt on a cold winter day and frozen to death. There he saw reeds and miscathus with new buds, and a frog croaked and jumped into the water. There was a desolate shrine in the woods. From a corner of the woods Mt. Fuji was visible, and sometimes he saw rice paddies that seemed covered with beautifully blooming lotus plants. Then, after he had lived in the village for a while, various stories about the village came to ear without his asking anyone. There was the story about a woman who drowned herself in a reservoir because of worry about money; the story of a nurse who was tricked by a traveler and taken into the woods and raped; about three robbers who went into a rich farm house with drawn swords, tied up the family head and his wife, and took their money; about a silk-cocoon agent and a waitress who committed love suicide, and on and on. The more he heard, the more he discovered the sad, heart-breaking life of the people in this village that he had thought was so peaceful. People were divided into landlords and tenants, and there was a wide gulf between rich and poor. He had thought the people in the countryside had a clean, ideal life, and that they rested in the peaceful bosom of nature, but gradually he found out that this place, too, was an arena of struggle and a world of greed. Furthermore, he found out that the countryside, contrary to his expectation, was a place of obscenity and filth.

It is probably more accurate to say that Katai, the author himself, discovered this, than to say that the country teacher did. This teacher was unable to find "pride" and "meaning in life" by living in the village. But he was also unable to abandon his good parents. One day he took his students to the bank of the Tone River and on that night he wrote the following poem in his diary:

> The sun sets far beyond the pine grove—
> Amidst the gentle flow of the Tone,
> I view this desolate village,
> Here I'll spend a year of temporary hermitage,
> Abandoning vain love and floating world,
> I desire nothing, I am all alone.
> Sadly, I sing my lonely song
> So painful is it, that I cannot bear to listen.

After the Russo-Japanese War, a kind of grief expressed in words like "tears," "loneliness," "wandering," and "uncertainty" became general in Japanese popular songs. How similar this poem is to those songs! In the eyes of this young man, the pastoral scene reflected nothing but loneliness. For him, love and success were flowing away like the river's stream, and his dwelling was a temporary lodging. Here we find his desperate desire to wander made explicit. Why is he so miserable and unhappy? Why can he not live a vigorous life, full of hope? Neither this schoolteacher nor Katai knew the real reason; that is why this novel ends in "grief." No doubt that accurate portrayal of feeling is the reason the book produced a sensation among teachers and rural youth when it was published. In tracing Katai's work another thought comes to mind. Compared with farming villages in the 1880s, how gloomy this village seems! Twenty years earlier that village, like other villages in the Kantō region, had been in ferment over the

People's Rights movement, but now it was completely stagnant. The magnitude of this change is shocking.

Readers will recall the earlier chapters. The villages described there were all in the Tama district (present-day Musashi of Tokyo), but similar things were going on throughout the Kantō region—in fact, everywhere in Japan. Several hundred political learning associations, all of which opposed arbitrary government, were established then, and villagers discussed all sorts of issues from self-government to the drafting of a national constitution.

Horiguchi Noboru of the Kokuyūkai (Association for National Fraternity) attended a lecture meeting at Fuda in Northern Tama district (present-day Chōfu) in March 1881. According to him, there were about two hundred in attendance. After the lecture, a discussion session began; when one speaker stated that "the people should participate in drafting our country's constitution," Others argued in the negative, and "the argument went on interminably."

A year later, Horiguchi went on a second lecture tour to the Tokyo-Kanagawa area. Of this trip, too, he wrote that "political enthusiasts in the two counties competed in their eagerness to go up to the rostrum to present their ideas." Those attending stayed on even after a call for adjournment; "they were still arguing at midnight."[11]

The outpouring of opinion was like "water gushing out." This was an expression used by people like Suehiro Shigeyasu, Horiguchi Noboru, Kusama Tokifuku, Hizuka Ryō, and Nomura Motonosuke, who went on hundreds of lecture tours to villages all over the eastern part of Japan and wrote about them in their newspaper stories. These city journalists visited rural areas in response to requests from villages, and not on their own initiative, and they were involved in political controversies wherever they visited. The 1882 travel account of Tochigi by Kusama Tokifuku of the *Tokyo-Yokohama Mainichi* and another about Iwaki (in Fukushima) by Aoki Tadasu that same year spoke of political trends there "that cannot be

---

[11] Horiguchi Noboru, "Busō kikō," *Chōya shimbun*, March 24, 1881 and May 7, 1882.

controlled by human power." They wrote almost the same thing:

> In our contemporary society, the spirit of political con-
> solidation in local areas is a force that is like torrents of
> water running downhill, and it is almost impossible to
> control by human power. Moreover, the areas where this
> consolidation has succeeded most, where it reaches even
> small and remote mountain communities, are the two
> counties of Shimo-Aso and Tsuga of Tochigi Prefecture.[12]

Political thought develops day by day and month by month. Is this not like water flowing downhill? Lately, the people in various localities, realizing the need for improvement of knowledge and the cultivation of politi-cal thought, hold political lecture-discussion meetings and at other times lecture-study meetings on government and law. At times, they invite *shishi* from Tokyo to listen to their political views. By so doing, it seems, they are trying to initiate ambitious projects. In response to the invita-tions from those people, I went to a number of these lecture meetings held in several places in nearby prefec-tures, and now I have covered almost the entire Kantō region. I have long hoped for the opportunity to make a tour to more distant regions and to find similarly minded persons there, too. In early March 1882, the brothers Yoshinari Kenshichirō and Eishichirō of Uedanʾura, Hi-gashishirakawa-gun, Fukushimaken, wrote a letter to our *Ōmeisha* organization and asked us to attend a political lecture-discussion meeting to be held there on the 16th day of March.[13]

How stagnant the Kantō farming villages Nagatsuka Taka-shi described in *Tsuchi* were by comparison! How dark and dismal the villages Tayama Katai describes along the Tone

---

[12] Kusama Tokifusa, "Tochigi kikō," *Tokyo-Yokohama Mainichi shimbun,* February 4, 1882.

[13] Aoki Tadasu, "Iwaki kikō," *Tokyo-Yokohama Mainichi shimbun,* April 11, 1882. Ei Hideo, "Jiyū minkenka no enzetsu kikō," *Gakkai shi,* no. 64 (Tokyo Keizai Daigaku, 1969), discusses and analyzes travel accounts by lec-turers.

River are! Mayama Seika, in *Minami Koizumi-mura*, and Shimazaki Tōson, in *Hakai*, also portrayed "the hopeless farming villages of Meiji," and they corresponded in content to Natsume Sōseki's *Kōfu* (The Mine Worker) and Kunikida Doppo's *Kyūshi* (Death from Suffering). Meiji writers published works that responded—though unintentionally—to the stagnation and changed consciousness of the populace at the bottom of society. This probably was because the lowest classes were on the verge of collapse, and portents of an impending upheaval began to surface here and there. "The vague anxiety" of intellectuals who stood on this rumbling earth crust was most keenly delineated by Natsume Sōseki, but the poet Ishikawa Takuboku also had a real understanding of the nature of young intellectuals of this period. This can be seen in the following excerpt:

> Look! Where do we go from here? . . . The air that surrounds our young people has stopped circulating. The power of authority has now permeated the country. Contemporary social organization is complete, to the corners of the land.

"The air that surrounds young people" was moving rapidly, almost violently in the 1880s, but now it had stopped. Why? Because, says Takuboku, the power of authority extends to every nook and cranny of society. For this reason, young intellectuals discreetly avoided the problem of powerful authority. "They did not know what to do with their strength, which had been pent up for a long time in a state of lost ideals, lost direction, and lost escape routes." More and more they tended "toward internal conflicts and self-destruction," he asserted. "We young intellectuals should concentrate all our energy on the consideration of tomorrow; a systematic consideration of our own age."[14]

This perceptive view surpassed the general level of understanding that most writers had of social institutions. Takuboku was able to understand the problem of authority, but even he was unable to realize the power the thought-control

[14] Ishikawa Takuboku, *Jidai heisoku no genjō* (1910).

network had over the consciousness of the common people and the constraints it placed on the development of their thinking. Takuboku was poor all his life. His experience ranged from jobs as a country teacher in his native Shibutami village in Iwate Prefecture, an itinerant newspaper in Hokkaido, and destitution after he came to Tokyo; through almost his entire life he was in close contact with people in the lower class. Though he could criticize young intellectuals for their lost ideals, even he, it seems, was unable to grasp the desperate consciousness of people in the class like Endō Hisaharu. Why was this? The question is difficult to answer. For one thing, Takuboku left behind him when he was still young the popular consciousness that was based on conventional morality. His boyhood romanticism, in *Kumo wa tensai de aru* (The Cloud is a Genius), was opposed to conventional morality. His affiliation with groups of Epicurean poets (the Myōjō and Taitō groups) also probably stemmed from this revolt against conventional morality. In short, both his literary composition and philosophical development came while he was surrounded by intellectuals whose minds were oriented toward the modern West. On this point, Takuboku seems similar to his forerunner, Kitamura Tōkoku; like him he also died early. But in reality they were quite different.

Tōkoku's philosophical development took place while he was participating directly in the People's Rights movement as an activist. He personally experienced not only incidents and uprisings connected with Jiyūtō and Konmintō but also the failure of these and the popular timidity that resulted. After that, Tōkoku, like Takuboku, spent his life in honorable poverty, maintaining close contact with the populace at the bottom of society. He joined a group of romantics, but it was quite unlike Takuboku's Taitō romanticism of the late Meiji era. Tōkoku's romanticism stood for an "inner life" that was based on criticism of the People's Rights movement: he argued that modern man should resist all forms of oppression imposed from without, including communal restraints. Although Tōkoku did not have a weapon that would attract the populace with a real feeling for their lives similar to Takuboku's *tanka* verse, he was the first to warn of the deceit in Meiji civilization, to contrast its "tears of blood in the background" with the "shouts of joy on the surface," and to point out the human degeneration, illness, and poverty that were being created behind the scenes. At one time, he was shocked to see a poor woman kill her own child and go mad; at another he saw "diseases of the modern age" in Dostoevski's *Crime and Punishment*, to which he had a deep inner reaction. This was probably because he brought his thoughts down to the level of "the people of the lowest class." Tōkoku's literary activities began publicly with an article in the magazine called *Jogaku zasshi*. It begins with the following accusation:

On the surface, Meiji civilization manifests truly immeasurable progress, but do the majority of the people enjoy it? . . .

Go and carefully examine the actual condition of each house. On a cold day, when it is snowing, how many households contain families with rosy cheeks sitting by a warm fire? It is impossible to count the number of young girls without color in their cheeks and young boys without books who wander about the roadside. Even when a mother is ill and in bed, her son cannot remain at home and care for her; he must go out and work, but even so he is unable to earn enough money to buy her medicine. Together they wait for death, or they kill themselves, or they court death. Although society seems outwardly splendid and gradually approaches grandeur, on the other hand we see conditions of gradual deterioration, weakness due to illness, and destitution. Is this mere coincidence? In life not everything turns out according to one's wishes. Nothing, however, is more disastrous to a country than having its poor despised more and more while the rich become more and more arrogant and extravagant.[15]

[15] Kitamura Tōkoku, *Jizen-jigyō no shimpō o nozomu* (1891). See also chap. II, note 14.

By the 1890s, when Tōkoku wrote this, the vitality in farming villages seen in the 1880s was gone. The population of Tokyo, which was no more than 1,300,000 at the end of the 1880s, had started to increase rapidly; it became a mammoth city by absorbing millions of people from the farming villages. This demographic trend was accelerated by the government's policy of heavy taxation and domination by parasitic absentee landowners. Massive numbers of poor people poured out of farming villages to provide a cheap labor force that kept the machinery of Japanese capitalism turning. The tempo of this rotation was further speeded by successive wars, and both in cities and in the countryside the gap between extreme prosperity and extreme poverty increased relentlessly. Kitamura Tōkoku's criticism was a fundamental protest against such modernization, delivered from the standpoint of "the people" and in the name of a man who "honored the dignity of his life."

Japan's agricultural crisis worsened in the 1900s due to its imperialistic wars. At this stage, the problem was no longer just that farming villages were losing vitality. As mentioned earlier, conditions there became desperate; certainly they seemed so to the villagers.

Such desperate conditions were manifested in all aspects of people's lives, not only crop failures, starvation, and bankruptcy, but also in filth, hunger, apathy, resignation, ignorance, trachoma, rheumatism, asthma, tuberculosis, insanity, alcoholism, prostitution, water blisters, abortion, starvation, flight, and suicide. Such "uncultural" conditions, according to the old political philosophy of Confucianism, stemmed from the sovereign's dereliction of duty, from his refusal to follow the "Way of the True King"; in short, they resulted from the crime of the emperor system. What is terrifying about the emperor system, however, is not just such tragic external phenomena but rather the "logic of voluntary internal restraints" with which the people bound themselves. If this is so, the horrors of the emperor system make any mere dereliction of the Way pale by comparison. If we imagine this emperor institution to be looking at us with a faint smile, yet in a cunning way, from behind the stolid and pressed-down faces of Tōhoku farmers, its horror can make people's hearts freeze in broad daylight.

Takeuchi Yoshimi once stated that he saw the emperor institution itself in Takamura Kōtarō's "The Country of Netsuke" (Netsuke no kuni).

> Cheekbones protruding, lips thick, eyes triangular, with
>   a face like a netsuke carved by the master Sangorō
> blank, as if stripped of his soul
> not knowing himself, fidgety
> life-cheap
> vainglorious
> small and frigid, incredibly smug
> monkey-face, fox-like, flying-squirrel-like mudskipper-
>   like,
> minnow like, gargoyle-like, chip-from-a-cup-like;
> Japanese[16]

"The extremely unpleasant tone of this poem, enough to make one vomit," as Takeuchi says, "grasps by intuition the nature of the emperor system."[17] When I read the following paragraphs in Mayama Seika's Minami Koizumi-mura I experienced a similar, shivering feeling.

> The skin of both old and young is thick, with the sallow, pale, and dry look of poverty. Generally their teeth and cheeks are big and their faces are flat. Their eyelids are flapping as if they have tapeworms. Their hands and feet are so huge and unsightly—eight out of ten have no arch in their feet. Their chest and shoulders are limp. Their stomachs sag sloppily. . . .
> Their lips are ugly and noses gross. Especially dis-

[16] Reprinted by permission of the University of Hawaii Press, from *Chieko and Other Poems of Takamura Kōtarō*, trans. Hiroaki Sato (Honolulu: University Press of Hawaii, 1980), p. 3. An alternate rendition by Donald Keene can be found in *Modern Japanese Literature: An Anthology* (New York: Grove Press, 1956), p. 206.

[17] Takeuchi Yoshimi, "Kenryoku to geijutsu" (April 1958), cited in the Introduction, note 10 above.

tasteful is the expression of their eyes. They look just like the eyes of an animal afraid of people. When I see a person who has a faintly stupid smile and continually moves his very small brown eyes restlessly in a cunning manner, I cannot help but recall the eyes of the gypsies, the lowly people who are said to live mainly in Turkey.
. . .

I do not want to believe, no matter how much I efface or humble myself, that the blood flowing in those miserable peasants also flows in my body. At one time in the past, I cursed ugly-looking things as a sort of sin. Ugly, ugly, the farmer's life is nothing but ugly.[18]

For shame, Mayama Seika! That same blood flows in your body!

If the emperor institution shrouds the entire Japanese people as a total mental structure, then to foreign eyes no distinctions will be evident; all Japanese will appear the same. Although his clothing and nutrition have improved, even now, on New York street corners or in lobbies somewhere in Calcutta, the average Japanese will still "have a faintly stupid smile" as he "continually moves his very small brown eyes restlessly in a cunning manner"; he still has "the eyes of an animal that is afraid of people." Other people observe him with piercing eyes.

(Translated by Noburu Hiraga)

[18] Mayama Seika, *Minami koizumi-mura*. A recent work that draws on the large body of Japanese literature emphasizing the social costs of Japanese modernization is Mikiso Hane, *Peasants, Rebels, & Outcasts: The Underside of Modern Japan* (New York: Pantheon, 1982).

· VIII ·

THE EMPEROR SYSTEM AS A SPIRITUAL STRUCTURE

INTRODUCTION

In 1889 the Meiji Constitution established a political system in Japan that has come to be known as the modern "emperor system" (*tennōsei*). The term includes not only the constitutional framework but also the entire constellation of political, economic, and educational policies by which the government undertook to rule the people in the period that lasted until the end of the Pacific War. In the most general sense, the emperor system is regarded as the wellspring of Japanese nationalism, the source of the wealth and power that transformed Japan into an independent modern state in the face of Western pressure. In Japan even the development of capitalism depended on its successful accommodation to the dictates of *tennōsei*, and those Marxist scholars who deny the emperor system this role have let their hostility toward it cloud their historical vision.

There is no doubt the emperor system achieved its power by means of an illusion. My subject here is how this illusion insinuated itself into the hearts of the Japanese people. Thus it is something more than what is called "*tennōsei* ideology," since that describes the phenomenon from an exterior point of view. I am here concerned with the illusion of national community that operated from *within* the popular mind. It is my contention that the emperor system succeeded in controlling the people because it became part of the way in which they saw their world, and for this reason I have labeled it a "spiritual structure." Although I know this is not an easy domain to explore, I think someone is fated to try it, if only once.

The emperor system as a way of thinking was like an enormous black box into which the whole nation, intellectuals as

245

well as commoners, unknowingly walked. Once within its confines, the corners of the box obscured in the darkness, the people were unable to see what it was that hemmed them in. To my mind their fate was more terrible than that of the dissenters who were hanged for treason in 1911; they at least knew the reason why. Like the farmer who starved to death in a Tōhoku village in the same period, most Japanese lived and died without comprehending their fate. Their internal fetters prevented them from grasping the illusion that bound them, simply because they themselves had become a part of it. The emperor system roused them not only to the murder of Chinese and Koreans in the name of war but also to the acceptance of a different kind of destruction of their own countrymen—the nihilism responsible for the fate of Sunaga Renzō and Inoue Denzō during the popular rights struggles of the eighties.[1]

The emperor system gradually became part of the landscape, disappearing into the Japanese environment until people thought it was a product of their own village community rather than a system of control imposed from above. Takeuchi Yoshimi has said that the emperor system was not "something confronting us directly, but all wrapped up like a bundle." Shrouded from sight, it nevertheless left an indelible mark on the Japanese, turning them into a nation of *netsuke*, as repellent and unredeemable as the figures in Takamura's poem.[2] In the end the nation was badly scarred by the experience, and the habits of mind that made the idea of the emperor system so persuasive remain difficult to exorcise, even today.

Yet to denounce the emperor system as evil will not help to vanquish or explain it. It must be confronted on its own terms, and however hazardous the enterprise, transcended from within its own tradition. Scholars like Ichii Saburō have recently begun the task of tracing the development of the

[1] See chap. V, and Irokawa Daikichi, *Shimpen Meiji seishin shi* (Tokyo: Chūō kōronsha, 1973), pp. 343-52.
[2] See chap. VII, p. 243.

emperor system and exposing its inner logic.[3] My intentions are similar, and to understand *tennōsei* as an illusion within the popular mind, one has to begin with the very heart of that illusion—the concept of *kokutai*.

THE LEGACY OF *Kokutai*

In 1936 Itō Tasaburō introduced his first historical study of *kokutai* with the question, "What is *kokutai*?" and the answer, "Since every Japanese knows its meaning perfectly well, there is no need to dwell on it here."[4] Now, only a few decades since its meaning was self-evident, the same word brings to the minds of most Japanese the national athletic competitions held each year and called *kokutai* (short for *Kokumin taiiku taikai*). Surely few ideas have fallen as far and as fast as this one. In the years up to 1945, "the eternal and immutable national polity (*kokutai*)," unlike the easily changeable political system (*seitai*), was nothing less than "the concept of national morality grounded in the rational consciousness and religious psychology of the people."[5] It was the "spiritual force behind the activities of the state" and "the principle of national unity."

Distinguished from the political system, *kokutai* was a spiritual force, a moral concept that constituted the very essence of the state. More concretely, it was derived from "the harmonious unity of the ruler and the people, the whole nation as one family under the rule of the emperor, his line unbroken for ages eternal."[6] Itō Tasaburō does not suggest that the definition itself was immutable, but that as a result of the policies of ideological indoctrination since the Restoration, the awareness of *kokutai* had entered "an era unprecedented in its history." No longer monopolized by "the ruling few," *kokutai* had become "the precious possession of each and every

---

[3] See Ichii Saburō, *"Meiji ishin" no tetsugaku* (Tokyo: Kōdansha, 1967).

[4] Itō Tasaburō, *Kokutai kannen no shiteki kenkyū* (Tokyo: Dōbunkan, 1936).

[5] Ibid., p. 5.

[6] Ibid., p. 6.

Japanese."[7] This does not mean, however, that the Meiji oligarchs created it single-handedly, or that the Meiji period was the first time *kokutai* had been called upon to act as a kind of spiritual axis for the Japanese nation. It had been important in the imperial system of ancient Japan, in late Tokugawa loyalism, and even in the early policies of the new Meiji government. (Indeed the stated aims of a new government academy established just after the Restoration had been "to elucidate *kokutai* and make clear the obligations of the subjects.")[8]

It would doubtless be a good deal simpler if *kokutai* could be regarded solely as a Meiji product or as part of the superstructure of Japanese capitalism and the parasitic landlord system. In that case the Marxist explanation offered by the *kōza-ha* historians in the 1930s would suffice to combat its ill effects. One could explain (and denounce) the emperor system and *kokutai* as the "magic cloak" of class oppression donned by the elite—landlords, the bourgeoisie, and the bureaucrats—and be done with it. But this criticism of the emperor system faltered at the very wall that must be scaled: it failed to penetrate the popular mind and ended up isolated from the people. The critics were reduced to cowering submission and underwent "mass conversions" (*tenkō*) to the orthodoxy they had once reviled.

In fact, the Marxists of the early Shōwa period had seriously underestimated the power of their opponent's historicity. *Kokutai* had had a more or less continuous tradition for over a thousand years. Even without Itō Tasaburō's tutelage, we know that "the center of *kokutai*" lay in the eighth-century *Kojiki* and *Nihon shoki* and that scores of historical works later took up the same theme. Adapting it to their own times

[7] Ibid., p. 252.

[8] *Kokutai o benshi, meibun o tadasubeki koto.* This was the motto of the *Kōgakusho* (for Japanese studies) and the *Kangakusho* (for Chinese learning) that were established simultaneously at the court in Kyoto in October 1868. Discord between nativist and Confucian scholars as well as the move of the capital to Tokyo brought the new academies to an early end, and they closed in August 1870.

and to their own theories of legitimacy, some of these interpretations influenced the course of historical change.[9] The
Edo period saw a resurgence of *kokutai* studies, in both neo-
Confucian and nativist versions. The neo-Confucian idea of
kokutai began with the unity of Shintō and Confucianism advocated by Yamazaki Ansai and Yamaga Sokō in the seventeenth century and culminated in the works of the late Mito
school in the bakumatsu years. Among the nativists, Motoori
Norinaga and Hirata Atsutane developed theories of *kokutai*
that later combined with Mito neo-Confucianism to inspire
many of the *shishi*, the late Tokugawa loyalists.

By the time a modern national consciousness emerged in
the Meiji era, the legacy of *kokutai* was impressive indeed.
It was embodied in a vast accumulation of works of history,
literature, and art, in laws and in legends—from the *Manyōshū* in the eighth century to *sonnō-jōi* thought in the nineteenth. Mingling with beliefs from Shintō, Confucianism, and
folk religion, the idea of *kokutai* had long since entered the
popular mind, defining the very categories of thought and
culture. It had become almost indistinguishable from the Japanese sensitivity toward nature, part of the special *fūdo*, or
climate, of Japan, and inseparable from the indigenous beliefs
of the traditional village community. Indeed *kokutai* had been
virtually transferred into a Japanese folkway.

Because Japan was an island country isolated from the rest
of Asia, the legacy of *kokutai* was a long and uncontested one.
Never invaded or dominated by a foreign power, it was easy
for the Japanese people to subscribe to the illusion of "an
imperial line unbroken for ages eternal." Historical accident
fostered an insular mentality that, lacking a sure center of its
own, sought to gain stature by identifying with the powerful—in this case, an imperial family that could claim the lineage of greatest antiquity in the land. It is true that for most

[9] As examples, the *Jinnō shōtōki* of Kitabatake Chikafusa (1339), translated
by H. Paul Varley as *A Chronicle of Gods and Heroes* (New York: Columbia
University Press, 1980); *Chūchō jijitsu* by Yamaga Sokō (1669); the *Dai Nihonshi* begun by the Mito domain in 1657 (completed in 1906); *Kōchō shir-
yaku* by Aoyama Nobuyuki (1827); and Rai San'yō's *Nihon gaishi* (1827).

of its long history, the idea of *kokutai* remained submerged at the level of custom, a part of the nation's subconscious. But the moment Japan was confronted by a crisis or a change in political structure, *kokutai* would suddenly reemerge, its more than a thousand years of historicity ready in the service of the empire. Thus the Meiji concept of *kokutai* began with this entrenched if inchoate tradition and then added to it the new and modern values of post-Restoration Japan.

The modernization of *kokutai* began with the Charter Oath of 1868, which proclaimed that "all base customs of former times shall be abolished and everything based on justice and equity," and also that "knowledge shall be sought throughout the world." This enlightened spirit found expression for its modern enthusiasms in phrases like "the equality of the four classes" (*shimin byōdō*) and "one ruler, many subjects" (*ikkun banmin*).[10] These ideas in turn were then introduced into the *kokutai*. The Meiji government began to use *kokutai* to justify everything from the centralization of political and military power to the cultivation of respect for "public opinion" and the progress toward "constitutional government." The emperor system had begun to expand, embracing within its bailiwick the massive reforms of the early seventies—the abolition of the *han*, the education act, the conscription law, tax reform—and expelling from its domain the People's Rights movement and the opposition that it represented. Combining absolutism and a modern functionalism, the emperor system enlarged its borders in a single-minded pursuit of ideological perfection until it had grown large enough to encompass Fukuzawa's rationalism, the Social Darwinism of Katō Hiroyuki and Inoue Tetsujirō, and the nationalistic pan-Asianism of Tōyama Mitsuru, Tarui Tōkichi, and Uchida Ryōhei. As the emperor system expanded, *kokutai* became a strange composite—fragile, self-contradictory, but at the same time the most formidable idea in modern Japanese thought.

[10] Both phrases emphasized the abolition of Tokugawa class status and the national unity of all the people as equal subjects under the emperor. See Ichii Saburō, *"Meiji ishin" no tetsugaku* (Tokyo: Kōdansha, 1967), pp. 205-209.

The Emperor and the People

Possessed of an extraordinary flexibility, the emperor system was able to accommodate conflicting points of view and even to absorb the momentum of its own opposition. The Meiji Constitution sustained interpretations as divergent as Minobe's theory of the emperor as a political organ of the state and Uesugi's view of the emperor as transcendent and divine.[11] The 1890 Rescript on Education managed to combine Motoda Eifu's neo-Confucianism with the modern nationalism of Inoue Kowashi in an eclectic arrangement around the theme of *kokutai*. The emperor system suppressed the People's Rights movement at the same time that it succeeded in co-opting its leaders as the government's own rural base of support. Hostile radical religions like Tenrikyō, Maruyamakyō, and Ōmotokyō were disarmed by incorporating them into sectarian Shintō, which cast them in the mold of traditional, and therefore unthreatening, folk beliefs. Even Protestantism, its allegedly incompatible monotheism notwithstanding, was finally compelled to take its place within the emperor system. The tragic isolation and forced resignation of Uchimura Kanzō for refusing to bow before the imperial portraits and the Rescript on Education in 1891 was the exception; Christianity too, for the most part, entered the ideological cosmos. Only the Communists resisted the embrace of the emperor system and dared to call for its overthrow (*tennōsei datō*). The brutal suppression this earned them as "heretics" clearly revealed to others the lengths to which the regime would go to extinguish its opposition.

Although it possessed this seemingly magical power to transform all things to its own ends, *tennōsei* itself did not suddenly materialize in the space of a single night, as if in some tale from the Arabian Nights. Instead the modern emperor system was the historical product of a long process of repeated trial and error that began in the early Meiji period.

---

[11] See Frank O. Miller, *Minobe Tatsukichi: The Interpreter of Constitutionalism in Japan* (Berkeley: University of California Press, 1965), pp. 27-01, 40 72.

Thus we have first to consider the views of the emperor and *kokutai* that existed in the years before the Constitution, since these formed the background and the provocation for the ideology the government put forth in the later Meiji decades.

In the period before the Restoration few believed that "the emperor, as a direct descendant of the divine ancestor Amaterasu Ōmikami, is a sacred and absolute being." Aoyama Hanzō, the peasant protagonist of *Yoakemae*, Shimazaki Tōson's historical novel about the Restoration, may have regarded the reigning emperor as absolute. But he was a pious adherent of *kokugaku*, and that made his views distinctive.[12] Most of the samurai of the period had no such notion, nor did those nobles who stood close to the throne. Indeed one of the loyalist leaders at the court, Iwakura, had been sufficiently critical of Emperor Kōmei when he was alive to give rise later to the rumor that he might have poisoned his Imperial Majesty. And Ōkubo Toshimichi, who helped to bring about the restoration of imperial rule, argued openly that "an injust imperial command is not an imperial command" and need not be obeyed.[13]

According to one traditional political formulation, "the realm belongs to the realm" (*tenka wa tenka no tenka nari*) and not to the emperor alone. Imperial authority resided not in the emperor's personal possession but in his rule in accordance with the kingly way (*ōdō*), which implied the assent of the people. It was in this tradition that Iwakura asserted in 1865:

> National policy is on no account to be determined solely by the Emperor, for the realm is the realm of our imperial ancestors (*tenka wa sosō no tenka nari*), and His Majesty's decisions should be made on the basis of joint

[12] The novel *Yoakemae* (Before the Dawn), published from 1929 to 1935, recounted the events of the years before and after the Restoration through the experiences of a central character modeled after Tōson's father. The work is often quoted by historians as a moving re-creation of the hopes and disappointments the Restoration brought to the wealthy peasant, or *gōnō*, class in the countryside.

[13] Letter to Saigō Takamori, November 11, 1865. *Ōkubo Toshimichi monjo* (Tokyo: Nihon shiseki kyōkai, 1927-1929), vol. 1, p. 311.

deliberation of the merits of the issue by the ruler and the people.[14]

The old question of whether the realm belonged to the ruler or to the people was not resolved by the early Meiji leaders. Iwakura and others tried to minimize the theoretical contradiction by declaring that although the emperor ruled in principle, in practice the imperial way embodied the divine ancestral will, which meant in the political context of the 1860s that the emperor governed with the aid of public consultation.[15] Thus, from the beginning of the Meiji period the concept of *kokutai* included contradictory theories of imperial legitimacy.

In 1875 Katō Hiroyuki, later an ardent advocate of the family-state, criticized as a "base and vulgar custom the notion of *kokutai* that regarded the land and the people as private possessions of the emperor . . . for the emperor is a man, and the people, too, are men."[16] Katō's attack on the emperor-centered theory of legitimacy was not uncommon among intellectuals at the time. His interpretation of *kokutai* as consisting of feudal custom was shared even by a man as different from Katō as Yaginuma Kamekichi, an elementary school teacher from Fukushima. In 1882 Yaginuma was arrested for making a speech in which he said:

> All men are equal and have the same rights, and there is no difference whatever between the ruler and the ruled, the high and the low. Though an emperor or king wield unlimited power and treat his people like cattle, it is in fact only custom that produces their unquestioning ac-

[14] *Iwakura Tomomi kankei monjo*, ed. Ōtsuka Takematsu (Tokyo: Nihon shiseki kyōkai, 1927), vol. 1, p. 159. For a brief discussion of the *"tenka no tenka"* theory, see David M. Earl, *Emperor and Nation in Japan: Political Thinkers of the Tokugawa Period* (Seattle: University of Washington Press, 1964), pp. 10-15.

[15] See Matsumoto Sannosuke, *Tennōsei kokka to seiji shisō* (Tokyo: Miraisha, 1969), pp. 150-58.

[16] *Kokutai shinron* (1875), *Meiji bunka zenshū*, vol. 2: *Jiyū minken hen* (Tokyo: Nihon hyōron shinsha, 1955), pp. 111-12.

ceptance of the justice of their situation. . . . In Japan as well, this *kokutai* is based on custom.[17]

This statement is interesting, because both Katō and Yaginuma suggest that *kokutai* is based on custom. But if we read the Yaginuma statement backward, it is clear that in those days most people subscribed to the distinction between ruler and subject, high and low, as natural. What, then, were the "customs" held by the people that supported *kokutai?*

Tsurumi Shunsuke has recorded what Susaki Bunzō, a fisherman born in Amakusa in 1861, later recalled as bits of the talk among the old women of his village in the years before the Satsuma Rebellion:

> They say the emperor has taken the shogun's place, but I wonder what the emperor is like. I suppose he's like the people you see in a play, with a gold crown and broad sleeves of gold brocade. . . . I gather now that the emperor rules, the world will be different and every house will be taxed down to its last cotton gin. . . . It will be just like the play about Sakura Sōgorō.[18]

For the people the emperor seemed little more than an exalted personage in a play, a hazy figure who may have levied taxes but was somehow a person of great nobility. Those villagers who lived along the routes of the Meiji emperor's extensive provincial tours were greatly impressed with the honor

[17] Quoted in Ienaga Saburō and Shōji Kichinonsuke, eds., *Jiyū minken shisō* (Tokyo: Aoki shoten, 1957), vol. 2, p. 245.

[18] Tsurumi Shunsuke, *Nihon no hyakunen*, vol. 10: *Goishin no arashi, 1853-1877* (Tokyo: Chikuma shobō, 1964), pp. 272-73. Before the Restoration, Amakusa had been under direct shogunal rule, hence the reference to the emperor replacing the shogun as a levier of taxes. Sakura Sōgo (or Kinouchi Sōgorō) was a peasant in the mid-seventeenth century who led villagers in the Shimōsa area in protest against heavy taxes levied by their lord. Along with his wife and children, he was put to death for it. See chap. I, n. 19. By the end of the Tokugawa period he had become a peasant hero in tale and legend. The play referred to here is probably the well-known *kabuki* play, *Higashiyama Sakura sōshi*, first performed in 1851 and again, with revisions by Mokuami, in 1861.

and came to regard the *Tenshisama* in the same way as they did their local deities.

But this simple vision of the villagers of Amakusa was not necessarily shared by all the people, particularly not by the *gōnō*, or wealthy peasants. The village leaders and political activists of the period, the *gōnō* were educated, often in both Confucianism and *kokugaku*, and articulate enough to express their ideas in forms as difficult as Chinese verse. It was this class that produced so many of the grass-roots heroes (*sōmō no shishi*) active at the time of the Restoration, and it was again the *gōnō* who led the broadly based People's Rights movement in the 1870s and 1880s. Yet even the most outspokenly antigovernment leaders often exhibited an unexpectedly pure version of imperial loyalism and an authentic enthusiasm for *kokutai*.

In 1883 Hosono Kiyoshirō, one of the most active popular rights figures in the Minami Tama area, composed poetry in honor of the emperor's birthday:

> For more than 2,000 years, without bitterness,
> Has the unbroken imperial line reigned
> At the crown of the world.

> Today his subjects are granted this splendid feast,
> In which to celebrate
> The serenity of the throne.

Hosono added, "We are granted this splendid feast in honor of the emperor's birthday. Let us celebrate the eternal continuity of the imperial line." And again, "By the sacred virtue of his ancestors, the emperor protects our country."[19] Men like Hosono were careful to distinguish between *kokutai*, the unbroken imperial line, which he quite genuinely celebrated, and *seitai*, by which was meant the regime of the Meiji oligarchs. Thus, the People's Rights leaders demanded the overthrow of the Meiji government without directing any

---

[19] On Hosono, see Irokawa, *Shimpen Meiji seishin shi* (Tokyo: Chūō kōronsha, 1973), pp. 298ff.

criticism toward the unbroken imperial line, which was of course the essence of *kokutai*.

Examining the nearly thirty draft constitutions prepared by popular rights figures outside the government in the first half of the Meiji period, I was startled to find that private drafts, although more liberal than the official constitution, often began with precisely the same provision as to the nature of *kokutai*: Article I provided for the succession to the throne of the imperial line unbroken for ages eternal. This was true even of the earliest liberal version, the Ōmeisha draft of 1881, which began with the provision that "the imperial throne of Japan shall be inherited by the descendants of the reigning emperor in direct descent from Emperor Jimmu."[20] This article influenced Ueki Emori's draft, and Chiba Takusaburō adopted it verbatim. Fukuzawa Yukichi's group began the Kōjunsha draft with the statement that "the single, eternal imperial line, coeval with heaven and earth, is the source of the founding of the nation, and as such it is not a matter suitable for discussion among the subjects." The first section in the draft prepared by the Soaisha, a radical political organization in Kumamoto, was titled "*kokutai*," which was explained in the following terms:

> Our *kokutai* is different from other nations because the empire, composed of the emperor and the people together, came into being naturally, and not as an institutional expedient by which a government is established to meet a social need. Through *kokutai* the order of high and low is upheld, the obligations of ruler and subject clarified, and the happiness of the people under the eternal rule of the Imperial House preserved forever. Hence, while political forms (*seitai*) may alter in response to changes in the times, *kokutai* will remain the fundamental law, eternal and immutable.[21]

[20] See Ei Hideo, "Ōmeisha kempō sōan ni tsuite no kōshō," *Gakkaishi*, no. 61 (Tokyo Keizai Daigaku, January 1969), pp. 101-23.

[21] For a discussion of the private draft constitutions, see Inada Masatsugu, *Meiji kempō seiritsu shi* (Tokyo: Yūhikaku, 1956), vol. 1, pp. 352-425; for a

Japan's *kokutai* is thus not based on the idea of a social contract but represents a natural bond between the emperor and the people; it is distinct from the political system and remains immutable under imperial rule, however that political system may change. *Kokutai* is presented in much the same terms in many of the other draft constitutions,[22] and although the more liberal versions prepared by the Risshisha in Tosa and by Ueki Emori did not include an express provision for *kokutai*, it is disturbing to note that even there the imperial prerogative was substantially sanctioned.

How are we to interpret this? It is possible that the People's Rights activists felt it unwise to challenge an ancient "custom" that bore the intellectual authority of more than a millennium. They may have deliberately avoided a direct confrontation with *kokutai* and instead adopted the strategy of more gently ingratiating their progressive ideas into the minds of the public. For men as liberal as Ueki Emori and Nakae Chōmin I think this explanation makes sense. Though they spoke of a democratic revolution in the form of a constitutional monarchy, their real goal seemed to lie in the direction of the abolition of the emperor system and the establishment of a republic. Compared with most of the People's Rights activists, they were remarkably indifferent to the emperor. As political realists they undertook first to separate *kokutai* from *seitai*, raising the emperor and the imperial house above the political fray so that the government could be openly attacked and overthrown. The theoretical justification for this was provided by the traditional concepts of the kingly way (*ōdō*) and the removal of an unvirtuous ruler, although these

different view, see Irokawa Daikichi, Ei Hideo, and Arai Katsuhiro, *Minshū kempō no sōzō* (Tokyo: Hyōronsha, 1970), pp. 279-381; for texts of the draft constitutions, see Ienaga Saburō, Matsunaga Shōzō, and Emura Eiichi, *Meiji zenki no kempō kōzō* (Tokyo: Fukumura shuppansha, 1967); for a brief discussion of the well-known drafts, see Joseph Pittau, *Political Thought in Early Meiji Japan* (Cambridge: Harvard University Press, 1967), pp. 90-114.

[22] For example, the drafts of Fukuchi Gen'ichirō, Ono Azusa, the *Chikuzen kyōaikai* in Kyūshū, the *Tōkai gyōshō shimbunsha* in Ibaraki, and the *Kempō kōshūkai* in Hyōgo.

concepts have a long history in both China and Japan (*hō-batsuron*).[23] They argued that since concern for the people's welfare was the ancestral wish and the essence of the kingly way, it was their obligation (*taigi meibun*) as loyal subjects to destroy—in the name of the emperor—the government that oppressed the people. Thus they used traditional concepts of imperial rule as a wedge to drive the flawed notion of *kokutai* apart at the seams.

It is true that this political realism may also serve as a proof of the opposite: that the liberals were powerless in the face of the "imperial line unbroken for ages eternal" and its *kokutai*. Or it may be more accurate to say that history had not yet progressed to the stage where these two could be overturned. Little more than ten years had passed since the end of the Tokugawa regime, and, amorphous or not, perhaps only the "imperial house" and "*kokutai*" possessed the authority capable of unifying the nation. The People's Rights leaders may have acknowledged *kokutai* as the necessary prerequisite for national unity, hoping to use concepts like *ōdō* and *ikkun banmin* to work toward a democratic system within the imperial framework.[24] Indeed nearly all the liberal draft constitutions adopted the model of constitutional monarchy and contained, side by side with the article on *kokutai*, provisions for gradually limiting the prerogatives of the monarch.

At the end of his "Treatise on the Way of the True King" (*Ōdōron*) in 1882 Chiba Takusaburō wrote:

> His Majesty the Meiji emperor is a king, and he loves the kingly way. All his edicts are in accord with it. Among the enlightened and estimable people of the present era, only two or three in a hundred do not love the kingly way. This is truly the rarest of opportunities.[25]

[23] For an analysis of Yamagata Daini's understanding of *ōdō* and *hōbatsu* as the antecedent of the bakumatsu and early Meiji usage, see Ishii Saburō, "*Meiji ishin*" no tetsugaku, pp. 45-46 and 50-53.

[24] For *ikkun banmin* and the thought of Yoshida Shōin, see Ishii, p. 133; for its connection with the People's Rights movement, ibid., pp. 201-202.

[25] *Santama jiyū minken shiryō* (1969). For *Ōdō ron*, see chap. III above and Richard Devine, "The Way of the King," *Monumenta Nipponica* 34 (Spring 1979): 62-72.

By "the kingly way" Chiba meant a constitutional system that might be realized by seizing this "rarest of opportunities," the reign of the Emperor Meiji. Chiba both believed in popular sovereignty and shared the heartfelt reverence for the emperor that Hosono Kiyoshirō had expressed in his poetry.

The concern of the popular rights leaders with *kokutai*, which for us may be somewhat unexpected, was for the Meiji government a challenge it could not ignore. The liberals were using *kokutai* to separate the government from the emperor. To protect itself against such a fissure, the government responded with increased emphasis on the unity between its policies and the imperial will. Thus men like Ōkubo, Iwakura, and Itō, who in practice acted as if the emperor were but an organ of state, were always careful in principle to assert the importance of personal imperial rule. And when the People's Rights movement began to reach the people in the countryside through the activities of the *gōnō*, the government expended enormous ideological effort to bind these same people to the state.[26] The state appropriated the value inherent in the "imperial house" and "*kokutai*" and then tried to draw the people in by means of ideological fictions like *kunmin ikka* (the ruler and the people as one family) and *kazoku kokka* (the family-state). Both these slogans turned out to be double-edged swords, however, since they had to absorb interpretations that were at odds with their main purpose. The notion of the overthrow of an unvirtuous ruler, for example, or the theory of legitimacy that defined the realm, not in terms of the emperor alone but in terms of the emperor and the people, continued to plague the ideology from within. The idea of the family-state, in particular, encountered difficulty in reconciling two things that were as fundamentally different as the family and the nation. In order to explore this contradiction, which is of great importance in understanding the emperor system, we have first to digress and examine Maruyama Masao's influential analysis of the way *kokutai* operated in the ideology of the prewar period.

---

[26] See Irokawa Daikichi, "Tennōsei ideorogii to minshū ishiki," *Rekishigaku kenkyū* (May 1968), pp. 35-41.

A Tradition Without Structure

Maruyama Masao has made a lasting contribution to the study of *tennōsei* ideology, both in his own work and through his influence on scholars like Ishida Takeshi, Fujita Shōzō, Matsumoto Sannosuke, and Kamishima Jirō. Often known as the "Maruyama school of politics," their analyses of the structure of the emperor system and indeed of all Japanese thought from the viewpoint of modernism (*kindaishugi*) remain influential today. In the past few years the modernist methodology has evoked a good deal of criticism, most penetratingly from Yoshimoto Takaaki, Ichii Saburō, Tsurumi Shunsuke, and Yasumaru Yoshio. Although the critique of Maruyama's overall vision is not yet complete, the theoretical prospects suggest that the modernist methodology will eventually give way to a structural analysis of a different kind.

The most succinct presentation of Maruyama's methodology is provided in his *Nihon no shisō* (Japanese Thought), published in 1957. There he describes the intellectual character of the modern emperor system in terms of "unlimited responsibility" on the part of the subjects toward the system, which itself was characterized by "irresponsibility." An extreme intellectual "eclecticism" was subsumed in the "all-enveloping embrace" of *kokutai*, the axis of the nation. Maruyama traces these characteristics through the structure of Japanese society first to their origins in nativist thought (*kokugaku*) and further to the indigenous beliefs underlying it. He then contends that an intellectual tradition—in the true and systematic sense—never evolved in Japan. Maruyama's view is reminiscent of Weber's use of the intellectual order and ethos of Western bourgeois society as a standard to explain the character of Eastern thought. It is trenchant, but Eurocentric—a methodological "escape from Asia." Maruyama writes:

> It seems overly blunt when reduced to a single word, but what never developed in Japan was an intellectual tradition that could act—for better or for worse—as an *axis (zahyōjiku)* against which to coordinate all ideas and

theories of a particular period; to relate all positions, if
only by antithesis, to itself; and thus to place them in
proper historical perspective.[27]

Hence, any analysis of the Japanese mode of thought into its
constituent elements ends up in intellectual fragments—Buddhist, Confucian, shamanistic, and Western bits and pieces,
"all in a jumble, with no clear way of bringing them into
logical relationship with one another."[28] What was called traditional thought provided no true legacy for the future since
it was never "traditionalized" and so succumbed easily beneath the onslaught of Westernization in the Meiji period.
Because Japan lacked an organizing intellectual principle—a
spiritual axis like Christianity where authority was clearly
symbolized by an absolute providence—Maruyama speaks of
a "structureless tradition" (*mukōzō no dentō*), which he argues has been evident in the spiritual lives of the people since
ancient times.

After recalling Kobayashi Hideo's statement that "history
in the end is memory," Maruyama continues:

This proposition makes a good deal of sense, at least if it
pertains to the way ideas "succeed" one another in the
intellectual development of Japan and indeed of the individual Japanese. Since new ideas, even basically alien
ones, are absorbed one after the other without any ade-
quate confrontation with the past, the new triumphs with
astonishing speed. Instead of being sorted out against
the present, the past is shunted aside, or "forgotten,"
only to erupt suddenly at a later time as "memory." . . .
Which ideas that were "absorbed" in the past will be
"remembered" depends on the personality, education,
and generation of the person involved. The *Manyōshū*,
Saigyō, the *Jinnō shōtōki*, Yoshida Shōin, Fichte, *Haga-
kure*, Dōgen, Wen T'ien-hsiang, Pascal—the intellectual

[27] Maruyama Masao, *Nihon no shisō* (originally published 1957; Tokyo:
Iwanami shinsho reprint, 1969), p. 5.
[28] Ibid.

stock is rich enough to assure there will be no shortage of material. The scene changes, and it will be Tolstoy, Takuboku, *Das Kapital*, or Lu Hsün who will be "remembered" once again. Although this identification with the ideas of the past may seem extremely arbitrary to the outsider, for those involved it is a sincere effort to return to the "true character" of Japan or the "essential nature" of the individual, merely by rearranging and bringing to light aspects of the stock of the past that have always been there.[29]

This characterization of the way ideas succeed one another in Japan is a good description of the experience of many Western-oriented intellectuals of the modern period. The Shōwa modernists often proceeded in this fashion, and Meiji figures like Takayama Chōgyū were caricatures of the type.[30]

But was this also true of the people? Did the new also triumph with astonishing speed in popular thinking only to shatter again into fragments of "memory"? Is it not rather that beneath the superficial changes in attitude lay, like a deep and unchanging sediment, the essence of popular values, from whose solid tenacity Maruyama himself had once recoiled? Indeed many of the intellectuals who committed *tenkō* and abandoned their resistance to the government in the thirties have suggested that despair over the stolidity of the people was one of the reasons for their own loss of self-confidence.

Part of the problem here lies in Maruyama's understanding of the way an intellectual tradition ought to be formed. His is a purely European ideal that, when treated as a universal, leads to a negative view of the diverse patterns of traditionalization that existed in China and Japan and, for that matter, in Europe as well. How many peoples in the world possess a

[29] Ibid., p. 8. As an example of the sudden irruption of "memory," Maruyama cites the same passage from Takamura Kōtarō that is quoted in the introduction to this book.

[30] Takayama, as a young literary intellectual in the 1890s, proceeded from literary romanticism through nationalistic Japanism to Nietzschean individualism in the space of only eight years. He died in 1902 at the age of 32.

"structurally organized" intellectual tradition in which the past is consciously objectified and held up against the present? Although Japanese popular thought lacks an axis of the sort that Christianity provided in the West, it exhibits its own tenacious core of folk belief, which seemed to serve as just such a spiritual benchmark in Japan's modern development. A good example of this is provided by Sakurai Tokutarō's study of the *kō*, the associations within the village community that proliferated in the Tokugawa period to more than 300 varieties, each performing a different social function.[31] Sakurai has shown how the popular morality that underlay the *kō* demonstrated surprising tenacity in the face of foreign ideas and often determined the ways in which those ideas would be received. In Japan, then, one must look to this kind of popular morality, or to the enduring consciousness of the family, to reveal the strong patterns of traditional belief that operated among the people.

Here Maruyama would argue that the "structureless tradition" was not confined to the intellectuals but characterized the masses as well, and that the indigenous beliefs to which I have just referred were the very prototype of this shapelessness. He has pointed out that in indigenous Japanese belief "there exists no absolute being." Since the gods who are worshiped themselves worship other gods, the "ultimate object of religious ritual is lost to sight beyond the hazy reaches of space and time." Thus, "in these 'beliefs' there is neither the founder nor the scripture common to all universal religions."

Shintō, like a cloth container stretched featureless through time, was filled with doctrinal content by blending with the dominant religion of each successive period. The "all-enveloping embrace" and intellectual eclecticism of Shintō epitomizes the Japanese intellectual tradition as I have outlined it. Since Shintō possesses neither an absolute being nor a distinctive "Way" around which the world

[31] Sakurai Tokutarō, *Kōshūdan seiritsu katei no kenkyū* (Tokyo: Yoshikawa kōbunkan, 1962).

can be logically and normatively organized, it was defenseless against alien ideologies.[32]

Although, as Yanagita argued, the nature of the indigenous beliefs is more important than their ability to absorb alien systems, there is no question that Japanese in general have exhibited the tendency toward "all-enveloping embrace" that Maruyama defines. This tendency, exacerbated by Japan's late modernization, was surely responsible for Japanese intellectuals' penchant for imitation. But there was a great difference in the way the intellectuals and the people related to the indigenous tradition. The intellectuals roamed the world of Western ideas in pursuit of a replacement for a tradition from which they were alienated, whereas the people held fast to their traditional beliefs, which were still a vital part of their direct experience. Nor did those beliefs lack an absolute value around which the world could be centered. Both the popular morality of the Edo period and the new popular religions of the early Meiji period reconstituted the world according to their own distinctive "Way," whether it was the philosophy of the "heart" in Shingaku or the norm of the "gods" in Tenrikyō and Ōmotokyō. Of course in popular thought the principle that organized the world was not, as Maruyama rightly argues, normative and logical, but rather normative and apocalyptic.

It is this lack of logic that evokes Maruyama's rationalist critique, for his emphasis on the "structurelessness" of the Japanese tradition clearly derives from his belief in the scientific principle: "By separating one's cognitive self from reality as directly given, and standing for a moment in a relation of acute tension with it, one reconstructs the world logically, which is what makes it possible for theory to act as a lever to move reality . . . this is the logic necessary and intrinsic to modern epistemology."[33] And so indeed it is. Rigorous methodological awareness and the concern with verification are for

[32] *Nihon no shisō*, p. 20. Maruyama's words for "indigenous belief" are *koyū shinkō*.
[33] Ibid., p. 56.

us, too, the criteria of modern knowledge. They are not, however, the standard against which to judge historical tradition.
We must be careful not to project our own intellectual premises, even tacitly, into a past that may have operated on principles very different from our own.

Before the age of modern science, in the medieval and early
modern periods, it was far more common for the restructur-
ing of a new order to proceed not in logical terms but on a
religious or apocalyptic plane. The masses, for example, as if
exorcised from being possessed by foxes,[34] would suddenly
intuit a new vision of the world, make a mental leap, and rise
up to challenge the present order. This kind of religious apprehension of the world lay behind most of the popular rebellions and peasant wars of the medieval period. The spirit
of historic creativity took many forms, from the relation between Zen Buddhism and the samurai code of conduct to the
role of popular morality in promoting a new autonomy among
the common people. Thus there was neither a single spiritual
axis nor a general pattern for "the logical, or abstract, reconstruction of the world" but many diverse "reconstructions,"
each of which depended on the historical stage and folk customs of the people who created them. Shinran and Dōgen,
Kamo no Chōmei and Kitabatake Chikafusa, Ninomiya Sontoku and Nakayama Miki—all organized their world in a different way and each must be recognized as providing patterns
by which thought was "traditionalized" in Japan.

The same must be said of Tokugawa nativism, in which
Maruyama sees a "tenacious 'tradition' of anti-intellectual-
ism." Approached from my point of view, *kokugaku* acquires
a considerably different meaning. According to Maruyama's
analysis, the nativist critique of neo-Confucianism, which was
part of Motoori Norinaga's attempt at a "scholarly restoration
of the thought and sensibility of 'indigenous beliefs' before
Confucianism and Buddhism entered Japan," possessed the
following characteristics:

[34] Fox possession and exorcism were important and frequent concerns in
the world of folk belief that Yanagita and others describe.

1. an aversion to, or contempt for, ideology in general.
2. a denial of rational interpretation in favor of direct apprehension of objective reality (and hence the tendency to absolutize the intuitive interpretation of the individual).
3. a way of thinking that recognizes as authentic only the sure and palpable perceptions of everyday sense experience.
4. a critical style that undermines the credibility of its opponent by exposing the falseness of the pose he assumes or the discrepancy between his words and his actions.
5. a mode of thought that lumps together anything that has to do with reason (or norms, or laws) in history and then attacks these as contrived formulas.[35]

Here the object of Maruyama's critique is primarily the fifth characteristic, which he sees as the outcome of the first four. But I think it possible, without denying the obvious weaknesses in nativist logic, to point the arrow in the opposite direction and interpret this anti-intellectual tradition as an extremely effective and positive force for the "exposure of ideology" in the modern period.[36] Out of this general aversion to ideology emerged strong popular mistrust of *tennōsei* orthodoxy and of the arguments of the intellectuals, who were themselves discomfited by the people's skeptical apathy. The reliance on direct experience fostered the development of an intellectual method by which norms were derived, not from abstractions but from the people's daily life.[37] In the creation and preservation of this independent thought, the people were aided by Maruyama's fourth category, the critical style that exposed the discrepancies between the opponents' words and

[35] Maruyama, *Nihon no shisō*, pp. 20-22.
[36] Maruyama argues that *"ideorogii bakuro"* (the exposure of ideology) that is associated with Marxism in the West, though present in Motoori's criticism of neo-Confucianism, never reached the stage of "ideological critique" because of its resistance to rational norms and abstract logic. Ibid., pp. 17-20.
[37] See chap. VI.

actions. In this case the people exposed the illusion of national community by attacking the way the actions of the self-appointed leaders belied the theory that the people and the government shared anything in common. The preference for intuition over reason indicates the artistic nature of the Japanese without precluding their ability to employ inferential reasoning. Though the Japanese may never produce thinkers like Kant, Hegel, or Weber, this is insufficient grounds for doubting that they possess any scientific spirit at all. The rationalist critique thus fails to account for a Japanese "tradition" that, however different in nature from its counterparts elsewhere, had a very definite "structure" of its own.

MARUYAMA'S INTERPRETATION OF *Kokutai*

From the analysis of the "structureless tradition," Maruyama moves to a characterization of the nature of *kokutai* in the prewar period. He traces the origin of *kokutai* as the axis of modern Japan to a speech made by Itō Hirobumi before the Privy Council on July 18, 1888, on the occasion of its initial deliberations on the new Constitution. Somewhat startled by this assertion, I reread the speech, in which Itō explained the general principles of the draft put before the Council, and found that although it seemed in part to conform to Maruyama's interpretation, the word "axis" (*kijuku*) was used in an entirely different sense from the one Maruyama had imputed to it. For where Maruyama used the word to mean a coherent intellectual tradition against which all ideas must be measured, Itō was attempting to justify the absolute authority accorded to the emperor in the constitution. "In this draft," Itō argued, "imperial authority is the axis, which we intend shall not be compromised; the constitution is not based on the European notion of the separation of powers." Maruyama also cites the following passage from Itō's speech:

> Thus in establishing this Constitution we must first seek *the axis of the nation* and decide what that axis shall be. Without an axis, with politics entrusted to the reckless

deliberations of the people, the government will lose its guiding principle and the state will collapse. If the state is to survive and govern the people, we must see that it does not lose *the means to rule effectively*. Constitutional government in Europe has a history of more than a thousand years; not only are the people experienced in this system but their *religion has provided an axis* that imbued and united their hearts. *In Japan, however, the power of religion* is slight, and there is none that could serve as the axis of the state. Buddhism, when it flourished, was able to unite people of all classes, but it is today in a state of decline. Shintō, though it is based on and perpetuates the teachings of our ancestors, as a religion lacks the power to move the hearts of men. In Japan, it is only the imperial house that can become the *axis of the state*. It is thus with this point in mind that we have placed so high a value on imperial authority and endeavored to restrict it as little as possible in this draft constitution.[38]

Here Itō is simply pointing out that when the drafters of the document considered "the means to rule effectively" under a constitutional system, they could not hope to employ Buddhism to unify modern Japan as it had once done in ancient times, and a social and spiritual axis like Christianity was unavailable to them. To win the hearts of the people they had only the imperial house, which all Japanese revered and which they accordingly made the basis of sovereignty in the constitution.[39] The only novel element in this statement is Itō's assertion that in the West "religion has provided an axis" of the state. Since the context makes it clear that his was not a Weberian perception, it would seem that by "axis" Itō simply meant the means necessary to govern effectively and nothing as theoretically prescient as Maruyama suggests when he writes:

[38] *Nihon no shisō*, pp. 29-30. For a variant translation in which *kijiku* is successively "pivot," "foundation," and "cornerstone," see Pittau, *Political Thought in Early Meiji Japan*, p. 177.
[39] Inada, *Meiji kempō seiritsu shi*, vol. 2, pp. 567-68.

Itō clearly recognized from the beginning that "traditional" Japanese religion had failed to constitute a tradition that could function as an internal axis in the construction of the modern Japanese state.[40]

It is as if eighty years ago Itō Hirobumi had been aware of Maruyama's original concept of "an internal axis, a principle that orders the structure of values" and according to which "tradition" is constituted. Had Itō been aware of this, he might have entrusted to the imperial house "the enormous task of acting as a spiritual substitute for Christianity, which had been the 'axis' for a thousand years of European culture." He might have produced a unique, unified state whose "core of national order was also its spiritual axis."[41] Had he done so, he would have been a statesman of genius. And had Japan been ruled by such statesmen of genius, the popular resistance of the People's Rights movement and Meiji socialism would never have had a chance at all.

This image of Itō Hirobumi appears like a mirage on the historical horizon. In reality, men like Itō, Yamagata, and Inoue were politicians who worked by trial and error, and as they later admitted, made many mistakes in the process. Their "great success" was achieved with the aid of the creative powers of all classes and the luck of historical accident.[42]

In fact, the notion that the imperial house and *kokutai* must be made the pivot of modern Japanese unity did not originate with Itō. It was already present in the bakumatsu period, became a point at issue in the inner councils of the earliest Meiji government, and later, as we have seen, appeared in the private constitutional drafts of the People's Rights activists. In the sense that Itō's idea of using the imperial house as an axis for governing efficiently by entrusting inviolable authority to it was innovative, it was simply an extremely self-serving use of this hallowed institution. The People's Rights

---

[40] *Nihon no shisō*, p. 29.

[41] Ibid., p. 30.

[42] See Irokawa, *Kindai kokka no shuppatsu, Nihon no rekishi*, vol. 21 (Tokyo: Chūō kōronsha, 1966).

activists, for their part, had been led by their reverence for the emperor in precisely the opposite direction. Their constitutions had moved away from absolute imperial rule toward constitutional monarchy and joint rule between the emperor and his subjects. Theirs was a different but equally effective way of making the imperial house into the spiritual axis of the unified state.

Whether the modern use of *kokutai* originated with Itō is not, however, the point. What matters here is Maruyama's original and incisive interpretation of the nature of *kokutai* as it operated within the structure of the prewar emperor system. He begins his analysis with his own "acute perception" of the frightening magical power possessed by the "nonreligious religion" known as *kokutai*. The power to exact "unlimited responsibility" on the part of the people is the first characteristic of *kokutai* as Maruyama understands it. As an example he cites the Toranomon incident of 1923, when people only remotely connected to Nanba Daisuke, the would-be assassin of the Prince Regent, voluntarily assumed part of the responsibility for his treasonous act. Maruyama suggests that, at least in matters of collective responsibility, imperial Russia under the orthodox church demanded no more of the people than did the emperor system and its *kokutai*.[43]

The demands, however, were made in a distinctive way, and this Maruyama makes the second characteristic of *kokutai*. For at the same time that *kokutai* expected unlimited responsibility on the part of the people, it displayed a boundlessly benign facade and the same facility for "all-enveloping embrace" that had characterized Japan's indigenous beliefs. Since all academic theories discreetly shied away from delimiting or relativizing the *kokutai* ideology, it remained enveloped in layers of thick cloud that concealed its true nature.[44] Takeuchi Yoshimi used similar language when he described

[43] *Nihon no shisō*, pp. 31-32. Maruyama also points out that although unlimited responsibility was required of the subjects, the system itself was characterized by irresponsibility, which made it impossible after the war to define where responsibility had truly lain in the prewar years (pp. 37-39).

[44] Ibid., p. 33.

the emperor system, as "not solid, but a miasma that enveloped both itself and others." *Kokutai*, he wrote, was "a mysterious, transcendent being, possessed of an immense and uncanny power to render impotent any force that would oppose it." For Takeuchi, too, "the emperor system was not a single but a complex value system, and in some ways, not a value system at all, but a device for nullifying all other values."[45]

In Maruyama's analysis of *kokutai* the first two characteristics gave rise to a third: *kokutai* was more than an external system; it was a "spiritual axis" that permeated the inner life of the people. As such, comments Maruyama, Japan's emperor system possessed a facility for producing an "ideological homogeneity" (*Gleichshaltung*) that Hitler might have envied.[46]

The fourth and final characteristic of *kokutai* was its dependence on the village community (*kyōdōtai*) for its basis of support. The *kyōdōtai*, in Maruyama's words, was the "basic cell," the smallest unit in the structure of the emperor system. The *kyōdōtai* acted as a solvent for conflict and effectively blocked "individuation," the emancipation of individuals from communal restraints.[47] Reviving the kind of thinking associated with indigenous folk belief, the village *kyōdōtai* became the source of support for the emperor system. Hence Maruyama concludes that the structural dynamism of the modern Japanese state derived from this kind of unlimited reciprocal motion between the base of society and its apex. Modernization, which was initiated by the government bureaucracy, moved down and permeated the village *kyōdōtai* while the village in turn provided the social models that rose even to the highest levels of organization.[48]

[45] Takeuchi Yoshimi, "Kenryoku to geijutsu," *Shimpen Nihon ideorogii*, vol. 2 (Tokyo: Chikuma shobō, 1966), p. 378.
[46] *Nihon no shisō*, pp. 33–34.
[47] See also Maruyama, "Patterns of Individuation and the Case of Japan: A Conceptual Scheme," chapter XIV in Marius B. Jansen, ed., *Changing Japanese Attitudes Toward Modernization* (Princeton: Princeton University Press, 1965).
[48] *Nihon no shisō*, pp. 47–48.

From this brief summary it is clear that Maruyama considers *kokutai* to be the core of the emperor system and that the emperor system he has in mind is not that of the early Meiji period when the institutions were established but that of the 1930s when they had stagnated under fascism. Yet any analysis of the modern emperor system must surely take into account its entire historical course and not concentrate either on its establishment or on the period of its greatest deterioration.[49] Beyond this methodological defect, it seems to me that the first and second characteristics—the system of "unlimited responsibility" and the quality of "all-enveloping embrace"—are accurate representations of the prewar *kokutai*. I have profited from the interpretations of both Maruyama and Takeuchi on these points and have alluded to them frequently in earlier chapters. The third and fourth characteristics, however, which are asserted to have helped support the people and the *kyōdōtai* in the working of the emperor system as a structure, are another matter.

It seems to me that the notion of *kokutai* never penetrated the inner life of the people deeply enough to have become a spiritual axis. Although leaders like Itō Hirobumi strove toward this end, their attempts to win the hearts of the people got no farther than the ideological level, and they never got over their insecurity on this point. If the leaders had actually achieved their goal, there would have been no need for Japan to become a police state, as it did in the years preceding the war. Although people accepted the ficiton of *kokutai* to a considerable extent, they never relinquished their souls to the emperor system. The emperor system failed to capture the people's hearts, and *kokutai* never really became a spiritual axis. To substantiate this impression of the role of the people in the prewar system, I will try to show by what means and to what extent the fiction penetrated as far as it did. How the illusion of the family-state took hold is central to the case, but

[49] See Shimoyama Saburō, "Kindai tennōsei kenkyū no igi to hōhō," *Rekishigaku kenkyū*, no. 314 (1966), pp. 1-11 and p. 54.

before this link can be examined, a word must be said on the relation between the *kyōdōtai* and the state.

THE *Kyōdōtai*

Maruyama's contention that the *kyōdōtai* was the basis of the emperor system and the source of social stagnation, one shared by Takeuchi, is ahistorical in the extreme. It takes the village collectivity in its stagnant period—from 1905 through 1930, when landlord absenteeism was high and the villages had lost their vigor—and extracts from this specific historical situation a general definition of the *kyōdōtai*. Thus:

> The village *kyōdōtai* is based on real and fictive kinship bonds, shared religious ceremony, and the "old custom of mutual neighborhood aid." It is a group whose emotional immediacy and cohesiveness checks any overt conflict of interests, obscures the locus of decision-making, and disallows the autonomy of the individuals within it. It is also there that the tradition of "indigenous belief" originates. Through the control of irrigation and common lands and the web of personal *oyakata-kokata* relationships, the village produces an absolute unity of authority and feelings of mutual obligation. It is thus the very "model" of traditional human relationships and the smallest "cell" of the *kokutai*. In *kyōdōtai* at the base, as in *kokutai* at the apex, of society all ideologies—whether modern "totalitarianism," parliamentary "democracy," or harmonious "pacifism"—are necessarily subsumed. Thus liberated from the spell of "abstract theory," the *kyōdōtai* is enveloped in a world of perfect oneness.[50]

Takeuchi, too, has cautioned that unless the patterns that this *kyōdōtai* represents disappear from Japanese society the roots of the emperor system will remain.[51] Yasumaru Yoshio has already criticized this as too static and one-sided a view

[50] *Nihon no shisō*, p. 46.
[51] Takeuchi Yoshimi and Tsurumi Shunsuke, dialogue, "Jūnen no haba de kangaete," *Tenbō* 132 (December 1969): 16-34.

of the village community during one period of its history, and throughout this book I have introduced counterexamples from the *kyōdōtai* in its period of vitality to show that the village was capable of a social effect quite the opposite from the one Maruyama and Takeuchi suggest.[52]

Even if we consider only the last hundred years, there are at least three distinguishable periods in the history of the Japanese village community: first, the period of formation when, from the Restoration until the end of the People's Rights movement in the early 1880s, innovative attempts at change were made; second, the period of stagnation under the emperor system and the domination of absentee landlords, which lasted for the remainder of the prewar years; third, the period of dissolution and transformation when, after the war, the villages once again experienced turbulent change. The Japanese *kyōdōtai* was thus not wholly the property of the emperor system. Indeed, in the ideas associated with the Meiji Restoration, the People's Rights movement, and even the "Shōwa Restoration," the village demonstrated that it possessed internal forces capable of destroying that system. The *kyōdōtai*, in short, at the same time that it served as the institutional support of a premodern kind of control, was also able to function as an organization of resistance.

Although *kyōdōtai* may well be described as the smallest cell of *kokutai*, it does not follow that the village dissolved all possibility of conflict and destroyed all potential for change. Against such an interpretation stand the actual examples of the Chichibu commune and the mountain village communities that produced the draft constitution of Itsukaichi. With Ōno Naekichi's exhortation to fight the emperor "in all deference," the *kyōdōtai* became a base for insurrection, and the villagers attempted to change its very nature.[53] It was only when the communities were co-opted by the emperor system and robbed of this momentum for change that men like Ochiai

---

[52] Yasumaru Yoshio, "Kindai Nihon no shisō kōzō: Maruyama Masao cho *Nihon no shisō* o yonde," *Atarashii rekishigaku no tame ni*, no. 76 (1962), pp. 1-11.

[53] See chap. V, note 6.

Toraichi lost their sense of identification with the village. Though he had been a leader of the Chichibu rebellion and an indomitable guerrilla fighter, Ochiai later described himself as "imperial loyalist and constitutionalist *shishi*, Ochiai Toraichi." To justify his actions he had to resort in the end to the language of the government he had once rebelled against.[54] Thus began the period of stagnation under the emperor system when the *kyōdōtai* was indeed at its lowest ebb.

The term "village *kyōdōtai*" does not refer to any specific institution but simply to the ways the masses join together. It may take the form of a village council (*yoriai*) or any of the religious, economic, and social associations that proliferated on the village level (including the *kō, yui,* and *sha* described by Sakurai). Its essence lies in the illusion of community that carries with it definite powers of social regulation. So it is that when the *kyōdōtai* was vital, alive with the potential for change, men of leadership emerged and thrust the emperor system aside. When the *kyōdōtai* was stagnant, such autonomous men were cut off from the community, and the emperor system invaded the village. Ultimately it is these changes in the conditions among the masses that determined the way the emperor system was able to function.

If "autonomous individuals" (*shutaiteki ningen*) are defined solely in terms of European civil society, then the *kyōdōtai* may be judged deficient in producing them. But if we include in this definition those individuals who are aware of their autonomy and use it actively to affect the society in which they live, then in Japan, too, they are by no means uncommon. Ninomiya Sontoku, Nakayama Miki, Deguchi Nao, Deguchi Onisaburō, Tanaka Shōzō, Ōno Naekichi—these and others like them were products of the village *kyōdōtai* who, instead of being overwhelmed by their environment, attempted to change it. They, too, would seem to exemplify the "autonomous individual possessed of tenacious powers of self-discipline." Indeed, in many ways they were far stronger individ-

---

[54] Nakazawa Ichirō, "Chichibu jiken ni kansuru shiryō: Ochiai Toraichi no ikō o megutte," *Rekishi hyōron* 61 (November-December 1954): 28.

uals than the intellectuals of our time.[55] Even without adducing once again the examples of Itsukaichi and Chichibu, it is clear that there need be no contradiction between being an autonomous individual and wishing the *kyōdōtai* to survive. Those who were aware of their autonomy were not therefore bent on destroying their villages. It was because they perceived the crisis in the *kyōdōtai* and were concerned about it that they consciously turned toward preserving—and even toward developing—their local communities. Not only were there many such people in the Konmintō and among the People's Rights activists of the *gōnō* class, but the social activities of "conscientious" and "experienced" farmers (*tokunō* and *rōnō*) in offering agricultural guidance and the excellent leadership of the *Hōtoku* societies in these and other village matters showed the kind of creativity of which the villages were capable.

The new popular religions of the nineteenth century—Konkōkyō, Ōmotokyō, Tenrikyō, Maruyamakyō—arose out of a similar sense of local crisis and the resultant impulse toward change; and this tendency, or even "law," of popular autonomy and creativity was consciously taken over by the agrarianists (*nōhonshugisha*) of the twenties and thirties. The "law" involved a route traveled by countless of their forebears who had pursued the principle of *kyōdōtai*—fiction and all—with moral and ascetic conviction, until their critical awareness of social relationships had developed to the point that they could seize the opportunity for change.

For these people the spiritual axis of *kyōdōtai* was not the notion of *kokutai* but, as Yanagita Kunio perceived, the belief in ancestor worship and the continuity of the family and the village. It took a national emergency of the scale of the Russo-Japanese War, as I will argue, to introduce *kokutai* as a conscious fiction in the popular mind.[56] And even then the myths

[55] See chap. V, where I have tried to show the vast difference that developed between the intellectuals and the people in modern Japan.

[56] See below, p. 293. Yoshimoto Takaaki describes the phenomenon as occurring during the Pacific War, whereas I think it took place much earlier, during the war of 1904-1905.

of the emperor system could not easily penetrate the depths of these emotional recesses. Although both government and agrarian ideologues produced a steady stream of slogans that asserted "harmony" (*yūwa*) and "oneness" (*ichi'nyo*), these did not reach the inner soul of the Japanese people in the way that Hitler, the *tennōsei* fascists, or the modernist scholars have assumed. It was for this reason that the government remained afraid and insecure, reacting to even the slightest evidence of popular unrest with its distinctive ideological response. But since it was the government that was affected, it will not do to reverse the relationship and assume that the people were equally susceptible to the manipulations of the government.

That the modernist interpretation of the emperor system owes a great deal to admiration for Western civilization is clear—and understandable. I, too, have been inspired by the spirit of European civil society, by the internal disciplines that produced the culture of the Greek and Roman city-state, the independent cities of the medieval period, the Renaissance and Reformation, and the bourgeois revolution. I can well understand why this image of the West and its modern ethos so impressed intellectuals of the Meiji period that they developed an aversion to being Japanese and an impulse to total self-abnegation. The doctrine of natural law that runs through the history of Western civilization, the mode of action that "clearly establishes the locus of decision-making and responsibility," the "pattern of thought that conceives of the world as a purposeful creation of a single absolute deity," "the social contract theory that sees the state as a fiction," "the social barricades set up against state power"—for me, too, these historical achievements represent European civil society and Western individualism at their best, a masterpiece in human history.

To evaluate and learn from these achievements is one thing; to idealize them to the point that people possessed of a different cultural tradition are also judged by this standard is quite another. Yet this is what Maruyama has done in interpreting modern Japanese society in terms of Western social thought. He writes:

> The dynamic of modern Japanese development consists of a continual interaction between the processes of modernization initiated at the center, which then move out and downward into society, and the existing system of social relations modeled on the village, which, in its turn, is transposed upward into every national structure and organization. From the center comes rational bureaucratization as the organizational principle, not only of the government but of other functional groups, including those in the private sphere. From local society comes the social discipline that rests not on the system of straightforward reward and punishment but on paternalistic chastisement for the mutual good. Thus, every type of group or organization is an amalgam of the functional bureaucratization necessary to modern society (including the hierarchy of authority based upon it) with the system of paternal, factional, and personal human relationships that characterize village society.[57]

Although on first impression much of this description appears to be accurate, on reflection it seems to describe the contradictions that impeded modernization rather than the "dynamic" that produced it. In my analysis of the rapid progress made by the early Meiji state I have attempted to show how the desire for modernization among the people—"from below," as it were—worked in concert with the rationalization and modernization that proceeded "from above." I have also tried to stress the role played by the emerging middle class in linking these two impulses to the dynamo of national development. It was the "mediating energy" of the local elite that coupled the "energy of the leadership" to the "energy of the social base." Neither the mechanism of modern Japanese development nor the considerable propensity for moderniza-

[57] *Nihon no shisō*, p. 47.

278

tion can be explained abstractly without reference to this middle stratum on the local level.

By treating the government in its active mode and the *kyō-dōtai* only in its most stagnant one, it becomes impossible to discover any potential for political change within the system. It is also an analytical error. As Ichii Saburō has pointed out in his criticism of Weber, it is methodologically unsound to compare two systems from inconsistent points of view. Weber's comparison of progressive Europe with stagnant Asia depended on his understanding of Christianity and Confucianism, but

> his perspective on the two traditions was totally skewed. As a European, his discussion of Christianity was based on an ideal type that gave the Western religion every benefit of the doubt, whereas for Confucianism he fashioned an ideal type that systematically ignored all evidence of internal reform. . . . In short, Weber took the characteristics of Chinese Confucianism at its most traditional and retrograde and judged them the essence of the tradition, whereas for Christianity he took precisely the opposite point of view.[58]

What the modernists have done is to take European civil society and extract a superior ideal type from it, whereas from the Japanese village *kyōdōtai* they educe an inferior ideal type. Then from the heights of the former they proceed to try to root out the pathology of the latter. But why, if comparison is wanted, should not Japan and Europe be compared properly, superior to superior and inferior to inferior, since both types were clearly present in both places? If we do not proceed this way, we will continue to repeat the distortions of Weber and others who, being Europeans, pronounced arbi-

[58] Ichii Saburō, "Dentō to kakushin," *Shisō*, no. 544 (October 1969), p. 52. See also Ōtsuka Hisao, "Weber no 'jukyō to pyūritanizumu' o megutte," *Shakai kagaku no hōhō* (Tokyo: Iwanami shoten, 1966), pp. 133-85. Ōtsuka, one of the major interpreters of Weber in Japan, is himself an analyst of the *kyōdōtai* and open to similar criticism.

trarily from a Western perspective on the stagnation of Asian society.

THE "FAMILY-STATE" (*Kazoku Kokka*)

"So Japan is a family-state!" I thought. Even as a child I thought there was something phony about the idea. Had it meant that all Japanese were to join together *as if* in a family-state, I might have understood. But there was nothing I could see in the world around me that suggested a "familial harmony unparalleled in the world." And while they filled us with this at school our parents, on this subject anyway, held their tongues. In the early years of the Shōwa period, when fascism began to gain ground in Japan, it is said that even the German fascists envied the Japanese *kokutai* its status as a "family-state." But who invented the term in the first place?

After the defeat I found out: it appeared to have been created for the Meiji government by ideologues like Hozumi Yatsuka, Katō Hiroyuki, and Inoue Tetsujirō for the purpose of solidifying the emperor system. Ishida Takeshi explains it as "the union of familism (*kazokushugi*) and the organic theory of society (*yūkitairon*)." Although my own experience makes me feel that it could not have been that simple, Ishida's analysis of the "family-state" as "the most important ideological construct of the entire system of control under the emperor system" has gained wide currency since he first wrote of it in the 1950s.[59] Enough time has passed now that a reexamination of this concept, too, would seem to be in order.

I confess that I find the analogy between household (*ie*) or family (*kazoku*) and the Japanese state (*kokka*) insupportable. It is all well and good for families of ancient pedigree to bask in the sense of identity they feel with an imperial house that traces its lineage back "two thousand six hundred years," but it is too much to think that the nameless, propertyless masses

[59] Ishida Takeshi, *Meiji seiji shisōshi kenkyū* (Tokyo: Miraisha, 1957), p. 3. For familism and the organic theory of society, see pp. 21-104. See also Carol Gluck, *Japan's Modern Myths* (Princeton: Princeton University Press, 1985).

were ever admitted into this "family-state." Eligibility was restricted at best to those who could boast a single family line, whether nobles, samurai, old landlord families, the wealthy, or men of influence and reputation. The rest were no more than victims of that illusion.

Up to now the Japanese masses have survived without receiving the blessing of *kokutai* of the family-state. They have kept to themselves and lived according to their own ways of thinking. Their households needed no strengthening or protection from the Meiji civil code. The heads of their households had neither the need nor the power to pride themselves on the grounds of their rights as the family head, for husbands, wives, parents, and children all labored equally. Nor did they have the luxury of wrangling among one another over property rights. Even less, then, was there any family line or historical connection to make them proud of being associated with the state or emperor system. Were the history of their relations with the state to be uncovered, it would hardly be a record of blood ties to loyal and faithful retainers. It would more probably appear in the spectral shape of a grudge held against these loyal retainers at whose hands they were humiliated, sacrificed in war, and plundered. No discussion of the family-state can afford to ignore the earlier history of the relationship between the state and the people, which was likely to have as much impact on the understanding of the family-state as any theoretical basis laid down by the Meiji ideologues.

Yoshimoto Takaaki has written that the family forms a community based on the "illusion of pairing" (*tsui naru gensō*), an illusion not at all congruent with the supreme "illusion of community" (*kyōdō gensō*) that is the state. The shared familial illusion is based on the sexual and procreative bonds between husband and wife, parents and children, the most natural, the most physical and direct of all human relationships.[60] The only way the communal character of the "family" can be

---

[60] Yoshimoto Takaaki, "Kyōdō gensōron," *Yoshimoto Takaaki zenchosaku shū*, vol. 11 (Tokyo: Keisō shobō, 1972), pp. 179-203.

extended beyond itself is as a fiction, and this is true even on the village level. For the concrete familial illusion to be transposed first to the village and then further to the abstract community of the state requires a series of complex ideological leaps. A subtle ideological mechanism is necessary to forge the link between the family and the state in a way that will be emotionally persuasive to the people. The theoretical analogy of familism and the organic theory of society can never adequately explain the conjunction of two so utterly opposite values.

For that we must turn to the people and ask whether they would risk their lives for the state or the emperor in the way they would for their family. Not only is the level of abstraction different, but when the people's actual experience of the state is restricted either to the class pyramid bearing down on them or to an assemblage made up primarily of strangers indifferent to one another's concerns, the gap between the two is not easily bridged. What ideological grounds would suffice for the state or the emperor to ask millions of families to sacrifice their most important possession—the lives of their family members? Even feudal lords had found it difficult to extract loyalty from retainers whose families had enjoyed their patronage for generations. The state could hardly hope to evoke—and preserve—spontaneous allegiance from people who knew no such familiarity or favor from it. Although intellectuals might be lured by a theoretical import like organicism, the people, hardheaded and possessed of their own understanding of life (*seikatsu shisō*), could not be completely taken in, even by "familism." What then was the link that allowed two such disparate elements to be joined? Ishida proposes imported organic theory as the bonding agent, whereas his teacher, Maruyama, invoked the whole indigenous tradition since the Jōmon period to account for it. Neither approach, it seems to me, satisfactorily explains the connection established between the family and the state under the emperor system.

In my understanding four ideological intermediaries were used to join the household (*ie*) to the nation (*kuni*) in the

Meiji period: the imperial myth, the religious tradition of ancestor worship, the social structure of the family system, and the customary heritage of folk morality. Then, the ideological groundwork having been laid, the Russo-Japanese War provided the national crisis that cemented the bond between family and state. And in 1910, the product—the Japanese *kazoku-kokka*—was systematically formulated in the official government textbooks. Let me now pursue these elements one by one.

First, the imperial house (the core of *kokutai*) was drawn as close as possible to the houses of the people by making the Meiji emperor into a symbol of "the rare and enlightened ruler." Then the imperial illusion was continually expanded and invested with increasingly emotional content. To accomplish this, it was necessary to present the Meiji emperor as the symbolic hero of national unity who, even as a young boy, had selflessly "shared hardship with the people" so that the great undertaking of the Meiji Restoration might succeed. For these ideological purposes, the life of the Meiji emperor provided the perfect drama, both in plot and in performance. As a youth, he had overthrown the feudal government in the name of *ikkun banmin* (one ruler, many subjects) and *kōgi yoron* (public discussion). Later, victorious in several foreign wars, he had established the glory of the Japanese Empire. As "the head of the people" (*minzoku no osa*), he thus became the hero in the creation myth of modern Japan. The thousands of poems composed by the emperor made him familiar, not as a public figure but as a poet and a private person, providing him with direct and literary access to the emotional lives of the people. The "all-enveloping embrace of *kokutai*" needed no help from the patterns of indigenous belief—not when the emperor and the imperial house could be successfully brought into the households of the people. One has only to recall the symbolic sight of the portrait of the Meiji emperor that hung on the walls of most Japanese houses in the prewar period to realize how much the ideological basis of the emperor system owed to the person of the Emperor Meiji.

Ancestor worship, the core of the household and the very heart of the people, was the second means used to bind the family to the nation. Though the effort was on the whole unsuccessful, it did produce results of a kind. Among the ideologues of the Meiji establishment who had observed European societies at firsthand, there were those like Hozumi Yatsuka, who early identified Japan as "the country of ancestor worship" and suggested that this characteristic be utilized in building the nation. They intended that the ancestor of the imperial house, the Sun Goddess Amaterasu, be used to bestow a secular national unity on the ancestor worship customary among the masses.

As Yanagita explained again and again, Japanese spiritual life centered on ancestor worship in the household and festivals to the local tutelary gods in the village. Sakurai, too, has written that these were the oldest and most powerful beliefs among those who lived in the countryside. Although at times these beliefs seemed to have been overwhelmed by the power of the new popular religions, in fact the eclipse was temporary. In the end it was the local gods who survived, and the village beliefs remained essentially unshaken. The Ise and Fuji cults established themselves through the medium of the tutelary gods (*ujigami*) but were never able to replace the local deities in village life.[61] Their position was sustained by the belief that one's ancestors must not be neglected in life, since in death all become ancestors and can expect to be similarly honored. However unfathomable this idea may seem to the youth of today, it cannot be ignored if the popular consciousness of the Meiji period is ever to be understood.

It was here that the emperor system tried to plant its deepest roots. State Shintō was used as a device to establish Amaterasu as the ancestral deity of the imperial house (hence, the term *Tenshō Kōdaijin*, the imperial deity Amaterasu), as well as the chief god among all gods. Then the emperor, the direct descendant of Amaterasu, was deemed the "great father" of the people, thus enabling him to intrude into the people's

[61] Sakurai, *Kōshūdan seiritsu*, pp. 541-71.

worship of their own generations of ancestral spirits. Court ceremonies like the vernal and autumnal equinoxes, which are imperial offerings to imperial ancestors, became part of the calendar of national holidays. This was part of the attempt to incorporate the popular belief in ancestral spirits into the emperor system by associating it with the belief in the imperial ancestors and the myth of divine descent.

But the popular notion of *kami* (god) was particularistic and apolitical, shaped by social custom and natural climate, and based on the people's wish for peace and eternal life and a continuing sense of community with one's family after death. The *kami* of the emperor system, on the other hand, was universal, the lord of nature, and an artificial and political creation. Since these two disparate conceptions of the divine were not easily linked, the government labored mightily to paper over the differences between them. It tried to use the Ise cult (*okagemairi*) to reinforce the connection between popular religious beliefs and the imperial deity Amaterasu. It wielded public power to elevate the gods of the people to a national level by establishing a state shrine to the war dead at Yasukuni. It employed analogies like the comparison between the nation and the familial and emotional unity of the *kyōdōtai*, and it adduced imported theories like social organicism to support these analogies. And yet, for all this, as Yanagita recognized, the difference between the two notions of divinity was too great. The gods of the state were never able to oust the gods of the people nor, I think, to capture their inmost hearts.

A clear example of this failure was the attempt first to organize and later to merge the local Shintō shrines, where the masses of the Japanese traditionally worshiped. Originally the *ujigami* of popular belief were the domestic gods sacred to the communal ancestors of the village and had no relation at all to the gods of State Shintō. In the early Meiji period the government had attempted to establish such a relationship by organizing into a hierarchical system of national ranks all shrines at which these local gods were worshiped. Every shrine in the country was given a particular designation, and all were set under the Grand Imperial Shrine at Ise, which, by virtue of its status as shrine to the imperial ancestors, occupied the position at the top of the hierarchy.[62] Thus, every Shintō shrine was to be related to Ise in much the same way that branch temples are related to the headquarters of a Buddhist sect. This "rationalization" of the Ise shrine could not have been more removed from the popular Ise cults of the Tokugawa period that associated Ise not with supernal imperial ancestors but with the divine conferral of this-worldly benefits.[63]

After the Russo-Japanese War, when the government became aware of a structural crisis in the farm villages, it responded by launching a series of measures for rural improvement (*chihō kairyō undō*). These included the formation of town and village plans (*chōsonze*) for each locality and the merging of the nation's shrines (*jinja gappei*), a policy that touched on matters close to the hearts of the people. In order to strengthen control over the nation's Shintō institutions, the number of local shrines was suddenly and drastically reduced from 190,000 to 100,000 over a period of only five years from 1906 to 1910.[64] For the bureaucrats, one shrine to each administrative district, that is, one to each town or village, was apparently sufficient. As a result, in Mie Prefecture, 10,411 shrines were reduced to only 989, and in Wakayama Prefecture, nearly 80 percent of the 3,772 shrines were eliminated. Egi Kazuyuki commented: "it is said that when the shrines were merged in Wakayama, all the villagers cried as they saw the gods off to the edge of the village." Doi Gondai, a representative in the lower house of the Diet in the twenties,

---

[62] The ranks established in 1871 were government shrine (*kanpeisha*), national shrine (*kokuheisha*), prefectural shrine (*fukensha*), town or village shrine (*chōsonsha*), and at the bottom and the most numerous, the ungraded shrines (*mukakusha*). Yasukuni belonged to a small and special class devoted to heroes, primarily of the Restoration period, called "special government shrines" (*tokubetsu kanpei taisha*). See D. C. Holtom, *The National Faith of Japan* (New York: Paragon reprint, 1965), pp. 12-13.

[63] See Fujitani Toshio, *Okagemairi to ee ja nai ka* (Tokyo: Iwanami shinsho, 1968).

[64] See Wilbur Fridell, *Japanese Shrine Mergers, 1906-1912* (Tokyo: Sophia University Press, 1973).

suggested that the shrine merger policy was the reason that so many of those indicted in the Great Treason incident of 1910-1911 came from Wakayama. And in Wakayama, too, Minakata Kumakusu, the famous biologist and folklorist, was detained for questioning by the police in the course of his opposition to the shrine mergers and later received support in his protest from Yanagita.

The opposition aroused by the shrine merger policy was soon overshadowed by the shock of the Great Treason incident, which served as an important warning to the *tennōsei* state and its bureaucrats.[65] Neither protest, however, was able to stop the spread of the fiction of the family-state. The government persisted in its effort to make ancestor worship the mediating link between the *ie* and the nation, and people gradually became accustomed to the idea. Most compelling was the national dimension attached to the familial rites for the husbands and sons who had died in battle. As repeated wars swelled the number of spirits enshrined at Yasukuni, the original distance between the ancestral gods of the people and the gods of the nation was dramatically and persuasively narrowed.

"DOMICIDE" (*Iegoroshi*)

The third and fundamental ingredient in the ideology of the "family-state" was the crisis in the "family system," for the family illusion became an issue only when the actual family structure had begun to disintegrate. It was not until the early

[65] The "Great Treason incident" of 1911 in which Kōtoku Shūsui and twenty-three associates were sentenced to death for alleged complicity in a conspiracy to assassinate the emperor (twelve of the sentences were later commuted to life imprisonment) is described in F. G. Notehelfer, *Kōtoku Shūsui* (Cambridge: Cambridge University Press, 1971). Because of the severity of the sentences and the secrecy of the proceedings the trial marked something of a divide in the attitudes of some intellectuals toward the regime. "Nothing between the Meiji reform and the unconditional surrender of 1945 exerted the influence on the Japanese intellectual world that the Russo-Japanese War and the Kōtoku incident did." Shūichi Katō, "Japanese Writers and Modernization," chapter XII, in Jansen, *Changing Japanese Attitudes*, p. 427.

1900s, with the rapid development of capitalism, that the family system (*kazoku seido*) attracted the interest of the intellectual elite. Men like Hozumi Yatsuka, Inoue Tetsujirō, Ukita Kazutami, and Yokoi Tokiyoshi all spoke to the issue, and at the meeting of the Greater Japan Agricultural Association in 1906, Yanagita sounded an ominous note:

> Even if the living members of the family raise no objection, when one takes into account the descendants as yet unborn, then domicide, or the killing of the house, is not suicide—it is murder. If killing one's own children is homicide, then is it not equally criminal forever to deprive our living descendants of the awareness of their lineage? Is the *ie*, which is second to the nation in the length of its existence, to be destroyed overnight at the discretion of the head of the household? And yet, today, moving one's permanent residence to a big city nearly always results in just this kind of domicide, or *iegoroshi*.
> . . .
>
> In Japan, the connection between a person and his ancestors, in short, the awareness of the existence of the *ie*, is at the same time the link between the individual and the nation. Today, if we but probe a little, we realize that the faithful subjects and loyal retainers of history are our ancestors, and we are aware, not just vaguely but in a concrete way, of the intentions of our ancestors. The awareness that our ancestors have lived and served under the imperial family for thousands of generations forms the surest basis for the feelings of loyalty and patriotism (*chūkun aikokushin*). If the *ie* were to disappear, it might even be difficult for us to explain to ourselves why we should be Japanese. As individualism flourished, we would come to view our history no differently from the way we view that of foreign countries.[66]

From a contemporary point of view, Yanagita's statement is clearly retrogressive. The laws of capitalism dictate that

[66] Yanagita Kunio, "Inaka tai tokai no mondai," *Jidai to nōsei, Teihon Yanagita Kunio shū*, vol. 16 (Tokyo: Chikuma shobō, 1962), pp. 38-39.

agrarian nations become industrial and that rural population declines as cities grow. To defy the inevitable and lament the migration to the cities seems hopelessly sentimental. Why then did an intellectual of Yanagita's stature wish people to stay forever in the villages and perpetuate the single family line (*ikkei no ie*)? He condemns the loss of awareness of one's family lineage as the crime of "domicide" and suggests that losing the sense of family will mean losing the awareness of thousands of generations of service to the imperial house. He then prophesies that once they have moved to the city and the *ie* has ceased to exist, the people will even have difficulty understanding why they are Japanese. For Yanagita the *ie* was the basis of the loyalty and patriotism that were Japan's distinctive characteristics, and so he spoke of an awareness of lineage in which all our ancestors were "faithful subjects and loyal retainers." But this idea of the "*ie*-state," though characteristic of Yanagita, looks very different when viewed from the perspective of the masses.

Yanagita went too far in judging all Japanese through the eyes of the old landed families and the local elite (*meibōka*). Think instead of the masses who constituted most of the Japanese population and consider the reasons they might have for abandoning their *ie* to live apart from the families for whom they cared so much. Most of them belonged neither to old houses nor to the elite, and they knew nothing of "lineage" or "faithful subjects and loyal retainers." Yet they loved their *ie* and cherished their ancestors and wished to remain in their native place. But capitalism destroyed their houses and forced them to flee to the cities, breaking up their families in order to survive. To understand what drove them from the villages, we have only to recall once again the destitute farmers of the Tōhoku whom we encountered in the last chapter. Since neither the glory of the Japanese Empire nor the creation of a "wealthy nation and strong army" would have been possible without the massive hardships endured by the Japanese people, it is hardly fair to censure them for committing a crime against posterity by murdering their houses.

Yanagita, however, was not moved to speak of domicide by the tragic plight of "household dissolution among the masses."

What alarmed him, and others like him, were the signs of disintegration of the local elite class to whom they looked as the social and economic mainstay of the villages. These "old families," who did indeed possess a pride of lineage, were also feeling the impact of capitalism and were beginning to move to the cities. Yokoi Tokiyoshi put it more bluntly:

> The only people we can rely on are the farmers. . . . In contrast to the cities, which is where revolutions are always made, the country is always the opponent of revolution and protector of the social order. . . . I look to agrarian society, and particularly the landlords, as the heirs of Japan's samurai tradition (bushidō), the cultivators of moral discipline, and the sustainers of vital energy.[67]

Ukita Kazutami was also apprehensive lest the farmers, in changing their residence, weaken the bonds of ancestor worship and threaten the family system.

The establishment clearly expected a great deal from the local landed elite, hoping that they would function as the support of the family system and the link that would bind the *ie* to the state. Without this intermediary social class the idea— or even the illusion—of the family-state would have been impossible, and that is why Yanagita associated awareness of family lineage with the awareness of being Japanese. In the late Meiji period, when this important local elite class confronted the inevitable crisis, the state, which depended on that class for its base of control, could not very well remain silent. Since it was this sense of crisis that impelled the ideologues to amplify and systematize the communal illusion of the family-state, to ignore the social background is to obscure the historical dynamic that generated the ideology in the first place.

Typical of the ideologues who responded to this historical

[67] Yokoi Tokiyoshi, "Tokai to inaka" (1906); "Nōgyō kyōiku i o shushi ni tsukite," *Yokoi Tokiyoshi zenshū*, vols. 4 and 9 (1925). (Quoted in Ishida, *Meiji seiji shisōshi kenkyū*, p. 110.)

dynamic was Inoue Tetsujirō. The author of an official commentary on the Rescript of Education in the 1890s, Inoue stepped forth once again in the period after the Russo-Japanese War to try to link the family system to *kokutai*.[68] Although he had been trained as a Hegelian in Germany, in Japan Inoue was the scholastic heir of Katō Hiroyuki at Tokyo University. There he lectured in philosophy and influenced, among others, the young writer Takayama Chōgyū. This professor, taking social organicism for his model, came up with the simplistic notion of the "comprehensive family-system state" (*sōgō kazokusei kokka*). The individual family system he described as "the single family centered around and led by the family head." "When these individual familes aggregate into Japan as a whole, they form one large family system." This Inoue labeled the "comprehensive family-system state" and defined it as the structure of Japan's *kokutai*. Japan differed from a country like China, whose society was based solely on the individual family, because it united the individual family's ethic of filiality with the comprehensive family's ethic of loyalty. The result was the ethic of loyalty and patriotism (*chūkun aikoku*), the national watchword of the late Meiji period.[69] But what if the individual familes that constitute the whole were to be destroyed? This, of course, is what actually took place in the ensuing decades, accompanied by the government's continual and futile attempts to prevent it. According to Inoue's argument, the "unique and incomparable *kokutai*, coeval with heaven and earth," would also be imperiled, making of it a flimsy *kokutai* indeed.

However absurd the argument, the question here is how this nonsensical logic became the core of government ideology. Adopted in the 1910 textbooks, it eventually penetrated the hearts of the nameless, propertyless masses whose families had lived until then without reference to the *ie* (house-

[68] Inoue Tetsujirō, *Chokugo enji* (1892) in *Meiji shisō shū*, Pt. 2, Matsumoto Sannosuke, ed., *Kindai Nihon shisō taikei*, vol. 31 (Tokyo: Chikuma shobō, 1977), pp. 85-116; also *Kokumin dōtoku gairon* (Tokyo: Sanseidō, 1912).

[69] Inoue Tetsujirō, "Waga kokutai to kazoku seido," *Tōa no hikari* 6, no. 9 (1911): 2 (quoted in Ishida, p. 108).

hold) as defined by the Meiji civil code. For this ideological penetration to succeed, a fourth intermediary was required, and that was mobilization of traditional folk morality in the name of the emperor system.

The ideological attempt to absorb elements of the folk morality (*tsūzoku dōtoku*) into the emperor system began in the 1870s, when the government supported the *Hōtokusha*, the rural self-help societies based on the teachings of Ninomiya Sontoku. These and other aspects of the folk morality had originally evolved to foster the rigorous self-discipline necessary to revive the families and villages ravaged by the famines of the Temmei and Tempō eras (1780s and 1830s). By the middle of the Meiji period, however, conventional folk morality had become an end in itself, and its original human significance had receded to the point that people no longer knew why it was they were supposed to be diligent, humble, and self-disciplined. It was this loss of purpose that enabled *tennōsei* ideology to reinterpret folk morality to its own ends. The customary ethic was rendered newly significant as the morality of the family in service to the higher goals of loyalty and patriotism. This view appeared first in the Rescript on Education in 1890 and was gradually incorporated into the prescription for the Meiji version of worldly success (*risshin shusse*). As a result, the mode of thought characteristic of folk morality was absorbed into the emperor system at the same time that folk morality acquired a raison d'etre that it had hitherto lacked. Education, both inside and outside the schools, emphasized the importance to the nation of the practice of the folk virtues. Thus were the starving Tōhoku peasants bound by "internal fetters" to a state that placed so heavy a burden on them that they died a helpless death that was tantamount to suicide.

I know from my own youthful confrontation with the questions of life and death during the war that it could not have been easy for the masses living in their wretched individual *ie* to identify with and immerse themselves in the state, "the most abstract of all illusions of community." And yet, the leap of will required to cast one's lot with the nation had first to originate from the side of the people. This meant that the constant daily preparation necessary to secure ideological consent had to be followed by an "extraordinary national crisis," a drastic national shock, that would induce the people once and for all to make the "unnatural leap" into the state. At a moment of national crisis, the idea of the family-state took its first hold on the masses. Then the state had to sustain the fiction by providing additional war shocks at appropriate intervals to tighten the loosening bonds around the national psyche. With the aid of the powerful spiritual opiate of *kokutai*, the emperor system effectively employed this universal method of mass control until the "family-state" of the Meiji period swelled, albeit with an increasingly hollow sound, into the "total-war state" of the Shōwa years.

A Soldier's Feelings

I argue that the "fiction of the century" emerged with the Russo-Japanese conflict and burned itself out finally in the ashes of World War II. The war against Russia in 1904-1905 brought the people of the Meiji period direct experience of the state as a shared national fate, and this experience in turn first assimilated them into the nation. Ample evidence of the popular response appears in the wartime notebooks and diaries of soldiers, in the large number of letters they wrote from the front, and in the diaries kept by the families at home. I have already quoted from the wartime diary of Private First Class Ōsawa. The 1905 diary written by Sunaga Renzō, the former leader of the Busō Poor People's party, which was discovered in the Tama village of Kasumimura that Ōsawa came from, is another example of the richness of the popular materials available to us.

These sources suggest what major revisions are necessary to remedy the deficiencies in the currently accepted view of the Russo-Japanese War. The conflict has most often been treated in the context of whether or not it was an imperialist war. Those who think it was have concentrated on the relative power of the two nations, the character of their ruling classes, and the aims and wartime situation of their capitalist, military, and diplomatic sectors. Those who think it was not have restricted themselves to accounts of diplomatic relations or narratives of military strategy. Both the left and the right (for that is the division behind the debate) have dealt in abstract terms with—or rather ignored—the historical viewpoint of the soldiers who actually fought the war.

The Russo-Japanese War was a major war against an empire that possessed the strongest army in the world and that had posed a threat from the north ever since Putiatin's fleet established Russian supremacy in the Japan Sea during the bakumatsu period. Although the war against Russia was Meiji Japan's second foreign war, in terms of scale it was in a class by itself. The Sino-Japanese War of 1894-1895 had been a small localized conflict that produced battle casualties of only 5,000. The Russo-Japanese War, on the other hand, began with no assurance of success and concluded by exhausting Japan's national resources. It required the sacrifice of 118,000 dead and wounded, barely to wrest a difficult victory at the end. Soldiers went off from every village in Japan, and nearly half of them died or returned disabled. No discussion of the Russo-Japanese War can proceed in ignorance of the pain and grief that accompanied this national experience.

Although I agree that in an international sense the Russo-Japanese conflict was an imperialist war, in my view it possessed a character too complicated to be wholly subsumed under this rubric. To summarize briefly: the war succeeded only because three very different but complementary aims converged. The first was the intent of the Japanese ruling class; the military, in particular, had long hoped to establish a foothold in Korea as a basis for an advance into the continent. The second was the fixed strategy of British imperialism to block Russian expansion to the south by whatever means, which for Britain in the Far East meant having Japan block it for her. The third was the intent of the Japanese people, who regarded the clash between Japan and Russia as a fated "national crisis" that could only be solved by laying down one's life for the sake of the nation's survival. It is this third factor that I should like to emphasize here, both because this difficult war could not have been won without it and because the spontaneous upsurge of popular involvement gave the conflict something of the "character of a people's war" (*kokumin sensōteki na yōso*). If we overlook this phenomenon, we fail to grasp the significance of the change that occurred in popular thought and remain unable to solve the riddle of why the ideological fiction of the emperor system achieved victory.

Private Ōsawa Keinosuke, a farmer from a Tama area village, participated in the combined attack on Port Arthur in late 1904 and again at Mukden in the spring of 1905. In his diary, written in pencil and stained with sweat, he recorded in detail the situation at Port Arthur, the attack on Hill 203, and the excitement with which the troops greeted the first news of Japan's naval victory in the Battle of Tsushima. His record is remarkably unrestricted, suggesting that important military information was available even to the rank and file. This is in striking contrast to our own experience during the Pacific War, when even the highest officials were sometimes unaware of major military developments. It is said, for example, that Prime Minister Tōjō, who was both Army Minister and Chief of the General Staff, did not receive detailed information on the catastrophic defeat of the Japanese forces at Midway until a month after it occurred, and civil officials like Foreign Minister Shigemitsu Mamoru were not informed of the total destruction of the fleet until after the war was over.

Private Ōsawa, on the other hand, wrote just after Port Arthur had finally fallen in January 1905, at a cost of nearly 60,000 casualties. He and his unit were pushing toward the battlefields of Mukden, marching through blizzards seven or eight hours a day, and camping out at night. On February 10, 1905, his diary entry reads:

9 a.m. formation. Marched toward Hsiao-tien-tzu. A company dispatch at lunchtime reported that in the fighting near the Sha-ho from January 26 to 29, there were more than 7,000 casualties, both officers and en

listed men. One major general and three regimental commanders were killed. The enemy's losses were about twice ours.

The 7,000 casualties at the Sha-ho represented an enormous loss, and yet this information that could not but affect morale was allowed to reach even the soldiers who were moving forward as reinforcements. The army's confidence in the soldiers and their willingness to fight must have been considerable. The diary continues:

> They say that in the Russian capital there is no electric light, no coal, no fuel. The Czar's whereabouts are unknown, and the revolutionaries have fired on the Palace. Now that Port Arthur has fallen, Kropatkin has lost his objective and fighting will be hopeless. The Russian capital is temporarily in darkness.

> 3:30 p.m. arrived at quarters.[70]

Ōsawa was obviously referring to the Revolution of 1905, Bloody Sunday having taken place only two weeks before he wrote. News of the general strike and rebellion in St. Petersburg had already spread to the Japanese soldiers in distant Manchuria. Ōsawa even incorporated the speculation that since General Kropotkin had lost his battle objective and the home front was in darkness after the attack by the revolutionaries, the Russian army might possibly withdraw, an amazing prediction to find in the diary of an ordinary soldier. Although the two nations were engaged in the same imperialist war, Russia was fighting merely for territorial expansion, whereas Japan was risking its national fate in the contest, a risk that was understood even by the common soldier. It is because we have underestimated this aspect of the war against Russia—which was different indeed from the situation during the Pacific War—that we have failed to understand the internal

[70] For the full text of the diary, see Irokawa Daikichi, "Nichiro sensōka no heishi no kiroku: Ōsawa jōtōhei senchū nikki," *Jinbun shizen kagaku ronshū,* no. 24 (Tokyo Keizai Daigaku, November 1970), pp. 195-290.

process by which the masses of soldiers were drawn willingly into the illusion of the nation as their common destiny.

"Miles and miles away from home, here in far-off Manchuria"—so began the famous war song that is now just a nostalgic melody evocative of past times. For the people of the Meiji period, however, these were words and music that stirred the soul.[71] For the masses of Japanese, the war had been their first direct international experience. Viewing their ancestral land from a strange and distant place, they first discovered what Japanese "nature" (*shizen*) meant to them and experienced for the first time the emotional bonds that unite comrades-in-arms. The writer Tayama Katai drew on his own observations of the war to describe this profound psychological phenomenon in his story titled *Ippeisotsu* (A Soldier).[72] In the story soldiers who began as strangers from different districts and different regiments are thrown together on the vast plains of Manchuria, where they struggle and give comfort and encouragement to one another. But when the protagonist, after being wounded and rescued by two privates, dies a painful and solitary death on the eve of the battle of Liao-yang, his dying thoughts stray far from Manchuria and his comrades. He sees instead "his mother's face, his wife's face, the large house surrounded by familiar trees, the gentle beach that led from behind the house, the deep blue sea, the familiar face of a fisherman. . . ." He returns at the end to images of Japanese "nature."

Thus the soldiers died, pulled between two powerful illusions. They felt their fated identity as compatriots of the "na-

---

[71] "*Koko wa okuni kara nambyaku ri, hanarete tōki Manshū no,*" the first lines of the famous war song *Sen'yū* (Comrades-in-arms). The song was composed just after the Russo-Japanese War, became widely popular at the end of the Meiji period, and was sung throughout the prewar years. In the song a soldier stops to help his wounded comrade, a friend he first met on the ship leaving Japan. When the friend dies, the soldier thinks of his family at home and writes to them of their son's death. Both the nation (*okuni*) and native place (*kuni*) appear and are emotionally linked in the lyric. Horiuchi Keizō, *Teihon Nihon no shōka* (Tokyo: Jitsugyō no Nihonsha, 1970), pp. 122ff.

[72] Originally printed in *Waseda bungaku* (1908), *Tayama Katai zenshū*, vol. 1 (Tokyo: Bunsendō shoten, 1973), pp. 608-31.

tion," but they were drawn at the end by their affection for the solitary comfort of their "family" and "native place." The relationship between the two illusions was important, for it enabled the emperor system to make use of the people's attraction in both directions. Even a soldier who died a wretched and inhuman death on the plains of Manchuria—as long as the name of his village and family was stitched on the back of his uniform—would be registered as a guardian god of the nation at Yasukuni Shrine. There he would be reverently worshiped, even by the Emperor Meiji. The mutual acceptance of this process, by which personal and national fate were indissolubly linked, became the epic that symbolized the creation of the "family-state."

The Russo-Japanese War wrought still another important change in the popular psychology. More than a million Japanese returned from the battlefields of Korea and Manchuria with a distinct feeling of contempt for the Chinese they had encountered there. The letters the soldiers wrote home were filled with undisguised scorn and hostility for what they saw as the barbarity, poverty, filth, squalor, and servile nature of the people. As a result of fighting against white people for the first time, the Japanese had shown signs of acquiring an international perspective, whether expressed in the friendly feeling the Japanese army displayed toward the Russian troops or in Private Ōsawa's interest in the Russian Revolution of 1905. But this internationalism was soon reduced to the single point of racial prejudice against the Chinese. Popular nationalism was thus early perverted into a form that paved the way for the ultranationalism of the prewar years. As stories of personal experience in China circulated, they hardened into prejudice, and this prejudice became a chronic mental affliction. Later, in the Taishō and Shōwa periods, as Japan's imperialist invasion of China assumed greater and greater proportions and the Chinese became aware of the danger to their people, their disposition changed dramatically and they began to resist. The Japanese, however, were never able to acknowledge this change. The contemptuous image of the Chinese that had been formed in the Meiji period lasted until the end, contributing both to the moral atrocities of the China War and to the effective manipulation of the people by the Japanese leadership.

Perhaps this spiritual affliction was unavoidable. It had its roots in a habit of mind created over several hundred years of isolation and then burdened in the modern period with the strain of a nation making a belated entry into the ranks of world imperialism. It is also true that the people of every country have been warped in some way or other by history. We should not despair that we have not yet eradicated in these twenty-five years the roots of evil of a system that dominated Japanese ways of thinking for more than half a century.

THE POWER OF NATIONAL EDUCATION

I would like to conclude with a discussion of the role that education played in bringing about the domination of "the emperor system as a spiritual structure." Prior to the elementary school texts of 1910, which I regard as the first systematic presentation of *tennōsei* ideology, education in the schools had followed a rather uneven course.[73] Tokutomi Sohō's well-known report on his observation of a third-grade ethics (*shūshin*) class at the Atami Elementary School in the spring of 1893 provides a glimpse of the situation that prevailed in the years before the Sino-Japanese War:

TEACHER: Why must we be loyal to the Emperor?
PUPILS: Because the Emperor. . . . (*He stopped, at a loss; only titters were heard.*)
TEACHER: Because we are indebted to the Emperor. . . . Now why are we indebted to him?
PUPILS: (*Mumbling and looking around at each other.*)
TEACHER: Coming here to school, being safely at home— You owe all these things to the Emperor.

[73] The author's discussion here is based partly on his earlier examination of more than a hundred Meiji textbooks in ethics, Japanese language, and Japanese history. See Irokawa, "Meiji makki no kyōkasho mondai," *Rekishi chiri kyōiku*, no. 20 (August 1956), pp. 2-38.

SOHŌ: Children, you always hear about what is good and
   bad. What kinds of things are good?
PUPILS: To practice loyalty and filial piety.
SOHŌ: (*Silent, appalled at the mechanical response.*)[74]

Six years later the pupils in an elementary school in Okayama
Prefecture were asked about "the people we should take as
models." Twenty-six percent chose Kusunoki Masashige,
twenty-two percent the emperor, and twenty percent the
teacher.[75] Even in 1899 the emperor was still not the dominant influence in the minds of the pupils. Again it was during
the Russo-Japanese War period that the emperor was finally
established as the center of *kokutai* and the focus of elementary education. And at the same time, the legendary imperial
loyalist Kusunoki Masashige and his son Masatsura came to
the fore as the ideal models of Japanese loyalty and filial piety.
   The elementary school texts of the early Meiji period had
fostered quite a different image. Reflecting the enlightenment views of the time, the texts were largely unrestricted,
and books like Fukuzawa Yukichi's *Encouragement of Learning (Gakumon no susume)* were freely used in the schools.
Then, in the 1880s, the government and the People's Rights
movement clashed, not only over politics but over textbooks
as well. The result was that the stiffly written Confucian works
and baldly nationalistic tracts of the establishment competed
with the awkward adaptations and difficult political texts produced by the opposition. It is interesting to note that as the
government began its inspection of textbooks and gradually
eliminated Fukuzawa and other liberals from the schools, the
enrollment figures stagnated. During the same period the informal study associations founded by the People's Rights activists flourished. At their peak there were well over a thousand of these independent "political schools" around the
country offering a brand of political education that, from the

[74] "Atami tayori," *Kokumin shimbun*, April 7, 1893, here somewhat abridged.
[75] Tamaki Hajime, *Nihon kyōiku hattatsushi* (Tokyo: San'ichi shobō, 1954),
p. 95.

viewpoint of the emperor system, must have seemed threatening indeed.

Once the People's Rights movement was suppressed, the government took the offensive in education. It revised the School Act, issued the Rescript on Education, and instituted controls on anti-establishment education. The authorities also launched a thoroughgoing systematization of the curriculum, including the textbooks. But even in this period, which lasted through the nineties, the textbook inspection system allowed some variety to reach the schools. Mixed in with the number of sycophantic texts centered on loyalty, filiality, and *kokutai* were works that aimed at modern civic education. The best of these was Tsubouchi Shōyō's *Japanese Readers* (*Kokugo tokuhon*), published in sixteen volumes by Fuzambō from 1899 to 1901.[76] Tsubouchi devoted all his energies to these texts, which he wrote in the context of the heightened nationalism of the late nineties. Tsubouchi himself had been branded as unpatriotic in the course of his heated debates with Takayama Chōgyū, the leading advocate of the "Japanism" of the time, and he was profoundly afraid for the future of the nation. He poured his indignation, as well as his liberalism and considerable artistic abilities, into this series of readers, which I regard as the best of all his work. It is said that more than 100,000 copies were sold for use in the schools. In the end, however, the state would not tolerate critical trends in the classroom, and beginning in 1903, the use of uniform government textbooks became compulsory.

The 1903 textbooks were produced hastily in the same crude crambook style of the earlier texts, and as a systematic expression of *tennōsei* education, they were but primitive attempts. Revision was soon undertaken, and the result, after more than a thousand sessions of deliberation, was the second edition of government textbooks issued in 1910. This edition, unlike its predecessor, was a veritable exhibit of the "spiritual

[76] For the full texts of twelve of the sixteen volumes, see *Nihon kyōkasho taikei, Kindaihen,* vol. 6 (*Kokugo,* III), Kaigo Tokiomi, ed. (Tokyo: Kōdansha, 1964), pp. 195-385.

301

structure" of the emperor system. Here, for example, is Kusunoki Masashige as he bids his son farewell, refusing Masatsura's offer to accompany his father to fight what is almost
certain to be a losing battle:

> "Even though we die, as long as even one member of
> our family survives, he must raise loyal soldiers and con-
> tinue to serve the Emperor. You can show no greater
> filial devotion than this.
>
> "Although you are very young, you are your father's
> son and should at least be able to grasp this. . . . I send
> you back, not because I grieve at your dying young but
> so that you may grow up and serve the Emperor by rais-
> ing loyal soldiers and suppressing the rebels. . . . Have
> you forgotten so quickly?"
>
> A samurai like Masatsura, who fulfilled the demands
> of both loyalty and filial devotion, should be a model for
> the people.[77]

Thus Kusunoki Masatsura, like his father before him, faced a
great army and died a heroic death on the battlefield. It was
fortunate for the emperor system that history provided so many
exemplars of this kind of pure and willing loyalism. For the
people loved figures like Masatsura, who though he faced the
enemy alone would still stand faithful and, pitting himself
against the currents of his time, fight to the very end. This
symbolic historical image became the very soul of national
education in the prewar period.

Although the history and ethics texts have been much discussed, it seems to me that the essence of the emperor system is most clearly revealed in the Japanese readers, which
occupied a special position among the government textbooks.
Not confined merely to the study of the Japanese language,
these *kokugo tokuhon* were actually comprehensive readers
that ranged over a wide variety of subjects. Just the emotional

---

[77] For the 1910 readers (*Jinjō shōgakkō tokuhon*), see *Nihon kyōkasho taikei,
Kindaihen*, vol. 7 (*Kokugo*, IV), Kaigo Tokiomi, ed. (Tokyo: Kōdansha, 1964),
pp. 7-259. For "Masatsura," see pp. 106-107.

tone of the selections alone made them more effective than the didactic ethics texts. The crystallization of establishment wisdom accumulated over the course of a decade of deliberation, and the scope of the readers was as broad as the emperor system would allow. *Kokutai* was central, but not at all in a reactionary sense. Instead the readers were forward-looking, catholic enough in content to encompass the widely different orientations of the people of the period, and Japanese enough in form to be congenial to their accustomed ways of thinking. The editors adopted the literary tone of texts like Tsubouchi's, and the books were extremely well structured and organized. The style was emotional and familiar, part of the flesh and blood of the Japanese sensibility. One shudders to think of the impact this artistically presented and systematically administered education must have had on the as-yet blank minds of small children. And the lessons they read in class were reinforced by the numbers of historical songs they sang both inside and outside school. "Parting at Sakurai" (*Sakurai no ketsubetsu*), which recounted Masashige's farewell to Masatsura; "Kojima Takanori," whose protagonist, like Kusunoki, was an imperial loyalist of the fourteenth century; "Meeting at Shui-shih-ying" (*Suishiei no kaiken*), the account of the emotional meeting at which the Russian General Stoessel surrendered Port Arthur to General Nogi in 1905—all these well-known and widely sung songs dealt with episodes from the elementary school readers.[78]

Following the principle enunciated in the Charter Oath that "knowledge should be sought throughout the world so as to strengthen the foundations of imperial rule," the readers resolutely included "Lessons from Western History" and a chapter titled "An Awakening to the World." From the tales of the accomplishments of modern man and the presentation of new theories like evolution to the introduction of science and technology and the discussion of the rights and duties of cit-

[78] These and others appeared in the Mombushō editions of *Jinjō shōgaku shōka* that determined the songs that would be sung in music class. For the words and music, see Horiuchi Keizō, ed., *Teihon Nihon no shōka* (Tokyo: Jitsugyō no Nihonsha, 1970).

izens in a constitutional system, the readers assumed a posture of confidence in Japan's capacity to progress and an attitude of openness to the outside world. Since all this was intended "to strengthen the foundations of imperial rule," the first and second chapters of each graded reader usually contained material related to the emperor, the imperial house, or *kokutai*. This was reinforced in later sections on "family morality," "ancestor worship," "loyalty and filial piety," "love of native place," "model villages," and the like. In order to impress upon the people a sense of their common national destiny, there were lessons on "foreign wars"—from the Mongol invasion of the thirteenth century to the Sino- and Russo-Japanese conflicts. Tales of men who had saved the nation in time of difficulty were linked to these: the Meiji emperor and war heroes like Commander Hirose and Lt. Colonel Tachibana, General Nogi, and Admiral Tōgō. "The life of workers and farmers" was also included, but primarily with the intention of promoting conventional morality. On the other hand, some consideration was given to fostering the "ability to adapt to a capitalist society."

The structure of each volume was carefully considered, and the entire series was conceived with the aim of uniting feudal loyalty with modern functionalism, the imperial house with the people, the traditional with the modern. This effort at synthesis seems to have succeeded as long as it was based on the kind of "progressive" principles cited above. Indeed, were it not for this progressive quality, it might have been impossible to drag the Japanese people along this way of thinking for nearly half a century.

The upper division of the 1910 *Elementary Japanese Readers* (volumes 7-12, grades 4-6) contained the choicest pick of "matchless tales": "Masatsura" (vol. 7), "Ise Shrine" (vol. 8), "A Sailor's Mother," "Yasukuni Shrine" (vol. 9), "Meeting at Shui-shih-ying" (vol. 10), "Kojima Takanori," "A Sailor off to the Front" (vol. 11), "Poems Composed by the Emperor," "The Battle of the Japan Sea" (vol. 12). Of these, Kusunoki Masatsura, Kojima Takanori, General Nogi, and Admiral Tōgō were symbols of "the unity of loyalty and filiality" from the point of view of the loyal retainer or military officer. "A Sailor's Mother" and "A Soldier off to the Front," on the other hand, provided models of "the close relation between filial piety and loyalty" on the part of ordinary people and the common soldier. Indeed, "A Sailor's Mother" (along of course with Masatsura parting from his father at Sakurai) was the dramatic highlight of the entire series.

Most elementary school pupils in the prewar period had to recite "A Sailor's Mother," and it was an indispensable part of the repertory performed for the mayor and parents at the spring and fall exercises, which may make it the most frequently performed piece in all of Japanese theater. For the benefit of young readers who are not familiar with it, here is the story, so they can see the kind of emotional core their parents were brought up with.

It was the time of the War of 1894-1895. One day on our ship the Takachiho, a sailor was weeping as he read a letter written in a woman's handwriting. A passing lieutenant saw him and, thinking his behavior unmanly, said, "Hey, what have we here? Has life become so valuable? Are you afraid to die? Are you lonely for your wife and children? Don't you think it's an honor to become a soldier and go to war—What kind of attitude is that?"

"Sir, don't think that of me . . ."

[The officer reads the letter:]

"You said you did not fight in the battle of Feng-tao, and you did not accomplish much in the August 10th attack at Weihaiwei either. I am very disappointed in you. Why did you go into battle? Wasn't it to sacrifice your life to repay the emperor? The people in the village are good to me and offer help all the time, saying kindly: 'It must be hard on you having your only son off fighting for the country. Please don't hesitate to tell us if there is anything we can do.' Whenever I see their faces, I am reminded of your cowardice and I feel as if my heart will break. So every day I go to the shrine of Hachiman and pray that you will distinguish yourself in battle. Of course

I am human, too, and cannot at all bring myself to hate my own child. Please try to understand my feelings as I write this letter. . . ."

[The officer apologized:]

"I'm sorry. I can only admire your mother's spirit."

The sailor, who had been listening with lowered head, saluted and, smiling, left.[79]

The writing here is skillful, an improvement in both form and content over the initial version in the 1903 *Reader*. There the climax had been heavy-handed:

"Whenever I see them, I am reminded of your cowardice and my heart seems to break. I wish you would try to understand a little of what I feel."

As he heard this, the Lieutenant's eyes welled with tears in spite of himself.

"Oh, pardon. I'm sorry. You have a good mother. You must come from a good family."

The sailor left, smiling.[80]

The Russo-Japanese War had taken place between the first and second edition of the government textbooks, and it turned the sailor's mother out of an elite "good family" into the ranks of the nameless masses. The war also supplied the image—still unforgettable for me—of the poor sailor's mother standing on the shore calling out for her son: "Ichitaro-o-o!" In the context of the life-and-death crisis of war, the emotional association between the world of "mother," "family," and "village" with the world of "emperor" and "state" was a powerful one. It created a monument of mass nationalism with a core, perspective, and pathos sufficiently persuasive so that, once incorporated into the schools, it could influence the thinking of a whole generation of Japanese.

The 1910 *Readers* expounded a modern civic ethic in chapters that bore imposing titles like "The Dignity of a Great

[79] *Nihon kyōkasho taikei*, vol. 7, pp. 150-51.
[80] Ibid., vol. 6, under the title "Kanshin no haha," pp. 528-30.

People" and "The Spirit of Self-Government" (vol. 12). The same volume, however, also preached selflessness, thrift, harmony, and obedience in lessons on the "Duties of a Housewife" and "Japanese Women," where it was said that "in general the woman's duty lies in helping her husband to manage the household and in educating her children to raise the family name." Humanistic stories from abroad—"Street Music" (France), "A Brave Girl" (England), "The Drummer Boy" (Italy), "Columbus" (Spain)—were mixed without apparent contradiction with the heroic military tales of Chu-ko Liang, Torii Katsuaki, and Commander Tachibana. The poem in Volume 11, "I am a Child of the Sea," began with a delicate lyricism and then ended with the lines, "Now on a battle ship I will defend our country of the sea." The material was thus superbly structured, and the *Readers* betrayed no signs of the eclecticism, structurelessness, or all-enveloping embrace Maruyama has described. And when they sang out the aspirations of the nation, their confidence in the victory of the emperor system was complete:

Since the distant age of the gods,
The emperor and his subjects have stood in fixed relation,
The unbroken imperial line unchanged.

To the light shed everywhere
By the august virtue of our imperial house, we raise our
        eyes,
Here, we fifty million countrymen.

For wisdom we take the strength of east and west,
Our civilization the essense of the old and new.
Three thousand years since the founding of the nation.

Mindful of the departed past,
We move ever forward, never wavering.
Here, we fifty million countrymen.

The mission of the peace in the Orient
Lies upon our shoulders.
The forefront of Eastern civilization.

Japan's task is heavy.
The hearts of high and low united in perfect harmony,
Here, we fifty million countrymen.[81]

The face of the emperor system was everywhere visible in these comprehensive readers. It was present in the lesson on "Yasukuni Shrine" and in the selections on "Ise Shrine" and "Record of a Pilgrimage to Ise," where the meaning of the popular Ise cult was shifted from a folk to an imperial level. It was present in many more examples that one could name, but it is perhaps most important to point out that the presence of the emperor system necessarily meant the absence of material that had been included in earlier texts. Although the editors adopted the artistic approach of Tsubouchi's series, they rejected some of its contents, and a brief sampling of their omissions reveals clearly the limits of the "national education" of the period.

Tsubouchi, for example, had totally rejected the notion of the emperor as a "manifest deity" or a living god. He had presented the tale of Saho-hime, the consort of the Emperor Sujin, in terms of the humanism of the ancient Japanese. The heartless emperor who was willing to burn the palace with his wife in it was contrasted with the humane empress who, torn between loyalty to her husband and her brother, the rebel, first saved her husband and children and then followed her brother to death in the flames. The contrast was stark and bore no trace of the idea of the emperor as a living god. In his chapter on "Kinouchi Sōgorō," Tsubouchi commended the bold conduct of the peasant leader who had been put to death for resisting injustice on behalf of the people: "We cannot but be impressed with Sōgorō's fervent devotion to the village he loved." In a chapter titled "A Model Millionaire," he praised the integrity, independence, and social philanthropy of Andrew Carnegie, thus implicitly censuring the corruption of political entrepreneurs like Furukawa Ichibei,

[81] Ibid., vol. 7, p. 226. This song was sung throughout the prewar period, although as the population increased, so did the number of countrymen in the refrain, from fifty to sixty to seventy.

the owner of the Ashio Copper Mine. It is hardly surprising that these selections were left out of the government texts.

On the matter of Japanese attitudes toward the world, Tsubouchi included a chapter on "Racial Differences." In it he argued the fundamental equality of the races and criticized as erroneous the espousal of racial discrimination and superiority on the basis of the current level of civilization. When he treated the death in 1895 of the Chinese naval hero Ting Ju-ch'ang, Tsubouchi persuasively made the point that patriotism, humanity, and *bushidō* knew no ethnic distinction and that the Japanese contempt for China was nothing but baseless prejudice. In a lesson titled "Ezo Brocade," he used Ainu legends to show the meaninglessness of war and the value of peace. This posture, too, was completely absent from the official textbooks.

The government texts rejected the superb ideas of Tsubouchi and others like him and officially suppressed education on egalitarian or pacifist principles. And yet, the history of education in the later prewar years, especially at its most basic levels, suggests that the critical spirit that permeated Tsubouchi's readers was never altogether stifled. Despite the "family-state," and despite the government's best efforts to draw the people into it, the masses of the Japanese never wholly gave up their souls to the emperor system. They have retained somewhere deep within them the potential to rise up one day and free themselves from state control. Until that day, when the people can use it for their own liberation, the critical spirit of men like Tsubouchi—like the waters deep inside the dark earth—flows on as a subterranean current in history.

CONCLUSION

And so "the emperor system as a spiritual structure" was impressively established. We have detailed here the process of dextrous artifice by which tradition was "regenerated" in the form of *tennōsei*. But "as things rise, so they fall," and the emperor system was no exception. From the moment of its completion at the end of the Meiji period, it sounded its own funeral knell. When a frail young woman named Kanno Suga plotted to throw a bomb at the Meiji emperor and one of Japan's prominent thinkers, Kōtoku Shūsui, was hanged on the scaffold for alleged treason, the whole world learned of the profound unrest and contradiction that characterized the emperor system. The fate of Kōtoku and the others involved in the Great Treason incident of 1910-1911 revealed the truth: the emperor system was not a compassionate all-enveloping embrace but a tyranny that would stop at nothing to eliminate heresy, a self-contradicting system that concealed within the shadows of its harmoniousness a brutality that chilled men's hearts.

For the next thirty-five years, from 1911 to 1945, the emperor system held its grip on the Japanese. It became irresistible, inevitable, an object of fate; it framed people's lives, obstructed vision like a "weight upon the eyes," and pressed in on them like the air that surrounds all things. It was "thought transformed into sentiment," and it clung so tenaciously that no opposing theory could penetrate it. Thus it blocked the way to dissent, and the tragic succession of increasing isolation, conversions, and martyrdoms that plagued the social movement after the death of Kōtoku was part of the result.

But perhaps one should regard *tennōsei* as a historical trial that Japanese social science has had to endure to become independent. In that case the first task is to examine the emperor system objectively, to inquire into its entire history, from the conditions that generated it through its maturation and establishment, to the dissension that worked at it from within. For the emperor system will never lose its mysterious powers until the whole of its "spiritual structure" is thoroughly objectified and exposed. Then and only then is the next step possible: to root out one by one the causes of the intellectual twists and emotional distortions that, once traditionalized within Japanese, were responsible for their spiritual servility. We must root them out, reevaluate and retrain them, reject some, retain others, and thereby generate a new mentality, a new way of thinking.

310

To speculate about what concrete form this new mentality may take is beyond the scope of this book, although I do believe that we can look to some of the aspects of Meiji culture presented here for directions to the way out of this spiritual predicament.

(Translated by Carol Gluck)

INDEX OF NAMES CITED

313